I hope you will enjoy my father's story as much as he enjoyed life. I trust, too, that it will add fresh knowledge of those horrendous days in W.W.1.

And, of course, you have that spicy little memory of pulling Joe out of an old shell hole near the Ulster Tower, into which he fell as recounting a story. I can picture the scene!!.

With best wishes,
Michael A. Wilson   Dec. 1993.

# PETER

A Life Remembered
1894-1990

# PETER

---

A Life Remembered
1894-1990

---

Dr. A.G. Wilson
MC MRCS LRCP

---

Compiled and edited by
Michael A. Wilson

Published in 1993 by
Michael A Wilson

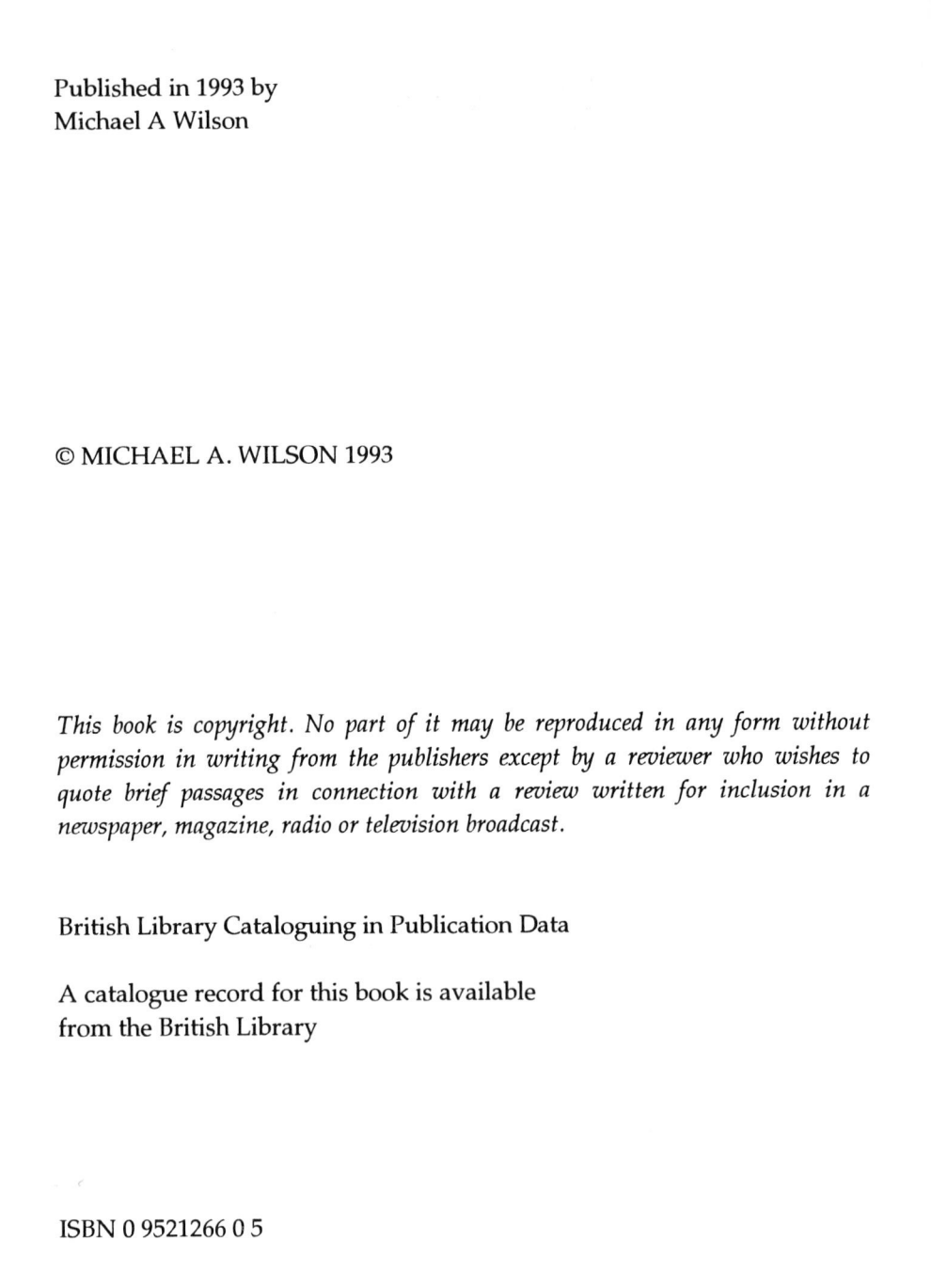

© MICHAEL A. WILSON 1993

*This book is copyright. No part of it may be reproduced in any form without permission in writing from the publishers except by a reviewer who wishes to quote brief passages in connection with a review written for inclusion in a newspaper, magazine, radio or television broadcast.*

British Library Cataloguing in Publication Data

A catalogue record for this book is available
from the British Library

ISBN 0 9521266 0 5

Designed and Produced by Images Publishing (Malvern).
Printed and Bound in Great Britain.

# Contents

| | | |
|---|---|---|
| Editors Note | | 9 |
| Acknowledgements | | 10 |
| Foreword | | 11 |
| Chapter One | IN THE BEGINNING ... A Yorkshire Childhood | 17 |
| Chapter Two | THE GREAT WAR ... with the West Yorkshire Regiment | 27 |
| Chapter Three | AN EARLY EXPERIENCE OF HOSPITAL LIFE | 67 |
| Chapter Four | BACK TO THE TRENCHES | 74 |
| Chapter Five | WITH THE ROYAL FLYING CORPS | 81 |
| Chapter Six | OXFORD 1920'S | 131 |
| Chapter Seven | ST THOMAS'S HOSPITAL | 165 |
| Chapter Eight | MARRIAGE, HONEYMOON AND A PRACTICE AT RADLETT | 175 |
| Chapter Nine | TAKING UP ARMS AGAIN ... With the RAF | 189 |
| Chapter Ten | BY TROOPSHIP TO SOUTH AFRICA Winter 1942 | 196 |
| Chapter Eleven | BACK WITH FIGHTER, BOMBER AND TRAINING COMMANDS 1942-1945 | 206 |
| Chapter Twelve | RETURN TO A GP'S LIFE ... Radlett 1945-1971 | 215 |
| Chapter Thirteen | RETIREMENT IN ROCKBOURNE | 251 |
| Chapter Fourteen | THE DECLINING YEARS OF OUR PATRIACH | 276 |
| Epilogue | | 283 |

# List of Illustrations

1. Peter. ................................................................................................ 8
2. Arthur George Wilson (father) in hunting kit, 1880s. ..................... 18
3. The Wilson family in the garden, Haxby c. 1903. .......................... 21
4. St Peter's School, York 1910. ........................................................ 21
5. May 1914. A proud young man joins the Territorials. ................... 28
6. Peter's platoon of lads from Knaresborough. ................................. 33
7. October 1916, Northern General Hospital. .................................... 71
8. Aerial Reconnaissance photograph of Front Line. ......................... 92
9. Proven 1918. RE8 Machine. .......................................................... 93
10. 7 Squadron Officers, Droglandt May 1918. ................................. 108
11. Peter at Buckingham Palace with his parents to attend the Investiture. ..... 125
12. Peter in Bristol Fighter at Mulheim. ........................................... 126
13. Oxford High Street looking towards Carfax, 1920. ..................... 132
14. Oxford Students. .......................................................................... 135
15. Peter marries Sheena Allan at Kilmahew, September 1927. ........ 179
16. Sheena with Michael and Fiona, 1934. ........................................ 185
17. Cranwell 1948. Doc testing Flight Lieutenant Lord's lung capacity. ..... 193
18. Michael and Fiona at the Caledonian Ball, 1950. ........................ 222
19. A fine catch. ................................................................................ 226
20. Grove House, Radlett. ................................................................. 228
21. Grove House gardens. ................................................................. 229
22. Peter poses among his dahlias. .................................................... 230
23. A favourite rhino enjoying Peter's pears. .................................... 231
24. A country doctor's lunch-time break. .......................................... 232
25. 1960s. Fiona's family grows. ....................................................... 234
26. Peter and Paula's wedding, 1961. ................................................ 235
27. Peter and Paula in the garden at Grove House. ........................... 236
28. Doc with Dick Bott, admiring one of the gifts at his retirement party. ..... 237
29. Michael and his family on a Brazilian beach in 1971. ................. 239
30. Fiona and her family c. 1972. ...................................................... 255
31. Michael and Rosemary in the Hebrides, 1979. ............................ 272
32. Peter's 90th birthday celebrations, 1984. ..................................... 277
33. Flanders with Lyn Macdonald, La Bassée 1987. ......................... 278
34. Doc at Walter Malthouse's grave after saying the immortal words. ..... 279
35. A family wedding group 1987. .................................................... 281
36. Peter with grandson Richard. The Last Photograph. ................... 282

# Dedication

*To all those valiant young men and women who sacrificed their lives or their mental or physical health in the Great Wars and who, thus, had no future to build, nor dreams to fulfil.*

"Not heav'n itself upon the past has pow'r,
But what has been, has been, and I have had my hour.

Dryden, Paraphrase of Horace.

# Editor's Note

Peter's life story has been printed here very much as he wrote it down. Due to the passage of time and his failing memory, he often resorted to copying straight from his old diary entries, and inevitably there are gaps, contradictions and repetitions in the writing. Nevertheless, the extraordinary vitality, sense of humour, Christian faith, courage and enthusiasm of the man shine through these pages, and it is easy to see how much he will be missed.

# Acknowledgements

I would like to thank all those who helped us to encourage my father to write his memoirs, most notably Margaret Facey, widow of one of his W.W.1. pilots, and Harold Ridley (President of the Intra Ocular Implant Club), fellow fisherman and his distinguished obituarist.

I am very touched by the spontaneous offer from all eight grandchildren to help me to pay for the publishing of the book. They are my sons Crispin, Andrew, Richard and Alistair and my late sister Fiona's children Rosalind, Sarah, Amanda and Jonathon.

It must have taken me nearly as many hours to prepare my father's memorabilia and read the texts, as it did my father to write his book. I must thank my family and friends, especially Christopher Guise, for encouraging me to keep going. Most of all my gratitude is due to my dear wife, Rosemary, for her invaluable help with our share of the editing and especially for putting up with my occupation of the dining room for weeks on end with enormous piles of photographs, documents and texts to sift and process.

Our special thanks are due to Tony Harold and his colleagues at The Self Publishing Association for their help and advice and to Catherine Whiting for her cheery and skilful help with the editing, which has reduced the unwieldy manuscript into a thoroughly readable book. I must also thank Pam Scruton, who entered so much into the spirit of the book, for her patient endeavour over the months deciphering and typing my own and my father's far from legible scripts.

# Foreword

In the churchyard of the lovely little village of Rockbourne in Hampshire, there is a newly-engraved stone which reads:

*In Loving Memory Of*

*"Peter"*

*Dr A.G. Wilson MC*
*1894-1990*

*Inspiring Patriarch*
*Dearly loved Warrior, Physician*
*Sportsman and Friend*

It is in loving memory of "Peter"[*] that I, his son, and his eight grandchildren have clubbed together to publish his remarkable story. It is at once ordinary, in that he lived through what hundreds of thousands of his contemporaries also endured in World Wars I and II, and extraordinary in that he lived to record his memories with a freshness and humour when of a great age.

The story really got under way after the death of his wife, Paula, in 1984, when he had to give up his garden and move into a retirement home in Headbourne Worthy. As a ploy to keep him occupied and interested, after a couple of earlier attempts had foundered, family and friends persuaded him to tackle his story in earnest. It was thus mainly written after his 90th birthday, and indeed the later parts show a little of the ramblings and repetitions of a very old gentleman.

Invaluable jogging of his memories and much excitement was provided by the invitation to join Lyn Macdonald as one of the veterans on her pilgrimages to the battlefields of Flanders. Lyn's meticulously researched trips with her coachload of Old Soldiers and enthusiasts provided a wonderful stimulus to my father as he rediscovered battlefields and billets fully seventy years after the horrendous events of 1914-18.

Sadly Doc had only reached 1942 when he died in 1990, but we have

---

[*] My father was called "Peter" by family and friends, though he was never able to explain to me quite how this came about. To those to whom he was not Peter, including his patients, he was "Doc".

partially solved this problem by including some chapters based on his letters to us in South America, relating his exploits with rod and gun, the progress of the seasons in his garden and some vivid descriptions of sporting events.

My father was a survivor, and as his story will reveal, he narrowly escaped death several times in World War I. In his first battle a shell killed his friend lying beside him in the trench; twice, the man he was talking to was killed by a sniper, and only a survivor would have come through his terrible multiple wounds of September 1916 on the Somme. In the Royal Flying Corps, many comrades were lost; on one occasion, my father's being the only plane from a flight of six to return to base. It was at this time that he won the Military Cross for vital reconnaissance work under heavy fire during the March retreat in 1918. I understand this was one of the last MCs to be awarded to an airman before the Royal Air Force was created and its Distinguished Flying Cross introduced. He also survived an eyeball to eyeball encounter with the dreaded von Richtofen. After the war, returning from a maternity case in the small hours, he ran full tilt into a steam roller parked without lights! In his seventies he was stricken by a strange disease which left him paralysed – the fact that he was the centre of attention, with squads of doctors gathering around his hospital bed in earnest debate, undoubtedly played a part in his recovery!

Yes, Doc Wilson loved to be centre stage, whether it was posing in front of the camera, or holding forth at a dinner party at some remote highland shooting lodge. What he had to say commanded attention, as he eloquently discoursed upon his philosophy, propounded his views on the way the twentieth century was shaping, or recounted his own personal stories. He had an incredible memory and even at ninety was able to recite poems and Shakespeare soliloquies.

He was charismatic, full of enthusiasm and an impish sense of fun. On one occasion on a visit to Yorkshire, he rang up his sister, Mary, and in perfect dialect pretended to be calling from the elegant firm of Hunter and Smallpage in York, advising that a large and expensive order of curtains was ready. Having nearly reduced the poor lady to hysterics, he admitted his leg-pull.

His irrepressible energy and optimism, even for hopeless fishing conditions was almost too much at times, and a number of his special friends and family (including me) admitted it could be over the top. As a young man, I believe he was a catalyst for maintaining morale, in the trenches with his native West Yorks Regiment and in his beloved 7 Squadron in the RFC, when casualties were severe, and the thought of the consequences of being shot down was ever present at the back of men's minds, the more so as there were no parachutes in those days.

During his years in the trenches he sometimes volunteered to work in the Field Dressing Stations and these experiences sowed the seeds of his calling to medicine. He volunteered to stay on in the Army of Occupation to help to finance his medical training. Upon demobilisation late in 1919 he put his vocation to the test and read medicine at Oxford and St Thomas's Hospital. At University, where his generation recaptured their lost youth and where he was immensely happy, he was one of the oldest undergraduates. He was asked to be Best Man to several friends eight or nine years his junior.

He was a popular visitor to my mother's family's homes in Scotland, where his enthusiasm and ability as a raconteur ensured repeat invitations for shooting, fishing and social occasions.

Sadly, his marriage to my mother, Sheena, was not a success and indeed broke up before the span of my memory. Loving them both, I can understand how great was their incompatibility, aggravated by the 12 year gulf between them and, no doubt, by the stresses of the recession. My father was a 33-year-old who had had a very full and adventurous life, desperate to earn his living and prove himself in his new practice; my mother, a 21-year-old on the threshold of life, yearning for fun after a somewhat strict Presbyterian upbringing. Countless outings were cancelled at the last moment when duty called, and temperamentally they were not suited.

After they separated in 1932, my father had a lonely life, lightened by his devoted patients, by wonderful friends who invited him to join them for sporting holidays, by cultural jaunts to London, and by glimpses of my sister Fiona and me on occasional weekend and school visits. His main therapy was his garden in Radlett, upon which he lavished the greatest care and attention, and which at every season of the year was a delight. A vital contribution to his well-being was a wonderful Cockney housekeeper, "Hawkie", who played an essential role in a busy doctor's household, not least sorting the urgent from the fussy calls.

My first memories of my father go back to the mid-Thirties, when he would fetch me from my mother's house in Surrey for a weekend visit. Suffering from fearful sickness (he was a dreadful stop-go driver), I remember asking "Tell me about the War, Dad." For many years both before and after the war I used to accompany him on his rounds with long spells sitting in his old Austin Seven by some country cottage or Radlett mansion while he went to visit the sick. He would get out of the car, grab his stethoscope and medical bag and trot up to the door, resplendent with a sprig of winter jasmine, snowdrops, cyclamen, a rose or sweet peas in his button-hole according to the season, and launch into his happy trilling whistle. However grave or deeply concerned the face that welcomed him, on his departure that same sad face would be brightened with Doc's legacy of hope, comfort and encouragement. Sometimes I would be summoned to see some intriguing pet or picture or new baby, and not infrequently just to be shown off. He was always the same whether it was to squire's mansion or ploughman's cottage; to Scottish Rugby Captain's or village footballer's home that we went.

I remember the peaceful routine of Sunday mornings. I would join him in his vast double bed and there would follow a companionable hour reading the papers, enlivened by his pithy comments on the political scene or the latest epic sporting event.

On half-days we would repair to the zoo, armed with a copious quantity of his pears and apples for his favourite animals. There were shrieks of mirth from bystanders, when, as a wee boy on my father's shoulders, I boomed, "Daddy, that baboon needs some ointment." On other occasions we would go to those marvellous Mickey Mouse and Silly Symphony movie theatres where we would sit enthralled, usually seeing the whole show twice round. At other times I would happily play in the garden with my lead soldiers for hours on end and would have a fine parade or major battle in the rockery (the Khyber Pass!) for inspection on his return from surgery or visits. I seem to remember spending most of my weekend leaves from the Navy high in his apple trees, pruning.

Small wonder that when the gathering storm clouds of World War II cast a shadow over his somewhat lonely existence he volunteered with alacrity as a doctor for the Royal Air Force Volunteer Reserve. It was his proud boast that he served his King and country from first day to last in both World Wars. He relished the companionship and the opportunity to participate in the Herculean task of defeating Hitler & Co. He was a much respected "Doc", and the Observers' wing and row of World War I ribbons on his chest earned him the respect of his youthful fellow airmen. He rose to the rank of Wing Commander and was awarded the Air Efficiency Award for his work as Senior Medical Officer of big Training Command Groups.

Apart from his garden, what kept his boundless energy and enthusiasm going were invitations to fish in Scotland, most often on those magnificent fly-fishing rivers the Brora and the Oykel in the far North. For this great privilege he was indebted to three very special friends: Huddy (A C Hudson, a bachelor and much-loved Harley Street and St Thomas's specialist who used to take the whole of the Oykel and its hotel for the month of June, as well as the Brora at other times); Miles Brunton, a friend and patient, and Jessie Tyser, a Boudicca-like character with a heart of gold, at whose impressive shooting lodge, Gordonbush, he had many a refreshing holiday when fishing the Brora. In early days my father is reputed to have made a skilful and timely diagnosis when one of Jessie's children was desperately ill.

He also enjoyed wonderful sporting holidays with his farming cousins, the Patersons at Invergordon. These four sets of people made the entire difference to his lonely middle years, from his separation in 1932 to his re-marriage in 1961. By including me and sometimes my sister these kind hosts enabled him to enjoy the company of his children. Patients also invited him for many a day's fine shooting in the Hertfordshire countryside. During the war we would patrol the remoter country areas near his base or my school in the car, armed with a .22 rifle and some brass neck and set about bagging an unsuspecting pheasant, partridge or rabbit for the pot. To his dying day he used to love to recount how, with adrenalin pumping, I had made him wait, rifle out of car window longer than prudent, for two partridges in a grazing covey to come into line – then "bang" and to my father's delight and astonishment, I ran out and collected two birds – one shot! Such fun, but on mature reflection it was quite a risk for a Wing Commander to take.

It was not until 1960, after nearly 30 years on his own and on the eve of his retirement, that he courted and finally won the hand of Paula Colyer, a nurse whom he had known for many years. She was a brave woman to take on my father after 55 years a spinster. She looked after him beautifully, fed him like a fighting cock, kept him in order, and enjoyed many holidays with him including four as our guests in Brazil.

After a few years doing locums and attending some private patients, my father finally retired in 1969 at the age of 74 and he and Paula moved to the Hampshire village of Rockbourne. There they created another superb garden – but harmony was only possible after Paula decreed that she would look after the flowers and lawns, and he could tend the fruit and vegetables! How well the system worked. They had 23 happy years together and her contribution to our family scene was enormous. She was greatly loved and respected. Their many friends relished the thought of Paula's culinary treats. Together they made a beautiful little home and guests loved to share the joy my father found in the many unusual treasures he had inherited, been given by grateful patients or which he himself had collected. These ranged from a silver-mounted Derby winner's hoof to a Roman ring! "He possessed them, but was not possessed by them." Throughout his life he had a keen interest in all things cultural. He knew London's museums and art galleries intimately and could describe his favourite pictures even in foreign galleries in great detail. He was especially stimulated by obtaining scarce tickets for Covent Garden, a major theatre or Promenade Concert and sharing the occasion with family or friends.

In the later parts of the book, I have filled out Peter's story by quoting extracts from his Game Book and letters. Our relationship during the 25 years I was working in South America was kept alive, nay enhanced, by a lively correspondence. We gave him details of our busy lives, his grandchildren's progress and of our adventures in remote parts of the Andes and Amazon, from which he could quote intimate details to his dying day; and he, for his part, gave us an enthralling succession of reports on his fishing, shooting and other activities, as well as delightful cameos about our children who visited him and Paula for *exeats* and also about my sister Fiona and her four children.

One final point, I must mention how my father's strong faith in God sustained him throughout his life. Due to his background as a choirboy in Yorkshire he knew most hymns, prayers and collects by heart and frequently headed his letters with the relevant Saint's day or religious festival, and always ended with *"Dominus vobiscum"*. How fitting that Reverend Tony Willmont took as the text for his funeral address "Blessed are the pure in heart, for they shall see God."

Enough of my views on Dad's life, let him tell you his story himself. I hope you enjoy it as much as I have done, sorting and preparing this account of the little man who "lived his life with courage and panache", was "game to the end" and "used to enfold us all with his love, affection and fun."

Michael Wilson<br>
Brasenose College Library and<br>
High Auchensail Farm, Cardross, Dumbarton. G82 5HN<br>
January 1993

# Chapter One

## IN THE BEGINNING . . . A Yorkshire Childhood

Ever since my retirement from General Practice, where I spent 48 years at Radlett in Hertfordshire, members of my family and many friends have frequently suggested to me that I should write my life story. Happily, I have a good memory and the unique experience of having taken part, from the first day to the last, in World War I and World War II. My life has been filled with thrilling experiences. Perhaps it was due to my extensive experience of treating the wounded in the trenches in 1915 that I was led to follow a career in Medicine following World War I. I was very reluctant to proceed with this venture as I felt so many writers had flooded the literary world with their writings. So it was not until I was in my late 80's that I took up a pen to relate my history.

I was born in December 1894 when my Father was Huntsman to the Atherstone Pack in Leicestershire and my earliest memories surrounded the closing years of the century[*]. I well remember seeing the wounded soldiers in Colchester, wearing blue hospital uniforms, who had returned from the Boer War in South Africa. My Father moved from the Atherstone to carry the horn for the Essex and Suffolk Hunt about the time of Queen Victoria's Diamond Jubilee, 1897, and he enjoyed a happy and successful period until his retirement in 1903. I remember that in his last day hunting the pack he brushed three foxes – a successful termination to his long career. He could now look forward to his retirement after being associated with a succession of famous packs. He commenced his hunting career with the Duke of Buccleuch's pack and was out with the hunt the very next day after the Tay Bridge Disaster when hounds in full cry passed close by the scene of this tragic disaster. He then joined his family who were living in Co. Waterford, Ireland, and was whip to the Marquees of Waterford's pack at Curraghmore, County Waterford. His next move was to take up the appointment of first whip to the Belvoir – the Duke of Rutland's famous pack. This period was certainly the golden age of hunting when huge fields raced across the cream of Leicestershire and there were no motor cars or farm tractors to dislocate sport or ruin scent.

---

[*] His father, Arthur George Wilson 1855-1935 mother Barbara Annie Wilson (née Hull) c. 1860-1929.

After many happy seasons in the mid-eighties he was offered the horn at the famous York & Ainsty Pack at Acomb near York. York was the large Military Centre of the Northern Command, and large and extensive barracks at Fulford accommodated a large Cavalry Unit and Infantry Battalions. Officers of the Cavalry Regiments greatly enjoyed hunting with the York and Ainsty, and famous cavalry regiments, e.g. 18th Hussars and Royal Scots Guards, were present in force throughout the hunting season to enjoy thrilling runs on the famous Ainsty country.

In 1901 Queen Victoria died and I was taken to her memorial service at Stratford St Mary's Church. I was then six years old and well remember the muffled peal of bells following the service, which greatly impressed me. Edward VII succeeded to the throne, but he died in 1910. He did not enjoy the best of health and it is interesting to note that he was the first patient to face the operation for appendicitis.

*Arthur George Wilson (father) in hunting kit, 1880s.*

After his final season hunting hounds, my father retired and the family moved north and took up residence at Haxby – three miles from York. We had a comfortable home, Ashtree House, with a delightful walled garden and my father soon acquired two hunters, as our residence was situated in the midst of three famous hunts, the York & Ainsty, Lord Middleton's and the Bramham Moor. It was a joy for my father to be domiciled in the heart of the York & Ainsty country, where in the eighties, he had enjoyed several seasons as Huntsman. So in the hunting season he could have three days hunting a week and he became Hunting Correspondent to the *Horse and Hound* and the *Yorkshire Herald*, and writing under the nom de plume of "Forrard On".

In my father's late 70s he was out with the York & Ainsty when hounds were in full cry and running over the country between Bessingbrough Hall and the village of Bessingbrough, heading for the River Ouse well below the confluence of the River Ure and River Nidd. My father felt fox and hounds would cross the River Ouse, so knowing that there was an operating sand ferry just below the junction of the river Ure and Nidd, my Father left the main body of the hunt and rode off towards the ferry. Happily on arriving he found the ferry stationary on the nearside bank with the Ferryman present. My father persuaded the ferryman to conduct him and his mount across the river to the opposite bank so he quickly led his mount on to the sand barge and they were soon across. On arriving at the far bank my father led his horse up the bank and quickly mounted and galloped off following the track where he felt the pack of hounds had pursued the hunted fox. Very soon he made contact with the hounds who were in full cry. What a joy for the old huntsman to be in the saddle again, hunting his pack. The hounds continued to follow the fox crossing many fields and heading for Marston Moor as did "Forrard On" and his mount in splendid solitude revelling in this unique hunt.

Incidentally at this point the hounds were hunting the fox over the very ground where in 1644, at the Battle of Marston Moor, Prince Rupert (King Charles I Master of Horse) fought so gallantly. I must mention here that the Master, Huntsman and all the Field were left stranded on the opposite bank of the River Ouse, now about two miles away!

Finally hounds rolled over the fox and my father dismounted and joined in the closing moments of this thrilling hunt surrounded by the whole pack of hounds. After securing the brush my father remounted his hunter and had the joy of seeing the whole pack of hounds following him as he led them on the long ride back towards the river where he joined up with the Master, the Hunt and the Huntsman and Whipper-in to reveal his thrilling story!

My father enjoyed a long retirement and continued to hunt until his 80th year and in the evening, after a glorious day with hounds he could re-live the excitements of the day writing his hunting reports.

In my very early days I always enjoyed driving in our trap round the country lanes and some of the local men had early types of "boneshakers" – a bicycle with one large and one small wheel which possessed solid rubber tyres. Then all of a sudden a thrilling appearance on the roads of the early types of motor cars provided me with much excitement. On at least two occasions I saw an early car with brass paraffin lamps and a steaming boiling corrugated radiator, stranded on a fairly steep hill. A local farmer was called upon to harness a heavy cart horse which had strong ropes attached to its massive body. After much excitement the horse towed the stranded car safely up the hill. Many children and several adults greatly enjoyed seeing this exciting episode as this dramatic new form of locomotion was launched on our metalled roads. On another occasion I saw a man walking in front of a slowly moving motor car (I think an early French Renault Car) waving a red flag, as it climbed slowly up a hill.

At this time all the roads were built-up by a metalled surface and sections were constructed by specially broken flints which were collected at various points on the road side. It was at these collecting centres that a "stone breaker" was constantly employed. Cart loads of heavy rock were delivered from local quarries and this sturdy Spartan labourer sat down on some sacks and, with his very strong hammer, firmly set about crunching the stone – this operation went on for months as the large rocks were reduced to a special size for laying on tracks of the road. It was quite an entertainment to watch a heavy steam roller in operation as it built up sections of the main roads. The stone breaker had to wear special spectacles which were constructed with a wire gauze frame: it was of paramount importance that his eyes should be adequately protected from minute splinters of flint which without protection would be highly dangerous.

I was very happy as a pupil at St Peter's School, York, one of the oldest schools in England which was founded in AD 627. I enjoyed the academic side of school life and cricket, rugby, and rowing gave me ample interest in the realm of sport. It is interesting to note that Guy Fawkes was a pupil at St Peter's School and I have seen his signature in the School Register as "Guido Fawkes".

Our family life was surrounded by great happiness and every Sunday we attended Church at 8 a.m. – Holy Communion where I acted as Server to our Rector – Matins 10.30, Evensong 6.30. There was also Sunday School in the afternoon and I sang solos at Whitsun and the Harvest Festival in the village choir. We had family prayers every evening with my father reading the prayers.

*The Wilson family in the garden, Haxby c. 1903.*
*From left to right on seat: Mary, Barbara Annie (mother), Peter, Barbara; with Arthur standing and Edward in the front.*

*St Peter's School, York 1910.*
*Peter behind headmaster in centre; his future brother-in-law, Eric Monkman, on his left.*

One Sunday morning after church, wearing my Eton suit and small bowler hat (which was a target for many snowballs *en route* for church), I went with my friend Eric Monkman for a walk to the River Foss. We were soon sitting on the parapet of the bridge gazing into the river below, looking for cruising fish. Suddenly I observed a Jack Pike swimming downstream and in my eagerness and enthusiasm I stretched so far that I lost my balance and tumbled in to the river. I collected my floating bowler and struggled up the bank looking like a sort of drenched hen. I had quite a long walk home which meant I had to face several parishioners returning from the mid-day Eucharist. Needless to say I felt I could not face entering my home by the front door so I quickly entered by the back door, just as lunch was about to be served. My sister soon discovered my plight and within seconds my father appeared and my story of the disaster stimulated him into action. He speedily collected his hunting crop and administered a fierce beating which seemed to be more intense through my wet trousers. No lunch for me that Sunday and I speedily discarded my drenched clothes and returned to my bed but not before twisting my torso in front of a mirror to observe some red herrings which had made impressions on my buttocks. I had not been in bed long when I received a visit from my beloved mother who brought me a slice of cake!*

We had a lovely walled garden and our gardener, Shaw (a grand old Yorkshire type), had been very active with the spring sowing of vegetable seeds. I wanted some worms for fishing in the River Foss – but had no luck from the well-established manure heap so I was tempted to investigate a newly planted pea row. This was an easy problem and provided me with a generous supply of worms, which I put in a tin with some moss which helped to clean the worms. Then I went to the river and spent a happy day but was not very successful. When swimming in the river I heard my reel whizzing so I climbed on to the bank and rushed to my rod and found I had a large eel firmly hooked, so completely naked I landed the eel – my only catch of the day. I was reminded of an early verse written about the time of Isaac Walton.

---

* It was about this time that Barbara Annie's sister Mary Elizabeth, lost her husband and the Wilsons took her and her daughter Florence ("Flopsy") into their home at Ashtree House. They remained here until 1935 when my father's father died. His daughter Barbara, then aged 45, who had faithfully run the home for many years, was then able to marry Harry Broughton (now a Canon of York minster), a much loved parson who still today (1993) holds services in the Dales, having had livings in Farndale, Thirsk and Coxwold.

> Armed cap à pie with baskets bags and rods, the angler early to the river plods. At night the woeful look the truth announce 'The baggage half a ton – the fish an ounce.'

Returning home in the early evening happy and weary I was greeted by my father who was in a state of considerable agitation and he led me to the vegetable garden and pointed out the disturbed pea row. I had no excuse to offer and admitted the pillage for worms and prepared for the anticipated punishment. On entering the house the hunting crop was soon produced and I was firmly beaten, a just reward for my thoughtless action.

In my early teens I became a Sunday School teacher and one Sunday morning attending Matins with my Sunday School Class of little boys aged between eight and ten, the Vicar and congregation were reciting the Litany. In the pew just in front of my class of small boys, the local Doctor's wife was deep in devotion and this venerable lady was always beautifully dressed and on this occasion was gently enjoying the comfort of a large muff held near her chin.

Suddenly the peace and sanctity of the devotions was interrupted by a most unusual episode. One of my wee boys had opened a match box which had enclosed a small frog. Swift to take advantage of a chance to escape, the frog leapt to freedom. In one bound he reached the shelf of the pew containing the hymn books and without delay made another vast leap and landed plum in the middle of Mrs A.'s muff. This action brought loud laughter from all the boys in the pew and Mrs A. suddenly observed the frog with throbbing throat sitting happily on her cosy muff. Mrs A. uttered a subdued cry and flung her arm upwards. This shot the frog into the air which cartwheeled into freedom. The uncontrolled laughter of the wee boys was responsible for causing considerable disturbance to the Litany responses and the Vicar and many of the congregation were totally unable to detect the cause of this unusual disturbance. I was naturally greatly disturbed and had a tense half minute in bringing the wee boys under control. My sister Barbara in the pew behind, sitting with her class of small girls, came to my assistance and it was a mighty relief when many of the congregation turned around from facing our pew and faced the altar and once again we could hear "we beseech Thee to hear us Good Lord".

On the Feast of the Dedication of the Church there was a delightful custom of all the children linking hands around the outside of the church and singing the hymn "We love the place O God." Incidentally, it was not long before the Organist inside the Church was at least two lines ahead of the singing children outside the Church. It was about this time we received a visit from Uncle John and family from New Zealand. Much excitement for all the family, especially mother. It was a thrill for me to chart the progress of the ship, which was reported in the daily newspaper.*

Our village of Haxby was only three miles from York – with its glorious Minster possessing half an acre of superb Mediaeval glass. The Chapter House, adjacent to the North Transept is circular and is used for special assemblies of the Dean and Chapter. All around the base of the large circular building the seats are constructed of stone and accommodate the Dean and Chapter during these special meetings. Several feet above each alcove there is a vast circle of mediaeval stone carvings which surrounds the whole building. This work has been most beautifully executed and records the wonderful talents of the carvers of long centuries ago. In one carving a man is seen with a monocle, in another a Matron washing a boy's ear, but by far the most exciting is one with a Monk tickling a Nun under the chin. The following story relating to this particular carving is quite true and most amusing. The Head Verger who conducted parties of visitors around the Minster told it to me.

During one tour of the Chapter House the Verger was conducting a party of visitors which contained a wide selection of society. Several of the usual tourists, a Yorkshire Farmer, a Roman Catholic Priest and some Nuns. During the course of the tour round the Chapter House the Yorkshire Farmer walked up to the Verger and in a very firm voice – in Yorkshire dialect – said," Eh Mister, wilt'er show us't Monk Tickling t'Nun under't chin?"

The Verger quietly said to the Farmer, "Yes, I'll show you the special carving, but we must be quiet about it as there is an RC Priest and Nuns in the party."

But the Roman Catholic Priest, who had heard the Farmer's request, said, "Oh yes, Verger, I would like to see that carving, too." So, quietly, the Verger told the Farmer and the RC Priest which alcove to visit and look up at the carving. So off they went and gazed up with much interest and delight at this masterpiece of carving. As the Verger joined the Priest and the Farmer, the Priest remarked to the Verger, "As it was in the beginning, is now and ever shall be."

On June 22nd 1911 the country celebrated the Coronation of King George V and Queen Mary and in our village there were great rejoicings. In a

---

* John Hull emigrated to New Zealand in 1891 and had four children William, George, Merville and Constance. On this trip Merville met Gladys Wilson at Ashtree House in Haxby . He was to marry her in 1920.

large barn most of the inhabitants sat down to a cooked lunch. The local Butcher provided a bullock, part of which was roasted and all the children were given a Coronation Mug presented by Mr Wood the Squire at the Hall.

There were sports for the Children and a special cricket match which I had the pleasure and thrill of playing in and I brought off a catch, after a mighty drive, which disposed of the Captain of the village XI.

After leaving St Peter's School, York, I entered Becketts Bank at Knaresborough in 1912 as it was planned for me to have two years training in banking, prior to taking up a career in Malaya. A friend of my Father's, who was an enthusiastic member of the York & Ainsty Hunt, had suggested this.

I greatly enjoyed my early days in Becketts Bank who issued their own £5.00 notes, which, incidentally, the local Yorkshire farmers preferred to the white £5.00 Bank of England notes. In those days there were no £1.00 and 10-shilling currency notes. These were introduced during the 1914-1918 war. It was a delight to shovel up the gold sovereigns and half-sovereigns. As they accumulated they were stored in the Bank safe and at intervals strong bags containing £1,000 worth of sovereigns and half-sovereigns were dispatched to the Head Office in Leeds, no doubt *en route* for the Bank of England in London.

It is perhaps interesting to mention here a feature of agricultural procedure which existed in pre-1914 days in England. Most of the farms were owned by landlords possessing large estates and once a year the rents were paid to the Estate Factor. The farmers paid these rents in £5.00 bank notes and were then given a Tenants' Lunch at a local hotel. The unmarried farm workers received their wages once a year and all lived on the farm in cottages. In this region of Yorkshire there were several small country towns, Knaresborough, Ripon, Wetherby, Thirsk and others.

In the late autumn, after the harvest, these small towns held an agricultural Fair called "The Statice" (Saxon origin) on the Feast of Martinmas, 10th November, commemorating Bishop Martin of Tours (circa. 397). The towns held their Fairs in succession and during the Fair all the farm employees: wagoners, cattlemen, shepherds, etc. congregated in the Market Place and, having received their lump sum year's wages, often fell victims to the tricksters (who regularly attended the Fairs) with the three-card trick or the gold watch sovereign trick. I noticed one crafty villain at work where he would drop three sovereigns into the open watch, before the eyes of the victim, snap the watch sharply and offer the watch plus sovereigns to the eager Ploughman who, on opening the watch, found it empty or holding a few halfpennies!

The reason for this ancient annual Fair was that the farm employees, who were "not stopping on" in the employ of their present employer, presented themselves in the local Market Square wearing in their buttonholes a tag of a certain colour which indicated that they needed new employment. If they already had work they wore a colour which meant they need not be approached by a new master. There was much activity in the Market Square as hosts of farmers were there on the look out for a new employee, be he wagoner, ploughman or cattleman, etc., and he would walk up to a likely man and say "Good morning, is t'a stoppin' on?" If there appeared to be mutual satisfaction a new contract for employment would be arranged and the date for commencement of work at his new farm would be fixed. If the farm worker did not succeed in finding a new post from one Fair he would move on to the next Market town – probably a few days later in the week – where no doubt he would succeed in finding new employment. As far as I remember, the full annual wage round about 1913/1914 would be about £35-£40, some young labourers starting at £20.

# Chapter Two

## THE GREAT WAR . . . with the West Yorkshire Regiment

As the spring of 1914 advanced, the whole countryside presented that glorious picture of nature which is unsurpassed anywhere in the world. All the gardens revealed the thrilling picture of the patches of colour from banks of daffodils, crocuses and the early flowering shrubs. Then the woods swiftly revealed that glorious eruption of nature from the dormant buds to the young embryonic leaves which were greatly enhanced by the sunshine. This scene when walking through the woods with carpets of primroses and bluebells is a delightful revelation and, as the avian chorus mounts with the added joy of the cuckoo, one halts to listen and somehow the voice quietly quotes "O how manifold are Thy Works." It was during one of these walks that I came across two soldiers in khaki uniform as they quietly strolled along with their young children, who were eagerly collecting primroses and bluebells. Already an atmosphere of anxiety had penetrated into the peaceful realm of England and many citizens were prompted to discuss the likelihood of war with Germany. I became engaged in conversation with these two soldiers and said "It looks as if Germany is preparing for war." Both sergeants, members of the 1st Battalion West Yorkshire Regiment, they were prompt to disagree with me and I told them that I had recently joined the Territorials – the 5th West Yorkshire Regiment – and started my martial training at Knaresborough, near Harrogate.

To enlist in the Territorial Force I had presented myself at the small West Yorkshire Regiment Drill Hall at Knaresborough and sworn my oath to our Sovereign King George V and received the King's Shilling. In the early summer the recruits paraded in a field near the Drill Hall two evenings a week and received training in marching and rifle drill and matters relating to army life. On Saturday afternoons all ranks proceeded to the Army Rifle range near Knaresborough and practised shooting with our Lee-Enfield rifles, .303 from ranges 200-500 yards. Here we carried out a full course of musketry and the Sergeant i/c the Depot was a Regular soldier, seconded for duty from the 1st West Yorks. Regiment stationed at York. All the early summer of 1914 we carried out most diligent training in preparation for the annual Territorial Camp to be held at Scarborough in early August. All the volunteer members of the 5th West Yorks. Territorial Force from York, Ripon, Harrogate, Knaresborough and Boroughbridge would join up at York and entrain for Scarborough.

*May 1914. A proud young man joins the Territorials.*

The mid-summer days of 1914 seemed to rush by and a pervading atmosphere of anxiety overshadowed the whole of Europe. There was much excitement at the local Territorial Headquarters in Knaresborough in the final week of July, as the troops were kitted up in readiness for the move to join up with the Battalion in York.

An early rise on the final Saturday in July found all the members of the Knaresborough Company on the local station platform, where they joined up with the larger contingent of troops who had boarded the special train at Harrogate. On arrival at York station there was much activity and with my platoon we were soon detailed to heavy fatigue duties in packing the railway vans with a wide variety of military equipment and stores. The colonel of the Regiment, Colonel C F Wood, the 2nd in command, his Adjutant and the eight Company Commanders were all supplied with horses and their mounts were soon securely packed into horse boxes attached to the train.

There was much extra equipment as all the troops were fitted with "walking-out" uniforms – glowing scarlet tunics, smart caps with a silver badge "The White Horse of Hanover," the West Yorks. Regimental badge. After about two hours of "hustle and bustle" the whole Regiment, fully a thousand strong, paraded plus the full Regimental Band and when all troops and the complete Regiment had entrained the heavily laden train steamed out of York Station *en route* for Scarborough.

After about an hour's journey through the rich agricultural Plain of York, where many cornfields had already been cut and the rolling acres of wheat were turning into gold, the train pulled into Scarborough Station. The Regimental Band was soon stationed at the head of the Regiment and the eight Companies "A" to "H" lined up outside the station. The holiday season was in full swing and Scarborough was packed with visitors so excited crowds watched the Regiment march off with the rifle at the slope, on the route to the Race Course where we would be in camp for a fortnight under canvas. The band led this long military procession with the Colonel and his Adjutant mounted on their horses. Each of the eight companies had a strength of about 120 and as the weather was gloriously fine, the citizens and visitors to Scarborough enjoyed the picture of the Regiment on the march.

The large marquees and lines of tents seemed to give us a welcome and very soon each company had taken up its allotted position. The Battalion Cook and his contingent had already been busy preparing a main meal for the troops and there was much rejoicing as the Battalion Bugler sounded "The Cookhouse." It was incredible how swiftly the various companies filed past the cookhouse benches and were supplied with a generous helping of roast meat, potatoes and carrots into their mess tins.

Our first duty was to parade with our palliasses and fill them with straw and it was quite a surprise to find we had to sleep fifteen in one bell tent – heads to the outside and feet towards the tent pole which was surrounded by fifteen rifles and our equipment.

The Adjutant and his Orderly Room staff had been busy quite early after our arrival in camp and by 6 p.m. Battalion Orders were printed up outside Headquarters, which gave details of the routine orders for the following day. At the end of the orders was a list of Regimental promotions and a friend of mine came up and told me the exciting news that I had been promoted to Lance Corporal. My Platoon Sergeant gave me instructions to parade at the Battalion Tailor's tent and have my stripe sewn on. I was then supplied with a list of names of those who were to be Privates in my section and this new responsibility added greatly to my regimental duties. I was amazed how well I slept in the crowded tent, although a few of my comrades were rather noisy, having been in Scarborough and celebrating. I turned in rather late as I had been on duty with my Platoon Sergeant and was somewhat surprised to find one of the Battalion cobblers had parked himself next to me. Apart from smoking black twist, he smelt very strongly of cobbler's wax and other disturbing odours and I'm certain Shakespeare would have been prompted to record that he was "Surrounded by a foul and pestilential congregation of vapours."

After the Battalion Bugler had sounded the Last Post there was much snoring especially from the fellows who had been celebrating in the local pubs but I was soon asleep and quite oblivious of my new domicile. The night seemed very short as the shrill notes from the Battalion Bugler sounded "The Reveille." Yet it was 6 a.m. and there was quite a rush to the Cookhouse with all troops carrying their mess tins eager to be supplied with "gunfire" (as Kipling quotes), which was tea and biscuits.

Already on parade to watch the troops was the Regimental Sergeant Major, looking immaculate with polished buttons and a swagger cane under his arm. The Regimental Sergeant Major is the only non-commissioned rank entitled to be addressed as "Sir" by all ranks. Sergeant Major Beale was a fiery character who had seen service in India and other stations abroad with the West Yorkshire Regiment. He was standing quite close to the large "dixies" which contained the tea and on tasting mine I noted that it was terribly sweet and most distasteful to me, so I promptly asked the Sergeant Cook who was supervising the Orderlies dispensing the tea, if I could have some tea without sugar. Here I received a spontaneous shock as the Sergeant Major's voice thundered in my ear, "Corporal, what do you want – a bloody nurse?"

Then followed the rush to the ablution benches – all splendidly arranged by the Pioneer Sergeant and his men. Water had been laid on and warm water for the troops who shaved. I was already quite efficient in using my cut-throat razor and with my portable small shaving mirror was soon spick and span and ready for the early morning parade, buttons and boots also polished.

Sunday morning in Camp was gloriously fine and the whole Battalion attended Church Parade, with the band assisting. All officers were stationed in front of their Companies and the Regimental Chaplain preached the sermon. After Church parade the troops were free to leave camp and, clad in their scarlet tunics, were soon marching into Scarborough to mingle with the packed holiday crowds. All the following week was spent in routine military training and daily route marches clad in full operational kit, plus rifle and pack. The weather was fine all our first week in camp and by the end of the week the whole Regiment was a smart body of men, who had obviously benefited from the training and the new experience of living under army conditions. On the Saturday afternoon I noticed on Battalion Orders I was to be Battalion Orderly Corporal, which meant I was to be in attendance at Battalion headquarters where the Adjutant, his Staff and the Regiment Sergeant Major were on the spot ready to deal with any emergencies. Also on duty was the Bugler for the day and he was ready to blow the various calls such as Cookhouse, Orderly Sergeants: Defaulters: Retreat: Last Post etc. Kipling, during his domicile in India was always devoted to the Army and several of the regimental calls were put to verse by him to match the bugle call, for example:

> Cookhouse: "Come to the cookhouse door boys, come to the cookhouse door."
> Sergeant's Mess Call: "Puddings and pies for the Officers' wives – the Sergeants, they get skilly." (mutton stew)

> Defaulters: Special pack drill in full kit found troops sentenced for defaulters' drill. The parade usually taken by a stern Provost Sergeant. (When in India under intense heat this parade was most exhausting.)
> "Left-right-left. You broke your Mother's heart. You can't break mine. About turn."

In the afternoon of my day on duty as Battalion Orderly Corporal, 4th August 1914, almost the whole of the Regiment was free to wander off into Scarborough and enjoy the manifold entertainments. I was reclining near Battalion Headquarters when I heard the thud of a motor bike and as it approached I could see the dispatch rider was from the Corps of Signals. After dismounting, he carried a dispatch case into the Orderly Room. Within the space of a few minutes there was a sudden burst of excitement and a tense atmosphere prevailed. The voice of the Regimental Sergeant Major boomed out "Bugler, sound Orderly Sergeants at the double." Each company A to H (eight) had a Sergeant "on duty" for the day and within a couple of minutes the eight Sergeants lined up in front of the Battalion Orderly Room. From the prevailing peace of a quiet, hot, sunny afternoon the whole scene was transformed into hectic activity. It was clear the dispatch contained orders of vital importance as the Adjutant gave orders for immediate striking of camp and plans were put out to collect the hundreds of troops enjoying their relaxation in the widespread coastal resort of Scarborough, which was divided into extensive North and South bays. As all the troops were in Scarlet they could easily be seen on the sea front. The Orderly Sergeants were soon in contact with their officers as there was much to be done in the striking of tents and with the returning soldiers hurriedly discarding their scarlet walking-out uniforms, all of which had to be packed and ready for store at the Drill Hall in York. There was much excitement in the air as all ranks realised that the crisis which had hung over Europe during the previous week had erupted and the country was on the brink of war with Germany. I shall never forget the scene in camp as the many "fatigue parties" were employed in the transport lines, heavily engaged in packing the transport wagons with the wide variety of military equipment.

Happily the weather was fine and by 8 p.m. the last stragglers from Scarborough had returned to camp and the whole Regiment was now clad in their khaki uniforms. I was told that, as Battalion Orderly Corporal, I was to carry the batch of "sealed orders" and would march between an escort of four soldiers with fixed bayonets, and that my rifle would be carried in one of the transport wagons. By 9 p.m. the whole Regiment was lined up on the Racecourse and the Colonel, mounted on his charger, headed the parade with the Regiment Band to lead the column through the streets of Scarborough to the station. The Company Commanders were mounted and led their platoons who marched at the slope, with fixed bayonets. I was somewhat surprised to find myself marching just behind the Adjutant's horse at the head of the whole Regiment, surrounded by my escort of four with their fixed bayonets and the vital "secret orders" closely gripped in my left arm. It is easy to imagine the electric atmosphere of Scarborough, with its population and thousands of visitors as they crowded the pavements to watch the impressive sight of the Battalion, a thousand strong, on the march with band playing and the prevailing air of tension owing to the imminence of war. By this time it was late in the evening and many residents were in bed but all the bedroom windows were crowded with people and children – many in night attire. In fact I saw many women in night gowns at the front doors and the pavements were packed all the way through the town to the Station. There was much noise and cheering as we marched along and in one street I heard quite clearly a broad Yorkshire lass – as she beheld me enclosed within my escort exclaim, "Oh! Look, that young lad's off to prison!!"

After handing my vital packet of sealed orders to the Orderly Room Sergeant at the Station, I collected my rifle from the transport wagon and joined my comrades in the crowded train and we were soon on the way to York. Much to my surprise we did not leave the train here but travelled on to Selby, where we constructed a new camp under canvas and were given several duties in providing guards for the vital railway bridge over the

River Ouse and the all-important arms magazine of the Northern Command.

*Peter's platoon of lads from Knaresborough rapidly becoming smarter and tougher. (Peter now a corporal.)*

*Also in group: Pte Mumford on Peter's right – killed at Turco Farm, buried at Essex Farm; Pte Walter Malthouse – killed at Aubers Ridge 1915, buried at Fauquissart Cemetery (see page 278 and chapter 13); Pte Peacock – "marvellous at wiring parties in No Man's Land" – killed at Turco Farm; also Mumford's brother and De Lacy.*

My Company was given the early 24 hour guard duty and I was Corporal of the Guard for this 24 hour spell. I mounted my guard at each end of the bridge with loaded rifles (live ammunition) and the troops had two hours on and four hours off. My Platoon officer, a 2nd Lieutenant, visited the Guard during the night. I was asleep between spells of duty and about 4 a.m., three or four shots from one of the sentries speedily called me to the alert and I dashed out, expecting that there had been an attack on the bridge and that the "enemy" was at hand. It was a dark night with much cloud and little moonlight. Here I should mention that just across the field, about 200 yards from the vital railway bridge, was a large advertisement on a wooden structure comprising two men walking and carrying a large wooden notice advertising "Halls Paint" and with a painted notice "London 190 miles." These wooden advertisements could be seen at frequent intervals on the railway route from York to London. When daylight arrived I made a trip over the field to inspect the "nocturnal enemy" and to my surprise found that one of the wooden men on the advertisement had a badly shattered thigh. Needless to say, there was much fun and ridicule in the various Companies of the Regiment on how the enemy had been repulsed! After a short spell of duty here the Regiment returned to York to be re-equipped and then moved on to the Strensal Camp, where we took over from a Regular Regiment who made a rapid move to join the BEF (British Expeditionary Force) in France.

The early days of the war, while at Selby were spent in special training exercises and daily route marches in battle dress helped to toughen us up. The end of August saw the Regiment installed in various billets in York and my Company was quartered in the large carriage works of the North Eastern Railway. As the winter days approached the weather became much colder and with a few comrades we decided to take a cold shower bath after the shrill bugle call of Reveille had called us to action. In December we carried on with this Spartan activity and in the darkness beneath the stars we felt quite lively and ready for the manifold sections of the long day's training. Each day after breakfast, the whole Battalion would march in full kit about three miles out of the city of York to suitable grounds, sometimes marching on to the famous Knavesmire Race Course for rifle drill.

On the morning of 16th December 1914, the whole Battalion was in the middle of battle exercises near the village of Copmanthorpe. The Brigadier and his Staff, mounted on their horses, together with our own Regimental Colonel, were busily engaged watching the lively activity of the troops when suddenly there was a violent succession of thunderlike eruptions, coming from the region north east of the city of York. The violent explosions seemed to rock the whole countryside and went on for several minutes. Within the space of a few seconds the Brigadier gave the order to his Bugler to sound "The Close at the double" and it was clear a Naval Bombardment was in operation about 40 miles away, in the region of Scarborough. It was amazing how swiftly the Battalion was assembled in marching order and *en route* for York Station where a train was in readiness to conduct the Regiment to Scarborough to repel the invader.

Incidentally, we did not entrain for Scarborough. History records that units of the German High Seas Fleet had slipped out into the North Sea and, one unit bombarded Scarborough and the other unit Whitby and Hartlepool. After a short bombardment with heavy shells, much damage was done. 119 were killed, mainly women and children and numerous casualties were inflicted. Incidentally, the German Fleet made a hasty retreat back to their home ports.

Training continued in the New Year with York as Headquarters. I decided to enter the Regimental Boxing competition and, with little training, I duly faced my opponent in my vest. To my surprise my opponent, quite six inches taller than myself, had a very marked squint. Having survived the first round, I faced up to the second and during the early moments I was wondering which eye was concentrating on my person; alas my doom was sealed as a smart left hook to my chin sent me to the boards and a cold wet sponge brought me back to reality.

In late January the Battalion moved to Strensal Camp, where we carried out musketry on the Northern Command Rifle Ranges. It was here that I took command of a large early morning parade of the whole Battalion, plus Junior Officers, in Physical Drill and my PT training when at St Peter's School, York, stood me in good stead. From this camp we underwent extensive Night Training, no doubt to prepare us for warfare thereafter.

In March the Battalion moved to the Lincolnshire coast, near Sutton-on-Sea where we had special training in manning deep trenches, where we spent all night, and this was extremely cold in the sand dunes.

All the troops received a course of injections in preparation for our service overseas. In early April, the Battalion moved to Gainsborough and we were kitted out for movement overseas. The arrival of a large number of mules from South America with limbers,* led us to believe that very soon we would be moving to join the BEF in France.

None of the troops had embarkation leave and my Father and Mother came down to Gainsborough to say farewell, which consisted of a short half hour on the station platform. It was 14th April when the Battalion entrained and we left for an unknown destination. Much activity was afoot as the Battalion boarded a special troopship of Dover and before long we moved out into the darkness of the English Channel, escorted by two destroyers and heading for France.

## To France with the Regiment

Happily we had a smooth crossing and we slowly entered Boulogne harbour at 10.20 p.m. It took about two hours to disembark all the troops and the mass of equipment. The whole Battalion paraded on the extensive quayside and then marched through the town to a large Camp which was a transit centre and each Company was provided with bell tents accommodating fifteen to each tent. By this time all the troops were hungry and we were soon paraded and marched to the extensive cookhouses where we received large buckets of hot tea, a tin of Bully Beef

---

* A limber was a horse drawn (gun) carriage.

and large hard biscuits. We spent the day in the Camp and were told we would move by train in the morning of 16th April up to the Front. I slept well for my first night with the BEF and we were paraded early in readiness for boarding the troop train. At the station there were several troop trains which consisted of large trucks which had painted on their sides "*8 chevaux + 40 hommes!*" We soon boarded the train and each truck contained 45 soldiers. We made slow progress through the countryside and after a long devious journey of seven hours we finally arrived on the night of the 16th April at Merville about ten miles from the firing line. We marched about three kilometres and arrived at a farm where we slept on straw.

It was a great shock for me to find that the latrines here were in full view of civilians who used a public path to and from the village only about 20 yards away. Slit trenches had been dug and along them tree trunks were suspended between cross wooden supports. There were no canvas strips or any protection to prevent the local civilians from having a full view of lines of squatting troops with shining bums in the operation of defecation. I found this enforced exposure of my nether regions most embarrassing and especially when one had to perform in the gaze of laughing French girls. I had to put up with this trying experience for several days and was greatly relieved when we moved up to the region nearer the front line where better latrines were provided by the Battalion Pioneer Sergeant, and we were far from the public gaze.

We had been in France a week and we were now much nearer the firing line and slept in barns which were partly destroyed. All villages were totally destroyed – some of the heavy artillery were frequently in action and long range enemy shells often fell in our vicinity. Two of our company Sergeants were detailed to proceed to the front line trenches for instruction in Trench Warfare. The Battalion moved on to Estaires and on 23rd, St George's Day, Gen. French inspected the Brigade. A fierce battle was raging for Hill 60 which was lost but a brilliant counter-attack by the gallant Indian Division re-captured the famous hill.

On Sunday 25th April I went to Holy Communion in a barn, conducted by the Battalion Chaplain and I received my first parcel from home containing boiled eggs, cakes, chocolates, butter and fruit. Then the first ration of cigs were dished out to the troops, 20 cigs per man. That evening we marched into the forward area and into the trenches where we had a hot reception from the enemy rifle fire. It was most exciting to find oneself in action for the first time and I fired several rounds at the Hun trenches only 200 yards away. But I soon learned that random sniping at the enemy was fraught with danger, as the German snipers were deadly with their telescopic sights. We were in the front line trenches between Laventie and Neuve Chapelle and one of my Corporal friends was shot by a sniper in the chest – our first casualty.

One night I was detailed for a patrol between the lines and took six of my section with me – this was a hair-raising experience and we manned a listening post only 120 yards from the German trenches. All the time both sides fired star shells which illuminated the region of No-Man's Land and often fell near patrols or wiring parties. The barbed wire defences which helped to protect both front lines revealed the tragic picture of the recent battle of Neuve Chapelle and were piled with the British dead which were entangled in the barbed wire, some could be seen wearing kilts. Even in our own small listening post there was the body of a dead member of the Essex Regiment. It was tragic that these gallant heroes could not be collected and buried. On these nocturnal patrols one could hear the constant screaming of rats which continued through the night – a most unpleasant reminder of the grim reality of war. After ten days in the front line my company were relieved and I had my first wash and we were told that we would be returning to the front line in readiness for a big attack – "Aubers Ridge".

On Sunday May 9th the whole Battalion went into action and a terrific bombardment of the German trenches at zero hour 5 a.m. raged. Very soon the German counter barrage was intense and no progress could be made. I had about ten of my section in my portion of the front line trench and we were taking what little cover we could from enemy shelling. Suddenly there was a terrific explosion and we all seemed to be blown up and the whole region was charged with the rank smell of explosive gases. I was partly buried by timber and trench debris and there seemed to be blood everywhere. One of my comrades, Walter Malthouse, (who was very close to me) was blown to pieces as he had received a direct hit from the heavy shell (high explosive) and was killed instantly[*]. I was greatly stunned and shocked but felt that I had not been wounded, although I was only a few inches from my comrade. I found that two other comrades had been wounded. This was a grim baptism to the reality of war and when I had been extricated from the gory shambles, I gathered up the shattered limbs and torso of my comrade (I knew his mother in Knaresborough,

---

[*] This story features in Lyn Macdonald's book: 1915 The Death of Innocence – to be published in 1993. My father was quite specific in relating the story to the author (and to me on a separate occasion): the shell was British. Indeed after my father had conducted a short burial service from his prayer book, when doubt was (naturally) expressed at Peter's opinion, he and some of the other Knaresborough lads dug until they found the nose cone. The W.D. (War Department) mark thereon gave all the proof that was needed.

Yorkshire) and put them in a sand bag ready for burial.* No stretcher bearers were available for this disaster so we cleared up the shattered trench and dealt with the wounded. As the news of the tragedy spread along the front line we were visited by our Platoon Commander who was stunned to hear the details, and he told me that our Company Commander had been wounded in the neck and been carried on a stretcher to the Forward Dressing station.

I had heard only a few hours before that Rupert Brooke had died on St George's Day in a French hospital ship in the Dardanelles and had been buried on the Isle of Skyros. Here surely his immortal words ring true, as I quote for my gallant comrade:

> If I should die, think only this of me:
> That there's some corner of a foreign field
> That is for ever England.

During the long march into Belgium we had no billets and slept in barns and sheds when we could and on one occasion I slept in a hen house with legs over the perch. I had a good night's sleep and in the early morning was amazed to see a large grand cockerel turn his head sideways to view his visitor. About 30 hens did not worry about my being there.

As each soldier only had one shirt it was impossible to keep the lice under control, but daily inspection of the shirt seams ended in a good bag. I frequently boiled my shirt in a large biscuit tin and found this helpful in controlling the fleas.

### Extracts from diary

### May 15th 1915

> *After Aubers Ridge the Battalion came out of the trenches for a rest and were only 4 miles from the Belgian border where we prepared to go into the trenches at Fleurbaix, N. of Laventie. The approach to the trenches was all sticky mud and waterlogged. But the trenches were worse – deep in mud and flooded, and there were no dry dugouts. We had to rest, eat and sleep on wooden platforms in the trenches. Rain made matters worse. In front a large number of our dead were lying in No-Man's Land. I spotted a modern rifle and*

---

* Through an article in the Independent in 1988 Peter was contacted by Walter Malthouse's, nephew who was born in 1915 and named after his uncle.

bayonet about 30 yards in front of our trenches, so took very careful observations and crawled out in the evening and succeeded in collecting this super rifle and bayonet in perfect condition. Heard that our Company Commander was making satisfactory progress in hospital.

I did some laundry and boiled my shirt in biscuit tin and went regularly through seams of shirt for lice. Barbara sent me out some powder (Boots Vermin in the Trenches) – very successful. I was in a billet at the farm where Durbar II was trained and who won the Derby in 1914.

The Company went to a brewery and had the first bath for six weeks. We bathed in large wooden vats – a real treat.

During a further spell in the trenches I was detailed for wiring parties – these operations were carried out in No Man's Land and the frequent firing of Star Shells demanded that all members dealing with the awful barbed wire had to lie flat immediately, or German snipers were very quick to spot any movement. I was always glad to get back to our trenches after these wiring parties.

I was also glad to be able to attend to casualties as stretcher bearers were not always available especially in isolated parts and deep down within my mind I had feelings that if I was fortunate in surviving this war I would like to train as a doctor. During one spell in the trenches we had a company of Gurkhas with us. I felt very secure and happy to have these gallant little soldiers with us and they were very friendly – they had British Officers in command of their unit.

When in the trenches at Fleurbaix, each morning at "stand-to" (at dawn) all the troops had to use a special gauze respirator covering the nose and mouth – this precaution had to be taken owing to the Germans using heavy tear gas, which they released if the wind was favourable – blowing the gas towards our trenches. Before being placed over the mouth and nose the gauze respirator was soaked in urine which had been contained in large tins which were used by the troops during the night. Much to the relief of the troops this vital period of "stand-to" only lasted for about 10-15 minutes.

In early July the whole West Riding Brigade marched northward and the long route marches, often 15 miles a day, in full kit were most exhausting. I was very careful with my foot hygiene and regular cutting of toe nails.

On the march we rested ten minutes every hour and frequently we had to face up to heavy rain and thunderstorms. During these early months I found great spiritual consolation in being able to attend services of Holy Communion, held in barns behind stacks and often with the roar of guns to accompany our devotions.

Our long marches northwards led us through Poperinge and Proven and we finally came within sight of Ypres with the shattered Cloth Hall and the ancient city in ruins. We crossed the Yser canal and could hear the incessant German bombardment of the city in progress.

We soon took over an advanced position of the trench system North of Ypres at Turco Farm[*], as our portion of the front line was known, about the most advanced station on the British Front. Here I was able to spot huge mortar shells as they tore through the air from the German mortar positions. I got quite expert in spotting these huge shells and soon learned that one must fix one's gaze well in front of the roar of the rapidly moving shell. At night the ration parties, brought up by gallant drivers with their mule teams, had an assembly point not far from the famous Bridge 4 on the Yser Canal. Of course the German Gunners were well aware that the assembled limbers with mules and mounted drivers made highly visible targets with all the rations and fresh water for the large numbers of troops manning the trenches in the Ypres Salient.

Frequently the fierce bombardment caused heavy casualties to the gallant drivers, their mules and the collecting ration parties. I went frequently on the ration fatigues and I was amazed to see the expert technique that accompanied them. The limbers were emptied with amazing speed and the organised parties collected their appointed rations and rapidly re-crossed Bridge 4 on the return journey to their various units, some two miles deep into the Ypres Salient. It was quite exciting to see how rapidly the mules with their riders commenced the return journey back to their transport lines, four to five miles back, greatly relieved that they had delivered the precious rations safely. Carrying the heavy ration packages was no simple matter in the pitch dark and often a member of a ration party would slip in the mud off a duck board and find himself wallowing in the deep mud, often up to the waist.

On one occasion I stumbled over a heavy sand bag in the dark and on getting up I collected a heavy sodden bag (obviously filled with rations). I carried my treasure quite a long tramp in the dark and finally arrived at my Platoon Headquarters in the front line. On opening the bag I found several tins of condensed milk – a packet of bacon, a bag of tea (alas very wet) but the greatest find was a huge tin of precious NZ butter, at least 14 lbs. There was also a big jar of sugar. This valuable ration was obviously not associated with my regiment as the Ypres Salient contained several

---

[*] Turco Farm – So called after the French Colonial troops in baggy trousers who had manned that part of the front. Also the sector where the Germans used gas for the first time in 1915.

Brigades of Troops. This supplementary gift of precious foods was greatly enjoyed by myself and members of my platoon and even the hard ration biscuits seemed to equal any Huntley and Palmer's with the tasty NZ butter.

Our spell in the trenches continued throughout the summer. We had many casualties and I lost several gallant friends. On one occasion we were 36 days holding an advanced position without relief. We were under constant mortar and rifle grenade fire, the latter being a lethal and devastating weapon of immense power. It could not be seen or heard, only sometimes a strange thud could be heard when the weapon was fired – a vague and anxious warning.

During rest periods, out of the trenches, we were able to make visits to Poperinge and enjoyed visiting Toc H where the Reverend Tubby Clayton gave us a great welcome and it was great fun to attend the Concert Party which regularly gave evening concerts. When our rest camp was near the Château at Elverdinghe I presumed to try my hand at fishing as I observed some large carp and other fish in the large lake. I wrote to my sister Barbara and asked her to send me a fishing line, some catgut and some hooks and these arrived in a very short time. I found a suitable tough willow which made an excellent rod and I ventured forth to the precious water. The fish quickly took my bait and I soon had some fine fish on the bank. But suddenly in the midst of my joy a voice thundered behind me, "What do you think you are doing here?" (I knew the Brigade Headquarters was quartered in the Château so I expected all the Brigade Staff would be in residence.) Immediately I recognised the Brigadier himself, so I jumped sharply to attention and found it hard to offer any excuse. The Brigadier suddenly seemed to mellow into understanding and asked how I had obtained the hooks and tackle. I told him I had written to my sister in Yorkshire and that the tackle and hooks had only just arrived. The Brig. carried on with a friendly conversation and put me at ease and I told him I would restrict my catch and was returning to my unit almost at once. He quietly walked away with a twinkle in his eye and the guilty poacher made his way back to his unit. I didn't return to fish at the Château de Trois Tours but did try my luck in the Yser Canal, but this was very difficult as the mud was so thick and deep – the Germans had dammed the canal some kilometres west of Ypres some months before. I did catch a few fish in the Yser Canal, mostly roach, but on one occasion when I attempted a swim with a friend, a German observer in a Kite Balloon must have observed us and given the warning to some German gunner who promptly shelled us. Four shells crashed into the canal, far too near us to be pleasant. Up sprayed the mud and water and about two dozen dead fish floated to the surface. We made a hasty retreat to the north of the canal crawling through the deep mud and arrived in a filthy state and then had to collect enough water to cleanse our bodies.

It was when we were in reserve positions adjacent to the Canal that I watched Bruce Bairnsfather painting at his easel and he was always friendly. How fortunate that I have a bound copy of all his war pictures entitled *Fragments from France* produced by the Bystander.

One day, when walking along the canal bank I observed the Brigadier, his monocle fixed in his eye, very diligently going through the seams of his shirt and dealing with the alien lice who had taken up residence in his garment. He seemed to be having a good harvest and I passed along leaving him in "full cry."

### *Extracts from diary*

*All August in trenches – many casualties and several friends killed, being on wiring parties and subject to counter-bombardments. Very frequent heavy rains and trenches very muddy. Had to share gum boots when on duty as some troops suffered from trench feet. (The whole foot and toes become swollen and inflamed and wearing gum boots made the condition worse – very painful and it was impossible to march.) Had several parties with Jimmy Ogden (member of the Harrogate Jewellers Firm) who had a succession of sensational food parcels.*

*Very heavy rains late August and September – mud and water in the trenches over tops of gumboots which had to be shared during duty spells when guarding parapets. Heavy bombardments often caused trenches and dugouts to collapse and some troops suffocated when overcome with fatigue and when sleeping in lightly built dugouts which fell in upon troops.*

*I found two splendid members of the Norfolk Regiment had died during sleep and only in a small dugout which collapsed upon them with no evidence of wounds. The earth had fallen in upon them and they were suffocated and had only been dead a few hours.*

I had several walks through Ypres and saw the tremendous destruction and devastation caused by months of relentless German bombardments. During all the late summer and autumn we were holding a long stretch of the front line and under constant German bombardment and even when in reserve positions, when we were resting, casualties continued to mount. At "stand-to" which was the period approaching dawn when all ranks manned the front line, our position, being in the advanced front of the

Ypres Salient, was subject to sniper fire and we suffered many casualties. There were several large trees which had been totally destroyed by the months of heavy shell fire and German snipers were crafty and skilful in constructing a sniper point in the shattered branches. It was when dawn was breaking they entered these posts, and with the accurate rifle fitted with a telescopic sight watched over sections of our trenches and waited for a victim as they came into the deadly sight of this lethal weapon. We were only 200 yards away from the German front line which was protected by belts of heavy barbed wire entanglements: it almost followed the contour and was usually well above our trench system. The enemy were able to pump out the water which accumulated in their trenches and directed the flow down the slope and during long spells of rain we had to face this added discomfort. The German snipers never used the same sniper post more than a few times and were probably 500 to 600 yards away. On one occasion I had a very near shave as, enthroned on a solitary latrine, a sniper's bullet crashed into the latrine bucket a few inches below my torso with a mighty thud. I jumped into action without delay and sought the cover and protection of the main trench to escape a further shot. The latrine was promptly moved to another site, well protected with heavily massed sandbags and totally beyond the view of any German observation post. As I mentioned earlier, I often attended to the wounded and assisted the regular stretcher bearers in helping to carry casualty to the forward dressing stations. There the Regimental MO with a Sergeant was accommodated in a specially protected dugout behind the reserve trenches. Every morning there was a special Sick Parade where the men received medicines, and some urgent cases, after examination by the Regimental MO were moved to a Casualty Clearing Station behind the lines.

During bombardments from enemy shelling casualties were numerous and the cry of "Stretcher Bearer – Stretcher Bearer" would pass along the trenches and it was amazing how quickly the specially trained SBs arrived on the scene. I saw the Reg. MO so frequently during the autumn of 1915 as I helped with the casualties, that he asked me if I would come and take over the duties of the Sergeant as he was required for duty elsewhere. The MO quickly arranged for my transfer from my Company to Sick Quarters. I was thrilled to be of assistance and quickly fitted into the manifold duties. Some casualties were so urgent that an immediate operation was necessary to save the life of a severely wounded soldier. A sniper's bullet (which had such incredible velocity) would sometimes just miss shattering the skull but would cause a fatal haemorrhage unless the pressure was removed immediately. The victim was unconscious within seconds of being wounded and after probably half an hour on the stretcher he would arrive at the dressing station. Quickly the MO diagnosed the severity of the wound and realised that to carry the victim two miles to an ambulance or casualty clearing station would have been fatal.

I had only taken over duties at the CC Station a few days when a casualty arrived and the MO decided on immediate operation. I soon had the sterilizer boiling and the operating instruments being prepared and I shaved the head. An immediate injection of anti-tetanus was given to safeguard serious infection later. Chloroform was in use as the anaesthetic and the MO gave me instructions how to supply this chloroform as he would be heavily engaged in a trepanning operation on the skull. It is perhaps important to report that this vitally urgent operation was carried out in a small dugout in the advanced section of the Ypres Salient, with the patient lying unconscious on a stretcher supported by a small wooden table.

I continued to administer the chloroform while the MO sterilized his hands and prepared the gauze and dressings. The atmosphere surrounding this dramatic event was most moving and after a few minutes the MO quietly remarked that we were ready to commence the operation. It was amazing how swiftly the MO performed the initial incisions and controlled any haemorrhage and he was soon busily engaged with the trepanning part of the operation. I was relieved to see the anaesthetic was going well and the patient breathing normally. The crux of the operation had now arrived with the removal of the small circular segments of bone from the central part of the skull. The dark oozing blood brought instant relief, and as it was drained from the interior of the skull, the vital pressure from the brain was relieved. The damaged tissue near the dented part of the skull was cleaned up and no further haemorrhage could enter the cranium. The MO breathed a sigh of relief. The change of colour in the face was evidence that there was hope and undoubtedly the patient's life had been saved. The MO quietly said to me that the casualty should survive the journey to the main Casualty Clearing Station. The MO quickly concluded the op; the sterile dressings to the head were applied and arrangements were made for the ambulance already waiting on the Yser Canal Bank to conduct the casualty to the Field Hospital near Poperinge where a full Surgical Team could administer what further treatment was necessary.

So all the late autumn I became more and more thrilled with my new duties and a steady stream of casualties continued to arrive at the Battalion Sick Quarters. Alas, several of my personal friends made the supreme sacrifice and their lesser Cavalries are strewn over the fields of Flanders, where the poppies bloom all the summer.

During the late autumn, with frequent spells of heavy rains, the trenches became waterlogged and the mud conditions were appalling. The gallant stretcher bearers had a mammoth task in carrying the wounded; the mud was sticky and in some sections was two feet deep. Six or eight stretcher bearers were often needed to get a severely wounded soldier to the Battalion Dressing Station. Progress was slow with the deep mud and frequent rests had to be made before the casualty was safely under the care of the Battalion MO. I would mention here that when visiting the Estaires War Cemetery I noticed the grave of Brigadier General J Gough, VC, CB, CMG who died of wounds 22nd February 1915. The inscription on the Cross read:

If thine Eye be single Thy Whole Body shall be full of light.

Surely this would suggest that this gallant officer had only one eye?

During all these months I received a wonderful parcel of food every fortnight, from my home in Yorkshire, superbly packed by my sister who always used a large Huntley and Palmer's biscuit tin which, when packed brim full of gastronomic delights, was sewn up in white linen and addressed in wonderful writing. One thrilling parcel arrived in September 1915 containing a brace of roast grouse and a tin of superb black Hamburg grapes from our own vine which, to prevent bruising, were intermingled with Quaker Oats, which I greatly enjoyed cooking in my mess tin.

*Yser Canal Bridge 4. October 1915. Sketch by Peter.*

On one occasion in late October, I happened to be with the ration party which was collecting rations and meals at Bridge 4 on the Yser canal. It was the night I always received my parcel without fail. The Corporal Postman of the Regiment said "No parcel for you tonight, Corporal," and I felt quite down cast. It would be about 10.00 p.m. and pitch dark. At the end of the bridge there was a strongly built dug-out always containing two sentries who controlled the traffic which passed to and fro over the bridge in daylight. This post was vital as only 4 miles away over the front zone, German Kite balloons, with their super German binoculars, could easily see all activity which occurred over the bridge as they were about 2,000 feet high. So I paused awhile as I dwelt on my disappointment and then commenced my long dark journey back over Bridge 4 to my Battalion lines. As I arrived at the bridge I noticed a faint light coming from the entrance of the deep dugout which was occupied by the two bridge sentries. I called out to them and a dog barked at my intrusion as I descended a few steps and entered the dugout. The welcome was friendly and I asked if anyone had found a parcel which may have been dropped from the regimental mail from the nearby ration assembly point. Almost before I received a reply I spotted my sister's parcel lying on a small bench but badly crushed as the wheel of a ration barrow had run over it and the white cloth cover was stained with mud. Imagine my delight as I recovered this precious parcel and I soon put my clasp knife into action as I ripped off the cover and shared some of the contents with my comrades.

Now I mention this dog who was well known to the troops and was of the collie breed, black with a white front. A few weeks later when I was crossing the bridge I was told that one of the sentries had been killed by a shell and that where he was buried about 50 yards from the bridge, the dog simply would not leave the grave with the small wooden cross. I went to see the evidence of canine devotion. The dog looked up at me and his body was stretched out with his head resting on the end of the small mound and the other sentry told me he took the dog food each day, but could not get him to leave the grave. I think the dog had been collected as a waif and had become a devoted companion to the two sentries for several months.

The weather continued to be terrible most of October and into November, with mud everywhere and conditions in the trenches appalling. HM the King made a visit to the army and returned safely to the UK on November 3rd. A DMS visited and I conducted him round the front line trenches where he saw the appalling conditions the troops had to face.

*Extract from diary*

> Advised to move most of valuable medical stores to dry dugout on Canal Bank. Carried this out – a useful and desirable move. Helped with more operations. One of the troops wounded by shrapnel in the neck and one by sniper in hand – both fortunate – evacuated to CCS. By this time I felt well in control of the main medical problems associated with my new post and was greatly helped by a splendid MO.

**November 1915 – Awarded Commission. Back To Blighty For Training**
One morning in November I was awakened from my slumber and told the exciting and thrilling news that I had been awarded my "commission in the field" and was told to report at Battalion Headquarters. The colonel gave me a cheery welcome and offered me his congratulations and later in the day I reported to the Brigadier at Bde. Headquarters when he signed my papers.

I was told I had to leave for England in the morning and had to arrange for someone to take over my duties at Sick Quarters. Happily I found a splendid relief and I said farewell to my Battalion MO and thanked him for all his help and advice during my spell of duty with him.

I reported at Battalion Headquarters next morning and the Adjutant told me that after a spell of training in England I would be returning to my Regiment. I was taken by car to the Rail Head at Poperinge and given a warrant for my journey to London. During the long train journey I had time to reflect on my good fortune. I had little time to wait at Boulogne but the crossing was very rough.

Arriving in London late that night I was told to go to the Westminster YMCA where I had a comfortable sleep. On the morning of the 12th November I reported to the War Office and I was given leave to telephone my home in Yorkshire to tell them the exciting news. Imagine what they felt like hearing my voice and that I was fit and well. Great rejoicings. Having little money I went by bus to the city to call on Glyns Bank, the London agents of my Yorkshire Bank, Becketts. The Cashier looked most surprised when I asked if he would give me some cash. I was still in my trench uniform and he asked me to see the Chief Cashier to identify myself. I soon confirmed my identity and my pre-war association with Becketts Bank at Knaresborough. My bank account was still in credit as my salary was being paid all the time. As I was able to answer all his questions he authorised the Cashier to cash a cheque for £3.00 and seemed highly amused by my enterprise. I returned to the YMCA for a "wash and brush up" and in the evening went to see *The Scarlet Pimpernel* at the Strand Theatre.

Collecting my kit I proceeded to Kings Cross Station and finally arrived at York where my father met me, but I did have the thrill, when passing over the Ouse Bridge at Selby, of seeing the "Halls Distemper" advert of the two painters carrying the huge advert with the notice "London 180 miles". This, as mentioned earlier, was where I was on duty with my platoon guarding the bridge and powder magazine only last year! – the second day of war.

What a thrill to be home again after nine months and to be with my dear family again.

All the family went to Holy Communion on Sunday and it was a happy service with the Vicar and many friends. I was given leave by the War Office and told to get measured for Officer Uniform without delay, so I called on Andersons in Colony Street, York who proceeded to complete my necessary kit. Leave had been granted to me pending instructions to report to the 3/5th West Yorkshire Regiment at Clipstone Camp near Mansfield. There was a letter from the Adjutant at Clipstone requesting me to report on Friday 10th December. I greatly enjoyed my leave and was able to meet many friends and had adequate time to be kitted up with my Officer Uniform etc. Notice of my being gazetted 2nd Lieutenant appeared in the *New London Gazette* on 2nd December 1915. It was a happy event to see the York and Ainsty hounds meet outside our home and many followers came in for a drink and to enjoy Barbara's mince pies, and seemed greatly to enjoy looking at the many coloured hunting prints. Incidentally whisky at this time was 3/6 per bottle. Such a change from the grim reality of war and the endless mud of the Ypres Salient. I enjoyed the warm company of our gardener Shaw and I helped him prune the fruit trees, build a new vine arch and plant several new roses. I loved these quiet days with my family and the peace of the evenings with the warm glowing fire.

My leave seemed to pass by so quickly. Friday 10th December arrived and I took leave of my family and with my kit I left York and journeyed to Mansfield and thence to Clipstone – back again into the welcome atmosphere of my Reserve Regiment. Clipstone Camp was a huge hutted military camp which accommodated a whole division of troops. I reported to the Orderly Room and after signing many papers I was told to report to "B" coy.

It was not long before I met many old comrades, including several newly commissioned Subalterns. Heavy snow falls during the latter end of December made conditions for training very unpleasant and a tough programme of training was carried out until March. Route marches, trench digging and musketry prepared the troops for fitness to supply much needed reinforcements to the front line 5th West Yorkshire Regiment in France. I was given a very warm welcome and met many old friends and my days with the reserve regiment were happy. During these months of training I received many letters from the Front line regiment in the Ypres Salient with tragic news of so many of my friends killed or severely wounded and victims of successive German Gas attacks.

In the middle of January (16th) I had instructions to proceed to Scarborough to attend Officer Training Course which included officers from all N. Command Units, especially the Highland Reserve Div. from Ripon. The special course was stationed at the Queen's Hotel Hydro and of the 120 attending, quite half were members of the Highland and Lowland Regiments. I greatly enjoyed this course which was very concentrated and we were given every aspect of military training including military law and map reading.

On the evening of 25th January, which was *"Burrn's Nicht"*, the Scots were our hosts at dinner and they produced two pipers from the Ripon Camp to pipe the haggis round the tables. It was a most entertaining evening and the commandant was called upon to propose the Toast to the "Immortal Memory" of Rabbie Burns. He caused much amusement by declaring that "do we as Englishmen recognise these tunes as different", in his reference to the Pipes!

In the final exam I did very well and felt I had greatly benefited from this excellent course. In early February German Zepps raided over the Midlands and five Zepps dropped over 200 bombs on Derby and Stafford. Sixty civilians were killed and over 100 wounded.

After concluding this course at Scarborough, I was granted a short leave which I spent at home with my family. As spring was well advanced it gave me much joy to see all the spring flowers and I greatly enjoyed working in the garden with Shaw.

On returning to my unit at Clipstone Camp, the Adjutant suggested that I report to the Div. Signal School and prepare myself for full training as a Battalion Signals Officer. I greatly enjoyed this new form of training and concentrated on mastering the Morse Code. As we had lectures each day I spent long hours in the evenings with the Corporal Signaller who brought me up to both transmitting and receiving 15 words a minute. I received instruction in the technique of all the Field Telephones, Heliograph and Lamp Signalling – this valuable instruction was to prepare me to take over the duties of Signals Officer with my regiment overseas. The course was most concentrated and went on for all March and April and in the final Buzzer Exam I got 99%.

Having finished the Signals Course at Clipstone, I was told by the

Adjutant that I was to attend the Northern Command Signals Course at Otley in preparation for duties overseas. So I was given short leave just before Easter and arrived home and was able to attend part of the three-hour service on Good Friday. It was a happy Easter with glorious weather.

At this time there was very disturbing news from Ireland of riots in Dublin with many casualties and troops in action in streets against the rebels.

**May 1916**
On 2nd May a German Zepp made raid on York – the Minster escaped but many of the civilian population were killed and wounded . All the family at home at Haxby had a clear view of the Zeppelin. I heard that most of the mediaeval glass – the priceless possession of York Minster – had been removed as a safety precaution.

At about this time the whole of the West Riding Division stationed in Clipstone Camp were in an advanced state of training and it was arranged that the whole division would be inspected by HRH the Duke of Connaught. So happily on a fine day, 12 Battalions paraded in a huge parade ground all in one long frontal line. My Brigade, consisting of the four Battalions of the West Yorkshire Regiment were posted on the extreme right. Then, looking down on the long front of the assembled Battalions, one could see the 12 Commanding Officers, each accompanied by his Adjutant, all mounted. In front of each Battalion the eight company commanders were stationed with the rank of Captain, and just behind the Company Commanders were stationed the Subalterns of each company. So it was a most impressive sight to see the whole West Riding Division. As it happened I was the 2nd Lieutenant on the extreme right of the tremendously long line.

A special Bugler was on parade and at the ready, so that as soon as HRH arrived he could sound a Royal salute. Kipling, as usual, had his humorous phrase already recorded in 'Whiskers like a field of barley." Obviously this was written round the personality of Field Marshal Earl Roberts, of the first Boer War.

Just before zero hour when HRH was due to arrive a most remarkable episode occurred. The Adjutant of my Regiment (in front of the whole Division) allowed his mount to dip his head and neck and commence grazing some tasty clover. Within a few seconds the Adjutant lost all control and slid down the neck of his mount and sprawled in the field. It is impossible to describe the immediate reaction and incredible embarrassment which was suddenly thrust upon the Regiment, in fact, the whole Brigade. The Adjutant quickly assumed the vertical, gathered up the reins of his mount – but did not mount again and stood by his horse at attention.

The Brigade sounded the Royal Salute and HRH was greeted by the Brigadier. The Inspection passed off without a hitch and it was a relief as the mammoth parade was dismissed and the Battalions marched back to their respective regimental lines. There was much humorous chat when the various Regiments assembled for lunch and the Badge of the White Horse of Hanover (West Yorkshire badge) was greatly tarnished. No doubt the lordly Elephant (Badge of the Duke of Wellington's West Riding Regiment) held his trunk very high!

**June 1916**
The Northern Command Signals Course was very concentrated and I made excellent progress with my buzzer tests and was thrilled to be able to take down and send 15 words per minute. I was fascinated to see all the types of Field Telephones and the Heliograph. On Saturday June 3rd I was invited by my Sergeant to go with him to the Signals Receiving Station and take down the incoming signals. With my headphones on I took down many messages and signals and then suddenly there was a dramatic episode when the first signals arrived announcing the Battle of Jutland. I received a frightful shock when I took down the list of our severe naval losses. The German High Command claimed a big naval victory. I continued to stay glued to my head phones and was to receive further shocks as I took down a list of our naval losses. In this great sea battle over 200 ships were engaged and 60 of these mounted guns between 11 and 15 inches. The British losses were 5769 killed in the battle. The German losses in ships and men were immense. It must be remembered that the German High Seas Fleet never ventured to sea again during the war and at the termination of hostilities the whole fleet surrendered at Scapa Flow, where they scuttled their ships. It was a most staggering experience for me to be able to take down these historic secret signals which were being sent to Northern Command, and as I returned to my quarters I felt deeply shocked to learn of our severe losses in this epic battle. Later, however when full details were released, the victory claimed by the German High Command was turned into a defeat, with their losses 18 to our 14.

After the blows of the Battle of Jutland we had to face another profound shock, in fact, almost the worst news since the war commenced: on June 7th 1916 the nation was told that Lord Kitchener and his staff had been drowned when HMS *Hampshire* struck a mine in a rough sea off the Orkneys at night. Actually, Lord Kitchener and his staff were on their way to Russia and the only survivors were a few members of the ship's crew.

I continued with the Signals Course at Otley and we carried out every form of signalling, Buzzer, Lamp, Heliograph, Flag, Field Telephones etc. In my final exam I passed with 92% in the written papers and 100% in buzzer with 99.5% in lamp. A signal from the Adjutant at Clipstone gave me orders to return at once to camp as soon as the course ended. I would not get any leave. I arrived back at Clipstone Camp on 24th June.

I expected orders for overseas any day and went to Sick Quarters to be vaccinated. Reports of numerous successful raids on enemy trenches in BEF suggests that the major attack (long expected) was imminent. On 30th June I was detailed to proceed to France with draft via Southampton. It was a good crossing and I arrived at Le Havre.

After handing over my draft of troops, I wandered round Rouen. I visited the superb Cathedral and climbed to the top of the high spire – at the top I came in contact with a solitary old French female, who was on her knees offering supplications to the Almighty. She informed me that her home had been burnt down so she wanted to be near heaven.

### *Extracts from diary*

> *At Station near the front, wounded on ambulance trains. Railway Transport Officer ordered me to escort wounded back to London. Crossed to Folkestone and thence to London, and back to Clipstone Camp. Was immediately ordered to conduct 200 recruits to York Depot of West Yorkshire. Learned that several friends had been killed and wounded on the Somme and Major Thomson missing. Father sent me some spurs and I had some delightful rides in the Sherwood Forest and expected to join BEF any day. Was granted short leave home and posted to BEF. My parents saw me off at York.*

### Somme 1916

Thus having been awarded my commission in the Field in late November 1915 I spent the next seven months at Clipstone Camp, training with the 2/5th West Yorkshire Regiment, and was finally posted back to the BEF in France in July 1916. On arrival at Le Havre I saw more casualties from "The Somme" battle front. All the Ambulance Trains were crowded with casualties, many coming straight from the advanced dressing stations at the front line. The walking wounded packed the platforms, many showing blood stained dressings. The seriously wounded were on stretchers and were transported to hospitals around Le Havre, Boulogne and Le Touquet for emergency operations before being evacuated by hospital ship to the UK.

I received instructions from the RTO to report back to my Regiment, the 1/5th West Yorkshire (146 Infantry Brigade), who were on a section of the Somme in front of Albert and holding a line of trenches in front of Thiepval. The final part of my train journey after leaving St Omer was in the usual French railway trucks. On arrival at the rail head I could hear the incessant roar of the heavy guns and on reporting to the RTO I received instructions to proceed to my Battalion reserve lines in Martinsart Wood. It was a thrill to meet old friends again, but there was an atmosphere of gloom as I heard my Regiment had many casualties and some friends, well known to me, had paid the supreme sacrifice. I had my evening meal with the Transport Officer which consisted of tinned kidneys and fried potatoes, with the inevitable tinned peaches to follow. As I was drinking a cup of Camp Coffee a Sergeant approached and said, 'Sir, Private Bradbury (from the Yorkshire Dales) is to be your batman and will join you and accompany you to the trenches tonight, when the Ration wagons move after dark and journey through Albert to the Reserve Lines."

On my introduction to Mr Bradbury it was grand to hear his Yorkshire dialect. I could see he was a man of action as he had already dealt with my valise and placed it in a hut where it would remain until the Regiment came out of action to take a spell of rest. Bradbury then sorted my kit, as this was my first spell in action as an Officer. I was supplied with a Tin Hat, skeleton equipment fitting over shoulders with my pack attached and my Webley Revolver loaded – leather Map case, and waterproof sheet to sleep on (necessary if no dugouts were available).

On this particular night I boarded a limber which was drawn by two mules with one mounted driver. All around on every side there was an incessant roar of guns. The noise was terrific as the heavies discharged their eight-inch and 12-inch shells on their way to the German lines and one could see the flash of cordite as the shells burst through the barrels of the mighty howitzers. The drivers of the transport were most gallant men and the mules behaved wonderfully as they pulled their heavily laden limbers through this inferno; they were frequently victims of ghastly injuries from high explosive shells and had to be shot.

As darkness fell the whole region resembled a mighty fireworks display as hundreds of guns, launching their shells, lit up the whole sky. As we gradually approached the front line region we passed through the lines of the lighter calibre guns, the six-inch howitzers, and the 18-pounders. Passing through the town of Albert – totally destroyed by the incessant shell fire from German batteries – we passed many ambulances which were transporting their casualties to nearby advanced dressing stations. Hundreds of troops were passed, marching through the stricken streets. I caught a glimpse of the Church tower with the large statue of the Madonna, still attached by the base to the top of the tower and the body of the Virgin bent down at an acute angle, steeply inclined towards the base of the tower and the street below.

Shortly after skirting the town of Albert we reached the assembly point close by the River Ancre and protected by a shallow escarpment. Here we joined a number of limbers which were busily engaged in discharging huge supplies of rations and equipment of all sorts – ammunition boxes etc. Standing by the limber were bodies of troops who had come up from the forward zone to collect the rations and equipment.

During this period German shells were in constant bombardment of the whole area, as their gunners were well aware that at this period vital supplies of rations and equipment were brought up to the forward zones each night. The enemy knew the roads they must use so they were a prime target.

The technique of this operation was intriguing to watch as an NCO was in charge of each point and the speed with which the fatigue parties collected their appointed rations etc. was amazing. The empty limbers moved away quickly as many other loaded limbers arrived to be met by other regimental parties.

The mules seemed relieved and moved off smartly as their wheels rattled along the cobbled streets and they faced the return back to their transport lines about five miles away into the comparative safety of Martinsart Wood.

My batman and I joined the returning troops and marched with them to join the Battalion who were holding a section of the line in Thiepval Wood. After a long march, with intermittent rest for the fatigue party to ease their weary shoulders, we finally arrived at the reserve line of trenches and I reported to the Adjutant at Battalion Headquarters situated in a deep dugout. He had been pre-informed from Brigade Headquarters that I was reporting to the Battalion and as I knew him during my 1914/15 spell with the Regiment he gave me a great welcome. It was another pleasant surprise when I met my old Colonel who had been C/O of the 5th Battalion West Yorkshire Regiment since August 4th 1914, when the Battalion mobilised. Quite a wonderful feeling came over me when I realised that I was back once again with my old Regiment and with so many of my old comrades. It must have been midnight when I left Battalion Headquarters. I was posted to D Company with Captain P Mandeville as my Company Commander. A guide led me through a maze of deep communications trenches and we finally arrived at D Company Headquarters which were in a dugout and consisted of four wire-supported wooden bunks, two wooden stools and a small wooden table where four could eat a meal. Two of my brother Officers were asleep in the dugout, which had two candles as the only means of illumination, and one Subaltern was out on duty visiting front line trench positions. Captain M. without much delay, after his welcome to me, said, "Wilson, I will take you round our Company front line as we are only 100 yards from the Huns and occupying an important 'Sap Head' (a 15 yard protruding trench surrounded by barbed wire and acting as a listening post, with a machine gun post at the head). You will take over your four-hour spell of duty at 4 a.m. until after 'STAND TO'."

Stand-to was the period of the dawn approach when all troops manned the fire platforms in the trenches and awaited full daylight – this period usually lasted about half an hour and enemy snipers often claimed a victim with their telescopic sights.

So off we started on this tour, having strapped on our revolvers and as we tramped over the duck boards one could hear bursts of machine gun fire and shells tearing through the air going in both directions, and see the ascending Verey lights as they illuminated the region of No Man's Land and provided a view of wiring parties or patrols. After our tour of inspection we returned to our Company Headquarters and Captain M. told me to get some sleep before my early tour of duty.

The German sniper, using a rifle fitted with a telescopic sight, was a deadly shot and often used a shell torn tree or partly destroyed building to take up a firing position which had a clear view of a short area of the British front line trench. He never used the same firing point twice and, as his carefully camouflaged position was almost ten to twelve feet above ground level, he was able to get a clear view of the British trench and obtain a view of the head and shoulders of the troops. I had the tragic experience of seeing three of my comrades who were quite close to me fall victim to a deadly shot and they were killed instantly. It was impossible to tell from which direction the shot was fired, as during 'Stand to" there was usually an uninterrupted inferno from shell fire and bursts of machine gun and rifle fire. I was once in a prepared Sniper Post which was protected by a special rim plate with a loop hole which allowed my rifle to protrude and allow me to align my sights on an enemy target 150 yards away in enemy front line trenches. I was in the firing position and lying prone with my rifle butt adjacent to my right shoulder when quite suddenly there was a metallic bang, and an enemy sniper's bullet had actually entered through the small hole in the metal plate and struck the back sight of my rifle – how it missed hitting me I do not know, but I must admit I was greatly shocked and promptly moved the protecting iron plate to a totally different angle. This demonstrates the incredible accuracy of the enemy sniper.

I tumbled into my wire bed, used my haversack as a pillow and to the roar of exploding shells outside I was soon asleep. I was reminded of the trenches in the Ypres Salient last year and how swiftly I fell asleep even during bombardments. I slept soundly until Bradbury, my batman, called me for my spell of trench duty. It was dark when I ventured forth and found my way round the front line limit of my Company boundary and eventually arrived at the advanced post which was near the German front line trenches defending Thiepval.

A sentry was on duty and I saw in the gloom that he was physically exhausted. I nudged his boot and asked him if he had anything to report. His spell of duty was almost over and another sentry was due to take over for a spell of two hours. I spent the rest of the night touring the front line positions and throughout the four hours the roar of the guns continued. I saw troops asleep and in each bay of the front line trench a sentry was on duty, where he could observe the region of No Man's Land adjoining his position and the German trenches 120 yards away. Intermittent bursts of machine-gun fire punctuated the night and as the dawn approached I was anxious to get my first view of the immediate surroundings.

By first light I could see that the whole of Thiepval Wood was a mass of shattered tree stumps, totally destroyed by months of shell fire. Within a few minutes the scene totally changed from lines of sleeping soldiers to intense activity, as 'Stand To" had arrived and all the firing positions were manned. Each Platoon Commander was with his troops and Captain M. and the CSM carried out a full inspection of the whole front line and reserve positions. During this period the artillery fire livened up considerably and continued throughout the whole of 'Stand To". It was far too dangerous for the troops to take "pot-shots" at the enemy trenches as German snipers lay in wait at prepared positions, and to expose myself was certain to result in a fatal disaster. The German snipers were probably concealed in the reserve line trenches 300 to 400 yards away. As the light improved rapidly the end of 'Stand To" arrived and the welcome call 'Stand down" passed along the front. All troops, except those on sentry duty, were soon engaged preparing breakfast which consisted of fried bacon or bully beef with ration biscuits and jam and tea, prepared in a mess-tin. With my companion officers I returned to our dugout to find breakfast had been prepared by our batman. After breakfast I shaved using my cut-throat razor and prepared to return to my section in the front line trench to carry out rifle inspection.

To my surprise my Company Commander Captain Mandeville said, "Wilson, I would like to have a word with you."

I thought this would be a helpful chat on trench warfare etc. We were soon alone and Captain M. said, "Wilson, a man cannot serve two masters." I replied, "Oh yes Sir, I know where that Biblical quotation comes from." But before I could realise the meaning of this remark Captain M. said, "When you carried out your tour of inspection I think you found a sentry asleep at his post, as it happened I was not far behind you in that trench."

I was astounded and was unable to offer a satisfactory explanation as, according to military code, I should have placed that exhausted sentry under arrest. In the grim atmosphere of the night, accompanied by incessant shell fire, I did not think the Private was asleep, just utterly exhausted!*

Captain M. gave me a just rebuke and sent me off to my Platoon to carry out the rifle inspection. But I slowly returned along those duck boards and pondered deeply on my "lapse" with a firm resolve to "uphold the right."

The ballistic symphony went on day and night with the German heavies tearing through the air like express trains. The screech of the 5.9s was so sudden one hadn't time to duck for cover. High above the roar of battle the airmen flew in their tiny machines and I saw several aerial combats with a machine crashing towards earth streaming flame and smoke, with no hope of salvation. Low flying machines like the RE8s, with the Observers doing a contact patrol only 200-300 feet above the troops, gallantly reported the up-to-date scene of the battle.*

Heavy rain caused much flooding in the trenches. With two feet of water and mud conditions were appalling and made evacuation of the wounded very difficult. With the artillery bombardments so intensive there were heavy casualties and I lost several friends in this way.

In late August I was interviewed by the Colonel of the Regiment and he appointed me to be Battalion Intelligence officer, so I was transferred from my Company to Headquarters. I was also asked to take on the duties of Signalling Officer and was, therefore, responsible for the trench system of hand telephones. The signaller had an appalling time trying to keep the telephone lines intact as the incessant bombardment continually destroyed communication and the repair teams braved the intense shell fire to repair the fractured life lines.

By this time Thiepval Wood was one mass of huge shell craters. They were half filled with water and all the trees were totally destroyed. One

---

* To fall asleep when on sentry duty especially in the front line, was considered an extremely serious offence as it endangered one's comrades and the allied defences. I understand that two men were shot by firing squad for this offence in the course of the war.

* Little did Peter realise then, that 15 months later, he would himself be an observer in an RE8 over the battle lines.

morning I was sitting on a shattered tree stump washing my feet in a tin hat when suddenly the roar of a German shell crashed into the earth almost on top of me and exploded with tremendous force and threw me off my seat. I was left almost on the top of a huge crater as an enormous shell hole was created just in front of me. It was a miracle that the whole force of the exploding shell was carried forward 100 yards and the wool of one of my socks completely unravelled. After I had recovered from the initial shock I put on my sock and boots and returned to Battalion Headquarters where the Adjutant said, "Wilson, you look very shocked" and I told him of my "near miss". I was given a strong coffee and just at that moment a Runner entered Headquarters and told the tragic story that the Company Sergeant Major had been struck by a splinter of shell in the heart and killed instantly. The Sergeant Major was at least 100 yards from the shell which exploded almost on top of me, but the force of the explosion carried the deadly splinter of shell until it struck the Sergeant Major with that fatal injury.

Since 1st July, there had been little progress in the front. Thiepval still remained intact, surrounded by terraces of barbed wire which were being constantly bombed by our shell fire. Just to the left of Thiepval there was an enormous German dugout called "The Wunderwerck" which was captured early in July. The war had been static for two years and this remarkably deep dugout was superbly constructed with lines of wire beds – it had excellent cooking stoves and was provided with fires, so during the winter months at least 200 soldiers were kept warm and dry every night. The British, on the other hand, had to exist in exposed trenches which were flooded as the slope of the ground drained all the water from the German lines downhill to the British positions. The British dugouts were small and only gave shelter from the winter storms and they often collapsed with the force of the enemy bombardments. I spent a few days in the immense German dugout which was deep down a specially built shaft – their engineers had spent many months constructing it. I went to sleep my first night in one of the officer's beds but had not been asleep for many minutes (free from the noise of the incessant bombardment above) when I was awakened by an intense irritation. On making a close examination, I found I was infested by dozens of large mud-coloured fleas and I decided to make a speedy exit from this inferno. Taking my waterproof ground sheet, I returned to sleep in the open for the rest of our spell in this section of the front line, but it was well into the next afternoon when, with a thorough examination of my underclothing, I got rid of the last fleas. I know I still had some lice in the seams of my shirt, but frequent inspections kept these well under control and I also frequently applied some more "Boots Vermin in the Trenches". This excellent powder kept me fairly free from the invading lice!

It was a great relief when our spell of duty in the trenches expired and I was appointed Billeting Officer. On leaving the trenches I was met by one of the Transport Section with a horse, about two miles from the front line. It was grand to be on a horse again, and we rode through several battery positions which were heavily engaged in firing salvos of shells at the enemy.

After about four miles with my groom we finally arrived in our allotted rest area and I interviewed the local village mayor and arranged for the billeting of about 700-800 which were accommodated in large barns and some in tents – protected by woods. I had most of the day in which to arrange the billeting programme before the Battalion – consisting of Headquarters staff and the eight Companies – arrived. Many of the Officers were billeted on civilians and were provided with beds. During the rest period passes were issued to Officers and troops, and transport was provided to convey us to the delightful city of Amiens. This city was beyond the range of the German guns and it was grand to be able to sit down to a superb meal in one of the excellent restaurants. I found the cathedral full of manifold delights, especially the Weeping Cherub, who looked down from the Triforium to the faithful below who were deep in their meditations.

It was of course, a great surprise for members of the BEF to see how the French Government provided state controlled Brothels in every town. After my visit to the Cathedral I joined up with my officer companion at the rendezvous with our transport, which would conduct us back to our rest-camp. I was somewhat surprised to see that my companion seemed gloomy and despondent, totally different from the moment we parted after our excellent lunch. It was not long before he revealed his tale of woe. He confessed to me that he had visited "The House of the Red Lamp" and had experienced his first intercourse with a female. He seemed so distressed that he had fallen from grace and what would his mother and sisters think of his moral crash? I did my best to console him and tried to explain the unique position of a young adult engaged at war – now here I would mention that I had discussed this problem with many of my friends.

It was clear that the vast majority of the young soldiers of the BEF had not had any intimacy with the opposite sex but being engaged in deadly combat, especially on the Somme, and seeing so many comrades killed, they had an inborn feeling that they had not proved their manhood until they had experienced sexual satisfaction. This latent feeling incubated the desire to satisfy these longings and the avenue was open to them when they were out in rest camp. Almost all the way back in our transport my friend continued to pour out his lamentation, and with the trust he conveyed to me I think my words did bring him some comfort.

I suppose with the strain of war and the prevailing tragedy surrounding the lives of all the inhabitants of that region's towns and villages, a unique situation prevailed. It was a common experience when walking through a French village for several little girls to rush up to a group of officers or troops and gleefully offer the invitation, "You jig a jig with my sister" and would lead any willing "gallant" to the open door of their home.

The State-controlled brothels were under medical supervision and venereal disease was unlikely to be contracted. But there was a grave risk of Gonorrhoea being contracted from the contact with females in the village houses. In fact, I well remember an incident where ten officers, lunching in a small hotel with much alcohol, afterwards indulged with the local "mamselles". Forty-eight hours later these ten gentlemen appeared on Sick Parade and all were consigned to the local Clap Hospital for treatment and all pay was stopped! Imagine the great shock for the CO of that Unit to find that ten of his combatant unit had been suddenly admitted to the special VD Hospital and this happened to be at the height of a raging battle!

On arriving back at rest Camp I received a message to report to the Battalion Commander. He briefed me for a special duty and gave me orders to proceed at dawn to the advanced zone to witness the mystery TANKS go into action for the first time near Ovillers and La Boiselle. I was mounted for this exciting enterprise and I had about two hours' ride through destroyed villages and devastated country. All the long ride I was accompanied by the endless roar of the mighty guns, and suddenly, behind some destroyed houses, I spotted several tanks all ready for action. It was early in the morning of 15th September 1916 that I saw Churchill's wonder invention go into action. All this time the German counter batteries kept up a fierce bombardment of all the British forward positions and I know I was most fortunate to escape injury with my gallant mount.

The Tanks rumbled into action through the lines of barbed wire and swept through the German trenches and continued their advance far beyond the reserve line. Follow up troops rounded up batches of prisoners and it was clear that the attack had been a great success. I had time to examine the large mine crater at La Boiselle, which had been created by the gallant miners of the Royal Engineers. The explosion was so vast, a whole hill had been blown into the heavens. My long ride home was filled with interest as I witnessed the advance forward of many batteries, masses of equipment and infantry. I was able to give my mount a rest, a much needed drink and a greatly enjoyed forage. I finally arrived safely back and reported to the Colonel and his senior Commanders on the unforgettable excitement of the day.

Next day we received orders for the Regiment to return to the Thiepval Wood area and we would move at dusk. I had just returned to my Company Headquarters for lunch when my batman brought in the usual parcel, which my sister Barbara had so carefully packed – a biscuit tin especially sewn up tightly with white canvas. What a surprise for my comrades and me to find the parcel contained a brace of roast grouse, some fresh farm butter and a large tin of Quaker Oats – only to find that a large bunch of black Hamburg grapes (still covered with that glorious bloom) was carefully interspersed with the Quaker Oats. Our party of four greatly enjoyed our banquet and the grouse was superb and we felt fortified for our long march back to the inferno of Thiepval Wood.

Throughout August and most of September the Regiment occupied the same quadrant of the Somme Battlefield and had short intermittent rests away from the front line. When in the front line regions the daily artillery battles raged and were so intense throughout the daylight hours that the Regiment suffered heavy casualties. It was interesting to note how the flights of wild duck, especially mallard, continued to make landings in the River Ancre even during dawn and evening bombardments. By early September the young flights had matured and I often saw ten to twelve mallard sweep in from the east, and land on the flooded areas.

The power of the enemy gunfire was so intense on our forward area that most of the overhead telephone wires were totally destroyed and it was impossible to make contact with Headquarters for urgent messages. Notwithstanding the havoc caused by the shell fire, the bravery and determination of the company signallers was incredible as they struggled to restore the destroyed lines of communication.

[My father drew a little sketch to commemorate a brave signaller whose death he witnessed and described thus:]

> "THROUGH"
> 
> *This sketch shows a gallant Signaller who goes out specially to mend the all-important telephone cable which has been cut by shell fire. After a long search for the broken line, he finally discovers the "break" and under heavy shell fire mends the cable. With his "tapping in" wire he joyfully establishes communication with his unit, and the Troops in the advanced post are again in direct contact with the artillery behind. Suddenly, a screech tears the desolated village and shrapnel finds its mark. Stricken in death he falls (his work completed as he is "THROUGH" to his*

*Headquarters) and as his vision fades, he gazes towards the little Crucifix with outstretched arms. Then "all" is peace.*

*The little Grotto even helps to support the German barbed wire – a reminder of the "Crown of Thorns" emblems of the first Calvary.*

*No mother or sweetheart will every know how her dear one met his end – They merely heard from the War Office "Regret to report your son Signaller ?? No. 02743 is "missing", believed killed".*

> No medal hangs from his brave chest
> But poppies bloom and in the trees, birds sing
> His gallant spirit claimed by God doth rest
> And as the sunset fades each day, bells ring.

*Sketch drawn by Peter after an incident which much moved him.*

*This sketch and verse is dedicated to the memory of a gallant "West Yorks Signaller" who fell 3 Sept. 1916 Thiepval.*

It was a great thrill for my Battalion Signallers to set up a special lamp communication with a Signalling Station almost two kilometres from the front line. Morse code signals continued with great success and vital messages were transmitted to Brigade Headquarters. No enemy observations could be carried out and they were never aware that all our vital messages could be safely transmitted, even during intense artillery bombardments. The vital long metal pipe allowed the Morse signals to be directed to the reception post and we could receive urgent messages from our reserve signal dugouts, and have the messages safely delivered to the Battalion or Company Headquarters. At one vital period my team of signallers were able to send coded messages by Heliograph (as used in the Boer War circa. 1900!).

We always seemed to have heavy days of action on Sundays and on one Sunday in early September the heavy artillery barrage raged all day and casualties were heavy. Darkness had fallen and I was having a short rest when my batman said, "A message, sir, for you to report to Battalion Headquarters."

Reporting to the Colonel soon revealed the urgency of his message. "Wilson, the Brigadier is anxious to obtain a German Prisoner and you will be required to conduct a raid into the enemy lines before Thiepval – you will take a raiding party of a Sergeant and 14 men and the artillery will put down a barrage to give you early protection."

After this long hectic day this was a profound surprise and great shock to me, and of course quite a new episode in my young military life. I wondered if I should write a short letter to my parents. I quickly interviewed my Sergeant and the 14 troops and had time for a short meal and hot drink. Bradbury, my batman, fixed me up with my loaded revolver and the raiding party prepared to assemble to the allotted point in the trenches. A quick survey revealed that the Hun had a most formidable line of barbed wire entanglement (Hun wire is very thick and strong). I had some final words with my Colonel and Headquarters Staff and then moved off down the trench towards the sap head, less than 100 yards from German trenches.

It was amazing what thoughts flashed through my mind during these waiting minutes – a prelude to the promised bombardment by our artillery. My raiding party was almost at the point of our sap head when suddenly up dashed a "Runner" in the narrow trench from Battalion Headquarters. "The Adjutant is on the way to see you, Sir." But before I had time to take in the message the Adjutant arrived quite breathless. It was only a quarter of an hour before "zero hour". "Wilson," he speedily gave me his message. "The raid has been cancelled." This message staggered me and through all the Verey lights and shell explosions my eyes penetrated the canopy of gloom and smoke, and all the stars seemed to encompass me with their celestial glory.

I quickly told my Raiding Party and we seemed to be walking on air as we wended our way back through the maze of narrow trenches to Battalion Headquarters.

The colonel was quick to welcome me back and handed me a whisky. He said, with a smile on his gallant countenance, "Wilson, a rather different job awaits you. After a rest you will proceed to Village X and prepare for billeting the Battalion. Your groom will meet you at Rendezvous X and you will ride about four miles and report to Brigade Headquarters for instructions."

No pen of mine is able to reveal the stream of thoughts which passed through my mind at this remarkable and dramatic change of plans. At about 0300 Bradbury called with a cup of coffee and handed me an envelope with my billeting orders. We both set off in a long tramp through the trenches of Thiepval Wood down towards Albert. At 0500 we met our Groom and my well-loved mount seemed to give me a welcome "nicker" of delight.

We had to ride through about three miles of roaring batteries of artillery which my horse greatly disliked. But the reeking smell of cordite and the incessant salvos of heavy gun fire could not take away my delight, as I rode through the dawn hours and reflected on the dramatic hours of the night. My mind refused to meditate on the grim reality of what that "Raid" might have finally revealed. It was a lovely sunny morning and just as I approached Brigade Headquarters I gazed into the heavens and could just hear the purring engine of a small reconnaissance aeroplane, as it flew eastwards to carry out a dawn patrol over the front lines. I received a warm welcome at Brigade Headquarters and after a short interview with a Staff Captain I was handed my instructions to billet the whole of the 5th West Yorkshire Regiment in a nearby village. The Battalion were coming out of the front line for a short rest. By early afternoon I had completed the task and awaited the arrival of the exhausted troops as they had an eight mile trek in full battle order. During the early afternoon the Sergeant Cook and his team had prepared a splendid meal for the whole Battalion (about 800 men).

It was grand for me to greet the leading batch of troops and I had a most energetic hour in allocating the eight Companies to their billeting zones. I received great help from the French Town Mayor and the local French inhabitants were kind and hospitable in offering accommodation for the Officers. The Army authorities provided cash payments for the locals, who provided excellent accommodation.

I enjoyed four days' rest in this most pleasant environment and spent long days in the saddle. It was a joy riding through miles of golden cornfields but I simply could not get away from the very heavy 12 inch guns.

The Colonel sent for me and said how sorry he was to cut short my rest. I would have to leave that very night to make a special visit to the front line forward observation post "Jacob's Ladder", which was at Beaumont Hamel. This post was unique as from its well-concealed position, it had a clear view of the German trench system at Thiepval and "The Triangle" adjacent to the Schwaben Redoubt, just the other side of the River Ancre. It was a long heavy tramp and I had Bradbury to care for my comforts. I slept on the floor of this small Ob. Post and shared the nearby deep trench with the troops.

I was very early on duty and from my small concealed peep hole I could see right into the German trenches and the massive Schwaben Redoubt. I had a complete close-up view with my telescope, and made observations on a special map on which I located strong concrete machine gun positions along the whole German Front Line. It was exciting to get long close up views of the German soldiers in their trenches and fortified strong points. I had been provided with an up to date trench map, with all German trench systems printed in red. I was able to plot several dozen machine gun points even back to the German Reserve line. After two days' intense and non-stop observations I made a detailed map, with all the vital posts and trench strong points carefully recorded and these were taken by special courier back to Brigade Headquarters. These vital points could assist the preparation for the coming big attack in a few days time. The companies carrying out the first wave of attack were provided with information on all the enemy concrete M.G. posts and the heavily protected barbed wire zones. I continued to make further inspections during my 3rd and 4th day in Jacob's Ladder and was able to dispatch my second detailed report on the Saturday afternoon to Brigade Headquarters.

**23rd September 1916**

As dusk fell on my fourth night in Jacob's ladder, I had just settled for the night after my batman had provided me with a meal and hot drink. I stretched out on the floor of this small O. Post, which had a protected roof and supported sides. Heavy shelling was going on and one could see the whole line of the battle front north and south by the Verey light spectacle and the hundreds of exploding shells.

I was soon asleep and without any warning there was a sudden tremendous crash and mighty explosion, as the whole O.P. structure crashed in upon me and buried me in a mass of heavy material. A mighty eight-inch shell had made a direct hit on the OP and the rank smell of cordite added to the grim tragedy. The heavy explosion had knocked me clean out and I could not feel my legs, or move my arms, with the weight of material debris over me. I could breathe with difficulty and eventually could hear voices and Bradbury was the first to make contact with me.

"Are you all right, Sir?" About six troops worked hard to remove masses of timber, iron girders and earth which had enveloped me. I was finally dragged from the destroyed post and gently laid on a stretcher. I could not move either leg and felt that there had been considerable injury to both legs. They were saturated with blood inside my riding boots and I knew blood was still oozing from the right thigh. One gallant Stretcher Bearer said, "There is a nail thrust deep in your right cheek." The SBs had a frightful time trying to conduct me in the narrow deep trenches. It was now pitch dark and I was hardly conscious of the true reality of my position.

It must have taken nearly an hour to reach the advanced dressing station, which was packed with wounded. The MO pumped a large dose of anti-tetanus into my chest as he said I had many wounds (I think 18 in all). He also said, "You will sleep on this stretcher all night under a hedge with many others." Another party of eight S.B.'s. and the faithful Bradbury were able to transport me about half a mile to a locality of small trees, and I could see quite a number of stretcher cases packed in a long line and waiting for the morning. By this time I was conscious of great pain in my legs and felt my breeches were sodden in blood. It was a great relief when a Medical Sergeant came along and gave me a heavy shot of morphine into my arm and within a few moments I was "out of this world". I must have slept five or six hours, completely free from any conscious suffering and the noise of great artillery fire.

When I woke, with Bradbury standing by with a cup of tea, I could see several small Ford ambulances busy with the evacuation of the stretcher cases. It was not long before I was given another injection of morphine and my stretcher, with one other stretcher case, was secured in the small Ford ambulance. We moved off slowly over the bumpy shell torn ground and I finally arrived at a Casualty Clearing Station.

I was hardly conscious as the injection had given me blessed relief. The Examining MO said, "You will not be dealt with here but will go to the rail head, where you will be taken by train to the nearest Field Hospital. A larger ambulance conducted me from the CCS to the rail head, where I was lifted into a truck with eight other stretcher cases.

I was trying to settle, in much discomfort, when a dear wee French girl, about five years old, presented me with a bouquet of flowers. After several trucks had been packed with stretcher cases, it was clear the train would soon move off. Here I had to part company with my gallant batman, Bradbury from the South Dales. It was a sad moment as we parted – he had to find his way back to the Regiment; I was on my way to be admitted to the Field Hospital for urgent treatment of my wounds.

# Chapter Three

## AN EARLY EXPERIENCE OF HOSPITAL LIFE

**24th September 1916**

The train – all army trucks – slowly chugged out of the rail head station and after about three hours we arrived at Asheux. There was much activity with dozens of stretcher cases and scores of walking wounded. At Gazincourt all the stretcher cases were packed into ambulances and there was a general inspection of the casualties by several medical officers.

Our ambulance, with four stretcher cases, moved off and travelled at speed along country roads and finally arrived at a large country estate not far from Arnes, with lines of huts and large tents close by a huge château. These tents were provided for operating theatres and X-rays. All the stretcher cases were examined by a team of doctors, and Army Nurses were in attendance. I found myself being wheeled into a large, lofty room (obviously the drawing room of the château) and was quickly dealt with by several nurses, who took off all my military clothing. For the first time I could see the extensive damage in both my legs. My wounds were dressed, I was washed and both legs were bandaged and supported by splints. Looking round the large room I could see at least another two dozen beds. The Army sister said, "You will go to the X-ray tent as the surgeons will require to inspect the X-ray films, so they can pin point the position of the shell splinters – a very necessary prelude to the operations on your limbs."

It was grand to be in pyjamas and I was refreshed by the careful washing the nurses had given me. I had not long to wait for the medical orderlies who conducted me to the X-ray tent, and within half an hour I had several films taken of the wounded regions of my legs and thighs. I felt greatly relieved to go back to bed and after a light lunch was soon fast asleep.

It was clear this large drawing room of the château was the main reception ward for Officer casualties, who were admitted here from the Somme battlefront. After their wounds had been dealt with and after a few days' post-operative nursing and rest, casualties were prepared for transport in the ambulance train to the channel ports of Boulogne and Calais and thence by the Hospital Ship to the UK, through the ports of Dover and Folkestone.

It was early evening when the Sister came and told me I was about to go to the Operating tent to have my wounds dealt with. I was given an injection to prepare me for the operation and soon felt drowsy. Two medical orderlies wheeled me into the anaesthetic tent adjacent to the operating theatre and the cheery anaesthetist made an early examination of my heart and lungs.

Very soon I was told to breathe into the mask covering my face and I could see the anaesthetist administering the chloroform from a drop bottle. I did not like the taste and potent smell of the chloroform and it wasn't long before I was wheeled into the main operating theatre and lifted onto the operating table. I could see the two surgeons looking at the several X-rays and I heard one voice say, "We'll do the left leg first."

Of course both surgeons and operating sister were fully dressed in operating gowns and face masks. By this time I was fairly well under the influence of the chloroform and the Sister was handing the surgeon his scalpel. He was directly above my prostrate figure on the operating table and I could only see his eyes. I was sufficiently conscious that I made an immediate alarm call by spluttering out under my anaesthetic mask, "Doc, I'm not under." The somewhat surprised Surgeon immediately remarked, "Pour on the dope, George." I felt a copious splash of chloroform on my cheek and a smarting discomfort – followed by speedy oblivion.

Late in the evening I returned to consciousness, when I saw two nurses attending to my physical requirements – but it was not long before I longed for sleep and an injection soon brought me that blessed relief.

It was early morning when I woke and was given a welcome cup of tea. I could now assess the extent of my wounds and the Sister and nurses said, "We must syringe the rubber tubes which we inserted into your thighs." This was not an unpleasant episode but I understood the tubes would be in position for several days. Both legs and thighs were heavily adorned with large bandages. The Sister remarked, "That German shell gave you a severe peppering and I think you have 15 wounds in your thighs and legs."

It was about breakfast time and I was now conscious of a great physical discomfort, as I had an enormous distension of my whole abdomen. It was, of course, an extreme distension of my bladder with urine as I had not passed any for well over 24 hours. The Sister made a superficial examination and was quite alarmed.

"I'm afraid, Mr Wilson, I must pass a catheter to give you relief." Very soon the Sister and Nurse approached my bed and arranged screens for privacy. I made an urgent appeal to the Sister to give me ten minutes grace, as I was most anxious and apprehensive of this new adventure into the realm of my privacy.

I was still sheltering under this dispensation when suddenly the drawing room door opened (close to my bed) and a young French damsel rushed in, shouting with delight," Two Zepps shot down in England." She was selling Continental Editions of the *Daily Mail*. As she passed near my bed, I snatched a copy and read eagerly how Lieutenant Robinson had shot down a big Zepp in Hertfordshire and had been awarded a VC. This unexpected and exciting news had a spontaneous effect on my nervous system, and I became aware of a soothing and tranquil sensation as streams of urine gushed all over my newly applied dressings and the bed. Nothing would stop that explosion of my waterworks and I could not avert the flow of urine until my bladder had discharged the last drop.

Up dashed the Sister and three nurses with catheter set, only to find that the worst had happened. No excuse could I find and I beheld the great upheaval behind the screen as the whole bed had to be stripped and all my dressings changed again. It took three nurses a full half hour to clean up my unconscious disaster, and didn't I enjoy my late breakfast and a thrilling read of the Continental *Daily Mail*.

I spent three days in the ward and required regular dressings and syringing of the tubes which were deeply inserted into my thighs. I also had to face a frequent bombardment from the Nurses as each time they passed my bed with impish smiles they remarked, "Two Zepps down, Mr Wilson!"

On the fourth day there was an early evacuation of about 20 stretcher cases from the ward, of which I was one. When we arrived by the ambulances at the rail head we were packed into a hospital train, which cared for about 200 stretcher cases and scores of walking wounded. The train spent most of the day on its journey to the coast and eventually I found myself in the Duchess of Westminster Hospital at Wimereux.

The tubes were now removed and I shared a ward with another wounded officer, Lt. Craig of the Royal Scots. I immediately recognised Lt. Craig, as I had met him on an Officers' Course at Scarborough in 1915. He had been severely wounded in the abdomen.

In the middle of the morning I had a rare and most thrilling experience. The door of the room opened and in walked a full General (all scarlet and gold) and his staff officer and the Matron. Matron introduced us both to the General and then he addressed Lt. Craig as follows: "Lt. Craig, it is my great pleasure to tell you that HM the King has awarded you the Victoria Cross for your recent gallantry in action."

What a unique experience for me! I had two happy days in company with Lt. Craig before I was evacuated again and this time I was transported to Boulogne, where I was put on the hospital ship *St Dennis*.

The crossing of the Channel was quite exciting as we had an escort of four destroyers, and it was not long before I had a view of the white cliffs of Dover. We crossed the channel smoothly in about one and a half hours. There was an abundant staff of nursing sisters on board the *St Dennis* and they were most efficient in getting all the stretcher cases ready for evacuation after the boat arrived in Dover harbour. It was incredible how swiftly all the stretcher and walking cases were evacuated from *St Dennis* and the heavily packed train was soon on its way toward London.

The Sister in our ambulance coach thought we would be going to a base hospital either in or near London. But after arriving in a south London station (Victoria), there was much activity on the platform and all light and walking wounded were evacuated from the train. Very soon a Railway Traffic Officer entered our coach and told us that we would soon be on our way for a three hour journey into the Midlands. It was now mid-evening and after a light supper, beautifully served, I was soon asleep as my legs felt more comfortable, especially with the tubes out.

It was about 11.00 p.m. when we slowly pulled into Leicester Station and found the platform packed with a large number of ambulance men and lady drivers. I was amazed at the number of ambulances. There must have been about 100 stretcher cases and the stretcher bearers were most skilful in lifting us from the beds onto the stretchers and into the awaiting ambulances with their lady drivers. Four stretcher cases were placed into each ambulance. There seemed to be a wait of about 20 minutes before the completed ambulance column was ready to move off. As we were waiting, I suddenly felt I was within shell distance of the firing line as I could hear very heavy detonation of bombs – we were told that German Zeppelins were carrying out a bombing attack on the Brush Electric Works at Loughborough, not far from Leicester. What a strange welcome for this array of wounded straight from the Somme, to arrive home to the detonation of scores of bombs, as they rained down on defenceless Loughborough!

It was well past midnight when we arrived at our particular destination of the Vth Northern General Hospital, Leicester. Quite a queer episode happened at this period of time. I was so comfortable on my stretcher, well wrapped up by warm rugs, that I fell asleep and the ambulance garage was locked up. I had not even heard the evacuation of the other three ambulance cases. The ambulance team felt quite certain that all the stretcher cases were well settled into the allotted officer wards. But a very rowdy noise just outside my ambulance soon brought me to action. Outside, the Night Sister was having quite an argument with several ambulance teams. She remarked, "There is an Officer stretcher case missing – we have only admitted 23 cases and my list quotes 24." At this juncture I loudly shouted, "I am in here!"

Quickly the ambulance garage door was opened – then they opened the ambulance door and found me lying in comfort on the top stretcher rack. The Sister had a few sharp words to address and I said I was asleep even leaving Leicester Station. The stretcher bearers soon transported me to the Officer Ward and within a few minutes I was in a very comfortable bed and after a hot drink I was soon fast asleep.

I was very impressed by the manifold comforts of this hospital and the nursing was excellent, especially by a splendid team of VADs*. My wounds required special nursing each morning and I was not allowed up for the first fortnight. There was a small splinter of shell in the left eye and the Eye Surgeon said he could not operate until a local infection had cleared up. However, after a few days of constant eye lavage and eye ointment I was put down for an eye operation. This was carried out most successfully and the scar quickly healed and there was no impairment to my vision.

It was annoying that my many wounds were prone to copious granulations and the excessive growth had to be burnt with applications of carbolic but as the weeks passed by I made good progress.

It was a great thrill for me when my beloved Mother and Father came down from York to visit me. I was delighted to hear all their news. I was much distressed to receive a letter from my Battalion in France that my Company Commander and several friends had been killed in the attack on Thiepval. Also of the great success of the capture of Thiepval and the Schwaben Redoubt.

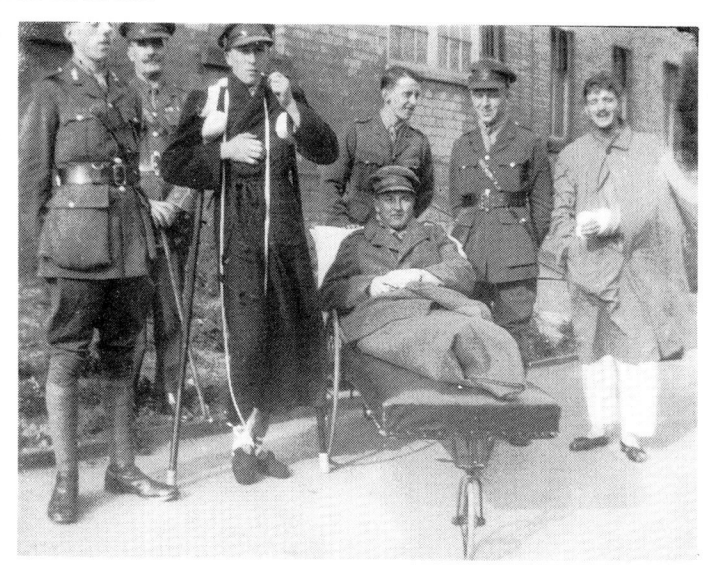

*October 1916, Northern General Hospital. (Peter on wheeled couch.)*

---

\* VAD = Voluntary Aid Detachment (auxiliary nurses).

My wounds made a rapid recovery and by mid-October I was allowed up each day and some friends in the ward took me for trips in my wheeled chair into the town. One of my friends, a Canadian Officer, caused me much embarrassment when he allowed some "ladies of easy virtue" to push me along and insisted on calling me "Darling." I could do nothing to check their approaches, and they seemed to delight in my shyness. I was glad that, although I couldn't walk yet, in late October I was able to go to Church in my "tank" and went to one excellent concert at the De Montfort Hall.

In early November I had special treatment to strengthen my legs and had regular physiotherapy, as my larger wounds were healing rapidly. I was thrilled with the help I received from the physiotherapy and massage. Many of the local residents of Leicester were most generous with their hospitality and the wounded officers enjoyed entertaining car rides into the surrounding attractive country.

During mid-November and all early December it was encouraging to find my legs were rapidly getting stronger and I was able to walk to the town and back. During afternoons I attended a small ammunitions factory and was very soon able to turn out Mills Bombs – this seemed a very profitable part of my convalescence. I was most happy on the Sabbath morn that I was able to walk to the early communion service, and by mid-December the strength in my legs had returned and my wounds almost healed. I had several medical examinations in December and the Senior MO at the Hospital said I would be able to go home to Yorkshire for Christmas but that it would be important for me to attend the Physiotherapy Department at the York Military Hospital, as my wasted muscles and limbs needed a course of treatment for two or three months.

**December 22nd 1916**
I was discharged from Hospital on Friday 22nd December 1916 and given one month's sick leave.

I said good-bye to the nursing staff and officers in the ward and to the Craven Family, who had been so kind to me ever since I arrived at Leicester in late September. Mr and Mrs Craven had entertained me most generously and their daughters, Nora and Phyllis, took me for rides around the countryside, including one visit to see their brother Frank play in a rugger match at Uppingham School.

My father met me at York Station and it was dark when we arrived home at Haxby at 6.30 p.m. What a thrill it was to be home again with my dear parents and my two sisters, Barbara and Mary. A severe frost was in control and on Sunday 24th I went to the village Church. It was delightful to enjoy the peace and beauty of the devotions again. It was Christmas

Eve and I went for a walk in the afternoon to see some of the locals revelling in the skating on Mrs Bradshaw's pond. We all enjoyed Christmas and went to the early Eucharist, where we greatly enjoyed the Christmas Carols.

I went into York, to the Military Hospital and arranged to attend the Physiotherapy Department three times a week. I made splendid progress and was able to carry out gardening activities with Shaw, our faithful gardener. Later in the month I was able to enjoy rides on Mulligan, Pater's hunter. I was given a month's extension of sick leave until early March. The Ouse at York was frozen.

# Chapter Four

## BACK TO THE TRENCHES

*Extracts from diary*

*Spring 1917*

Had distressing letters from my Regiment in France. My Company Commander reported missing and several officer friends killed in action. The Battalion had sustained enormous casualties all through the "Somme" – over 500 casualties. Went to a special memorial event in York Minster – Elijah – a superb performance.

The physios have done splendid work on my weak legs and at the end of February my medical board passed me fit for "light duty" so I was to report to the Reserve regiment, 5th W. Yorks at Clipstone Camp on Sat. March 3rd.

Report back to Clipstone Camp and given one month's light Duty. Was put in charge of messing and able to march round with aid of stick. A very busy Headquarters Cookhouse so I arranged uniforms (white) for all Cookhouse staff. Had an excellent Cook Sergeant and I planned to "screen" all the washing up water to collect the copious supply of fat. This fat most valuable for the production of TNT explosive and I sent many barrels to Northern Command Headquarters and received special letter of commendation for the valuable salvage. I greatly enjoyed my manifold duties as a messing officer and the troops were fed with "special diet charts" each day.

*15th March 1917*

Revolution in Russia. Reports confirmed that the Czar has abdicated. Riots in Petrograd.

Great activity on Western Front. Great advance Bayonne taken and many miles of enemy territory captured. A Zepp shot down near Paris all the crew perish. Great Anglo-French advance 240 sq. miles taken. Several Officers contracted measles and were confined to their rooms.

## 31st March 1917

*We had a thrill today, Col. Bousfield came and visited the 3/5 Regt. Able to limp round Golf Course – this very pleasant and beneficial. Big offensive both on British and French fronts in France.*

*Went to York to the Bn. Hqrs. to collect draft and brought large body of recruits back to Clipstone.*

*Going on Revolver Course tomorrow. This I found v. exciting and enjoyable.*

*Spent all week on the revolver range and finished with a good score of 330. Going to York (Fulford Barracks) tomorrow on messing course one week hectic activities.*

*Further Medical Board – given one more month of light duties, to continue with messing. Going to Leicester today to see the Cravens and the Staff at Hospital – most enjoyable visit.*

*Appalling list of Casualties in paper: 55 Officers killed or wounded including several of my friends.*

*Had an exciting day as I took all the Drummer boys down the Crown Farm Colliery – they were a bunch of young scamps – we walked right to the coal face – was greatly relieved when we returned to the safety of the surface.*

*The Adjt very kindly offered me his horse to ride and I graciously offered him my thanks and enjoyed frequent rides in the Sherwood Forest.*

*Went for ride at Welbeck to see Duke of Westminster's stud of race horses and arranged with his agent to do a deal – I had a surplus of sugar and I would do a swap with potatoes as we had none in camp at the present. This worked wonderfully and we bartered successfully.*

All June I continued with my messing duties and managed to buy a full size billiard table with the sale of the "collected" fats from the washing-up water. This was presented to the men's canteen and was a great success.

## *July 1917*

HRH the Duke of Connaught made a visit to Clipstone Camp and made an inspection of the whole Division – a most impressive sight. In early July I was passed fit for overseas, as the Regiment was very short of officers. I received orders to proceed on Monday July 9th.

I was rather anxious about the state of my wounds. I would find it difficult to sleep in the trenches, especially in newly captured trenches without properly constructed dugouts.

On St Peter's Day I left on Overseas Leave and arrived home p.m. I had arranged for the purchase of a Pekinese Dog for dear Mater from Sydney Smith's friend at Welwyn Garden City – so "Chang", a young bitch, arrived safely after a long train journey. A perfect pet, very affectionate. I greatly enjoyed this leave and visited many friends. I had a visit from Mr Craven and Phyllis who were staying at Harrogate.

I had an exciting day's fishing on Mrs Bradshaw's pond and caught 12 fish – mostly roach. My sister Mary had done some spartan work on the tennis court and we had games with the Fergusons and Masons.

**Extracts from diary**

*I had a new "Buck Eye Bee Hive" delivered and soon had it all fitted with honey frames and introduced strong colony of Italian Bees with new Queen – all working well next day. Now have four strong colonies of bees.*

*I received a Telegram from Clipstone to report at Port of Embarkation on Tuesday July 10th. Went to early service on Monday 8th July. Father came to see me off at York Station -stayed in hotel Grosvenor Victoria and called at Cox's Bank for some French money. Crossed from Dover to BEF very rough crossing – reported at Transit Camp and arranged for medical exam. for RFC. Passed FIT. Was posted to 2/5 W. York Regiment in trenches at Bullecourt. Went for swim in Channel – most enjoyable. Due to entrain tomorrow for Albert. Went to HC at the Camp church.*

**Back to the Trenches**

***16th October 1917***

*Tedious train journey to Albert via St Omer. Albert still in ruins and I was most interested in the journey along R. Ancre as we passed within easy view of Thiepval and esp. the very place where I was wounded in Jacob's Ladder Observation Post at Beaumont Hamel. Whole area still very desolate and utterly destroyed.*

*Thrilled to be back W. Yorks 2/5 Bn. Met the Col. and Adjt. Blanes White as Company Cmdr. Also met Samuel and others from*

> 3/5 W. Yorks from Bullecourt.
>
> Had guide to our sector and arrive in trenches at night – very rough trenches and few dug outs. In trenches for first time since I was wounded in September 1916. Up all night in trench digging and did not get any sleep. Officer Dugout just room for two wire beds and table for meals. First time I tried to sleep on wire bed – wounds v. painful and I could not lie on either side. Had to see Bn. MO as wounds not properly healed – all right in proper bed with mattress and sheets. All this first week went on wiring parties for all the hours of darkness.
>
> On 4th night ordered to take control of large Foot patrol in "No Man's Land". Sergt. and 14 men. Went on long 12 to 3 a.m. reconnaissance into No Man's Land. Very dark night and Verey lights often gave no help. V. slow silent progress and we did not bump into enemy patrol. I lost my revolver when crawling and had to make a diligent search in the dark. After long search actually placed my hand on the barrel of the revolver.

No Man's Land is very vague and we made a great long trek into the unknown and finally returned to our own zone of No Man's Land at 3 a.m. But here let me tell you of an exciting episode when out in No Man's Land. My Sergt. approached me, having mustered the full patrol about half a mile from our trench system. He said, "We must return this way, Sir," and to my surprise the patrol was facing due EAST – direct to the German lines. This night was clear, with all the celestial star system showing bright. I had studied the stars for several years and there to the SE was my favourite constellation "ORION" in all his glory. I told the Sergt. "Do sit down and listen to me," I said firmly. "If you go the way you suggest you will all be shot or taken prisoner before dawn." I pointed out Orion to him and said that position is SE and leads straight to the German lines. He didn't trust my decision – "We must go in exactly the opposite direction," I ordered. We then mustered the patrol and slowly made our way back and after half an hour found ourselves challenged by a Scots sentry. We were only three hundred yards from the West Yorkshire trenches. Dawn was breaking when we reached our own zone and all eager for that early cup of tea. We had been on patrol four hours in No Man's Land and now had to face half an hour of "Stand to" and waited until full sunlight had taken control. My Sergt. came up to me and apologised for his stubbornness about the route for the return to our own lines, and appeared grateful for the way I explained the crisis to him. I now had about three hours sleep in the front line trench. Later that day I had a message to report to the Battalion Headquarters, and soon the

Adjutant told me that he was instructing me to go to the Army Signal School for one month's course at Pas-en-Artois, when the battalion went out of the trenches. The Battalion MO agreed that my wounds on both thighs had not healed sufficiently for the tough conditions in the trenches. For the whole of the next week I spent the nights in No Man's Land, very busy on wiring parties from 11 p.m. to 4 a.m.

## Extracts from diary

### 28th July 1917

> It was amazing how hard all the troops worked on the wiring and on the trench building, as the Bn. were holding an advanced "region" which had only recently been captured from the Germans in the Battle of Bullecourt. By the time the Bn. went out of the trenches for a week we had constructed a splendid strong belt of barbed wire defences.
>
> Leave trenches at 5 a.m. for transport lines and taken by Mule Cart to Bapaume and then to Etaples. Had a bath on the way, with clean shirt and underclothing. Spent night at Abbeville. Had best sleep for month. Slept at Officer Club. Left early for Etaples – had delightful swim in sea.

### 1st August 1917

> Went to Base Commandant's Office for my interview re RFC. Result satisfactory and expect to get posting in near future. Move on via Amiens to Doullens and then to Army Signals School at Pas-en-Artois. Report to HQ. of School which is in the Château of the Comte de Pas. A fine building where we have class rooms – I have comfortable bedroom and mattress bed so more comfortable for my legs. Very busy on course, doing buzzer practice most evenings and lectures each morning. Share room with Lt. Cross RCA. Delightful companion – legs troublesome and wounds irritating. Given permission to wear slacks. Exam at end of first week on Lamp, Flag and Buzzer. We are worked v. hard. Met my friend of the Scarborough Officer Course (1915 Nov.) who won VC on the Somme, Lt. Craig, Royal Scots. Passed Entrance Exam to Signal Course. Met the Comte de Pas who showed me round his splendid garden and greenhouse. Gave me large sugar melon and other fruit – speaks good English.

*Now having many lectures and tests every day – most concentrated. Had help from Lt. Norman Skentlebury RCA with electricity circuits in Telephones. Earl of Malmesbury is Adjt. of the Signal School. Exam all day on 11.viii.17. Electricity in a.m. Signals in afternoon. Did well. Rest on Sunday.*

*On Monday 13th Buzzer exam. 98.5% most satisfactory and then forward to Flag and Semaphore drill and Field Telephones.*
*Canadian's splendid advance near Lens and Ypres.*

*Final Buzzer Exam registered 100%. My Sergt. tutor delighted. Had concert in Château. Skentlebury played Moonlight Sonata. He plays extremely well and from ear! Gave us a lively evening at Madame Morey's. H.C. on Sunday 19th in chateau – Sundays very restful and walk round château most delightful. Noel Terry now walking with crutches at home. Started on trench telephones and long days laying cable and fixing up transmitting pack – v. hard work. Complete circuits successfully. Had to give 5 minute lecture before whole school most trying – only 1 evening to prepare. Massed flag drill for the whole school: V. fine sight. Construct Field Telephone with Skentlebury – most successful.*

*Day off with Skentlebury and we go into Doullens. Went by lorry and enjoyed seeing some excellent pictures and met several delightful French citizens who entertained us.*

## 2nd September 1917

*Now all the school go to trenches and lay telephone lines and have wonderful day. Get lots of lovely fruit and meats from estate near front line. Back after midnight. Return to trenches next day and carry out full scheme of Trench Telephones with our circuits. V. hot busy all day until late at night.*
*Have final dinner with Staff and Guests. Sit next to Earl of Malmesbury. Have much enjoyed course and hear I do not have to return to 5 W. Yorks but proceed to Air Ministry London to complete transfer to RFC. Final dinner at "Hotel du Grand Cerf" with all my friends.*

### 15th September 1917

*Must mention here the partridge shoot of the Comte de Pas and his guns. The dogs used for retrieving at Pelline controlled by the Count's daughter. I saw them in action – most successful in collecting wounded birds. The guns walk in line and shoot most of the French Partridges running!*

*Leave Pas early and proceed via Merville and Amiens to Etaples. Had breakfast with Capt. G. Sowerby W Yks Reg. who lives at Haxby. Here I parted company with my excellent Batman Gallagher who gave me splendid service and attention. The Ideal Servant. Got my travelling voucher at Boulogne at 10 a.m. and arrived London at 2 p.m. – my interview at 2 p.m. tomorrow at the Air Ministry.*

### 18th September 1917

*Very friendly meeting at Air Ministry and accepted for RFC and given leave until 28th Sept.*

*Went to visit Mr Parsons in Vigo Street to get Mum and Dad's 25th Wedding Anniversary present – also got Vi Hunt 21st birthday present – finally arrived home at 10 p.m.*

*Mr Parsons provides me with lovely silver sugar muffineer for the silver wedding present. I greatly enjoy my leave. I plant a new vine in large greenhouse and commence a new rockery and happily hew some excellent natural rocks.*

*Went rabbit shooting with Mr Sharp and shot 6 and half couples bolting rabbits from thick hedges. Merville Hull cousin from NZ Forces on leave and comes to stay. Saw him as a boy ten years ago when he visited us with all the family from NZ. Went to Helmsley with Tim Mason for 2 days trout fishing – fly fishing above Helmsley very attractive water – fish mostly half pounders but very dour takers. I am due to go on Observer's Flying Course at Winchester prior to going overseas. Lovely to be with my family again and enjoyed the family worship in the Parish Church for Holy Communion.*

# Chapter Five

## WITH THE ROYAL FLYING CORPS

*Extracts from diary*

**28th September 1917**

End of leave, farewell to all at home. Pater came to York to see me off. Called on Vi and Reg Hunt and left York at 3.12. Met in Kings Cross by Mount-Somerly and stayed night at 32, Gt Ormond Street. On morning of 29 Sept, Feast of St Michael and All Angels I went to St Johns Church, Red Lion Sq. for Holy Communion.

Air Ministry ordered me to RFC Reading to be kitted up and after 2 days went to Winchester to Hursley to camp in tents. Started immediately on "buzzer" course and Musketry on rifle range, scored 4" group.

**12th October 1917**

After completing signals went to aerodrome at Worthy Down and commenced first flight as observer on RE8 machines. Greatly enjoyed early flights as I was taken over all the surrounding country doing reconnaissance over railways and down over Southampton. Mostly flying at 6,000 feet. Had two flights each day and much longer reconnaissance beyond Andover and main line routes.

Had excitement of aerial camera gun – this is highly entertaining and involves lots of aerobatics. My reports on results of aerial reconnaissance were judged highly satisfactory.

On 23 Oct we crashed on landing. I was thrown into flying wires and suspended upside down. No damage done and we were sent into the air again on RE8 and went on long reconnaissance.

Had day off and went into Winchester – greatly enjoyed visiting the glorious cathedral with Reynolds who was lieut. in 5th W York with me. This cathedral is a joy and full of interest. King Canute is *buried here and also memorial to Gen. Buller VC – enjoyed service with excellent choir. Had dinner at the God Begot, an excellent eating house and then walked the 4 miles back to our camp at Hursley. Went to the Harvest Festival in Hursley Parish Church.*

*Exam all day 26th and did well. 83% on main subjects and 96% on my signals. Going on leave for 10 days. prior to going overseas.*

*Arrive at home 31st Oct. found Eric Monkman\* also on leave from Tanks. Continue to work extensively on Gardens and Rockeries. Met Noel Terry (in 5th W Yorks) who was wounded in thigh near Thiepval Sept 1916. His wound most severe and he is walking with sticks. He was actually only in trenches for half an hour and he was struck in thigh by sniper's bullet (by reversed bullet) which pierced his cigarette case and smashed into his right hip. Leave very pleasant and greatly enjoyed days with family and all cheery; final day 9th November when left for RFC BEF. Arrived Kings Cross. Met by Mount-Somerly and Griffin. Stayed at 32 Gt Ormond St. Went to Carminetta for final night in London. V. good cheery show. Got Baptismal Shell for the Haxby Church font and had it dispatched to Vicar at Haxby.*

## 11th November 1917

*Instructions from Air Ministry to report to 2nd Wing RFC Boulogne. Left Victoria 7.35 and had comfortable crossing to Boulogne, thence to Hazebruck and Baillieu and reported to No 42 Squadron. On arrival at 42 Sqdn. there is much excitement as the Sqdn has orders to proceed to Italy on the morrow. When having interview with Adjt urgent message comes through from 2nd wing to say No. 7 Sqdn at Proven near Poperinge has lost several machines and needs replacement observers. Adjt asks me if I would not mind being posted to No. 7 Sqdn – I willingly agree, so my kit is packed and I leave by truck and driver and proceed to No 7 Sqdn at Proven. Arrive mid-evening and find a special dinner celebration is on for new C.O. Major B E Sutton DSO MC of the Cumberland Yeomanry.*

---

\* Eric Monkman later married Peter's sister, Mary.

**13th November 1917**

>  Reported to Orderly Room to Recording Officer Ft. Lt. Hall and then taken to the Mess where there is much merriment and many guests in for dinner. About 50-60 diners and many "shot away" before the meal. The dinner is very noisy and is followed by typical RFC games. Much alcohol dispensed and there appears to be a very ample supply of whisky. Games like "Stiff Man," Blind boxing and "Glass throwing." This latter is a wild affair where 2 partake and one partner throws the glass at the outstretched hand on the wall and throwing is in turn. (Awful destruction of drinking glasses). Happily aiming is poor and no broken glass strikes a naked hand. Then followed blind boxing. This is a fierce affair with much heavy punching and very wild combat. Dr Jim Birley from Wing in for dinner – was at Oxford Univ. with Bertie Sutton. By 10 p.m. several young "hearties" are down and out and I help to carry victims to their huts – much rowdiness. My batman fixes me up for the night in a "B" flight hut with Pilot-Officer R.V. Facey[*], Lt Ian Johnson-Gilbert (Royal Scots) and Lt Watson: all Pilots – all are very tight – Facey quite OUT. By midnight all is quiet and guests have departed and very soon I am fast asleep as I can now sleep in a wire bed in my flea bag and blankets. My batman brings early morning tea at 7 a.m. and I join my friends for breakfast.

**14th November 1917**

>  Report at Sqdn. Office to meet C.O. Maj. B E Sutton DSO MC apparently very fond of dogs and looks as if he was a real countryman. Fill in many forms and met Recording Officer John Vic Hall. Posted to the "Contact Flight B" and Johnson-Gilbert to be my Pilot. A dull day, unfit for flying so a party is organised for Poperinge with Facey and Durham. Tea at La Poupee where we meet "Ginger" who appears to be on most affectionate terms with Durham. Suppose she is with most of the BEF.

>  Go with Gilly to Stores to collect my Flying Kit and maps and then examine B Flight Hangar and our RE8 Machine. I make thorough examination of my "rear" seat position, examine M.G. mounting and wireless details and camera installations for vertical and

---

[*] Rex Facey became a doctor and also a life long friend.

*horizontal camera positions. Gilbert introduces me to Wilmott who is Mess President who then shows me round the Mess. I note an immense quantity of alcohol, especially whisky; what a dream for the poor infantry battalions! As it is a dull day Gilbert takes me to tea with Dr Leitch at the Army Bacteriology Unit. I note very heavy battery firing towards the Yser Canal. Dull weather continues so we play rugger match against 21 Sqdn. First time I have played rugger since I was wounded on the Somme in September 1916. Result – draw 3 pts ALL. Meet Equipment Officer Beaumont he arranges an amazing bed in his cubicle – so like all HQs. personnel. Meet Teale who is batman and official "hair cutter".*

*First fine day for ages. Told to fly with McClurg, a most unpopular Yank who is a typical hot-air merchant. We go on special photography flight over Canal in Passchendaele zone -take 2 boxes of oblique photos. I easily recognise the area where I was in the trenches May – July 1915.*

### 21st November 1917

*Flying again – repeat photos 500 feet over Salient and take low flying views of trenches. Hun machine guns pepper our machine but no damage. After flight I take machine gun practice on rifle range. British Army has success in the south, 5,000 prisoners and many guns – my old Bn. 5th W. Yorks in the battle. Orderly Officer today, have good opportunity of seeing men and their huts. Men have comfortable beds and good food.*

### 23rd November 1917

*Two flights today, more photos, verticals and obliques. Very thrilling – have Scout escorts.*
　　*I have opportunity at night being Ord. Officer, of making full examination of CO's card index system and many Sqdn. details. What a vivid contrast to the Infantry. I am very interested in seeing youthful aspect of RFC NCOs in comparison with the Infantry.*

### 24th November 1917

*Another "vertical photos" expedition well over "Hun Land" at*

8,000 feet. We have excellent Scout Escort of 29 Sqdn. Abundant Archie* but we complete our mission and photograph enemy counter battery area.

Have long chat with C.O. on Yorks and North Country people. Bertie's aunt, Mrs Richardson, lives in ancient home near Sutton on the Forest. I hear a rumour that I am going to be put up as Mess President when Wilmott goes.

## 28th November 1917

First shoot with RA up 3 1/2 hours with Gilly in wireless contact with 6" battery – great excitement. Use my wireless to the full and control battery on enemy target and finally get 6 gun battery fire on large enemy position. Take vertical photos before the shoot and after final battery fire – most successful – we totally destroy enemy target.

## 30th November 1917

St Andrew's Day. CO celebrates in real Etonian Style by inviting Cumberland Yeomanry to dinner. The full band arrive and a Mark I* is declared. Many of the Yeomanry pass out early owing to the potency of No. 7 Sqdn's celebration "camouflage" – this drink designed by John Vic and Geo. Gardner, splendid mixture of whisky and orange juice. Appalling noise during dinner, followed by Stiffman and blind boxing. Now "Stiff man" is played by members sitting on the floor in large circle, feet just far enough apart to permit one man to stand in the centre. This man holding himself perfectly rigid falls backwards on to extended arms of one of the "sitters" and is then hurled round at an alarming rate until somebody collapses under the strain. Stiff man and collapsed man exchange places. I have bout of blindfold boxing with Durham, an Australian. I get a very thorough plastering, but only one black eye. Geoff Cooper, Westmorland and Cumberland Yeomanry with Bertie Sutton have thrilling glass throwing bout. Gilbert and Facey completely pass out and Gilbert ends up in mud. Poor Teale looks on at the muddy tartan slacks.

---

* "Archie" was anti-aircraft fire.

* Mark I is a special party.

### 1st December 1917

Exam. in Wireless and Artillery Construction – passed both. Rugger match in afternoon against No. 9 Sqdn. We win 5-3. I convert Gilly's excellent try.

### 4th December 1917

Machine gun exam at Wing; very hard frost, tough on fingers. At end of day special party, 10 in all go to La Poupee. Facey soon goes groggy at the knees. Can't understand why he always goes groggy at the knees. He breaks a plate and reduces Ginger to hysterics by his failure to fit the pieces together by remarking "Il ne fittez pas Mamselle." Finally the tender returned to the Sqdn with several "silent" men.

### 8th December 1917

Another dud day and after heavy drinking Gilly and Wattie disappear into the night. I get alarmed and follow later in pyjamas and gumboots – damned cold – I make diligent search and hear strange noises. My torch reveals a priceless picture: in the ditch I find completely submerged, Gilly and Wattie tucked in each others arms and singing a Canadian song, entitled "Tickle." I return to collect Facey to help with the muddy rescue. What a job we had to get them home in the intense cold and we finally arrived back at our hut at 2 am. In the morning poor Teale has an appalling job cleaning the tartan slacks. That night I go on night bombing and drop 4 bombs on enemy position.[*]

### 10th December 1917

Hear news that my old Yorkshire batman the faithful Bradbury has been killed at Cambrai.

### 14th December 1917

Hear that our CO has been mentioned in dispatches. Splendid. Play in Rugger match against 21 sqdn. We win 13-3. I kick two goals.

---

[*] It may seem that the number of parties was excessive but one must remember casualties were very heavy and German planes at times superior. The RFC solution was to make merry rather than mope, and *"esprit de corps"* was certainly very high.

*15th December 1917*

> *Shoot with Gilbert – enemy battery positions and later go on vertical photography. Recognised old trenches I was in during summer of 1915, esp. Essex Farm and Bridge 4.*

*16th December 1917*

> *Up 3 1/2 hours on patrol with Gilly and return in fierce snow storm.*

*17th December 1917*

> *My birthday. Find it is CO's also. Have party in hut when learning from orders that I have been awarded "Observers Wing".*

*18th December 1917*

> *CO calls Facey and me to go on early morning run at 7 am. Hardly daylight. Gilly also joins in and he crashes on a gravel path and injures his knee badly and we take him to nearby hospital for admission and injections.*

*20th December 1917*

> *Go to hospital to see Gilly – Facey joins me.*

*22nd December 1917*

> *Gilly returns from hospital and Rex Facey adds to his broken undercarriages, with another crash on landing.*

*23rd December 1917*

> *Flying today with Wattie and we see crowds of Belgians skating on the flooded areas.*

*25th December 1917*

> *Christmas Day – snow everywhere, visited men for their Christmas Dinner – we have a splendid party and great night. Jones superb at*

*the piano and we had Sqdn songs at least 12 times.*
*John Vic sings "Yo ho my lads Yo Ho."*

## 28th December 1917

*Now extremely cold – my nose frost bitten. Up on Photos. Scout escort most successful. We go far East over Roulers and see Huns in tram cars. Up again in afternoon. Horrocks and Booth in crash. I see impact on aerodrome – looked slight but Booth incurred fatal head injuries and died in hospital. Letter from Pater who says all hunting is stopped in England on account of frost. Turkey arrived from home in perfect condition after long journey – followed by arrival of goose.*

[Michael Wilson's note: At a time when casualties were very heavy, Peter wrote the following letter in case he was killed. Happily it never had to be sent.]

*No. 7 Squadron,*
*R.F.C.*
*B.E.F.*
*December 28th, 1917.*
*Flanders.*

*"Be merciful unto me O God, be merciful unto me, for my soul trusteth in Thee, and under the shadow of Thy wings shall be my refuge, make this tyranny be over-past.* Psalms LVii V 1

*My dearest beloved Father and Mother and all my dear ones at home,*

*I now write you a final letter, which I trust will be a great comfort to you all, if it be the divine will of my dear Lord to call me to my eternal rest during this terrible War.*
    *You all know that throughout this fearful conflict my whole trust has been cast upon my precious Saviour. Through all these long and critical periods the unseen presence has been so near to me – an unspeakable comfort, a treasured and constant companion. I often thank my gracious Lord for his great blessings, which he bestowed upon me by granting me safe returns to you all on several occasions during this war. What a glorious thing Prayer is – a sacred communion with the Almighty and I know how earnest your*

*prayers are when before retiring every night you all join together in that beautiful Family Prayer which is so perfect in God's sight. What a blessing was bestowed upon us all last Easter, when the whole family knelt before the Altar of our dear little Parish Church. That surely was an answer to Prayer. May God grant that as a family here on earth may we worship together in the celestial courts above.*

*It is hard to find words in order to express my thanks for all your unceasing kindness to me during these long months. I often thank my loving Father for the blessed home he has given to me and my prayer is "May He grant me a safe return to my Home in peace". God be praised for blessing me with such Christlike parents and my dear loving Sisters and Brother. My dearest Father and Mother, how precious you are to me and may the Almighty shower down upon you his richest blessings for many years to come. Your tender words to me have always been carefully registered in my heart and have helped me to live a straight life.*

*Barbara and Mary my dearest Sisters, how sweet and devoted you have been to me and I know what comfort and joy you have given to dearest Father and Mother. Your labours for the Master will surely receive a reward and continue to serve Him and true happiness and joy will always be yours. Edward my dear brother, I pray that you put your whole trust in God. He will guide you in the path of the righteous – the path of life is no easy task – to live a clean, straight life is very hard – I feel sure you will fulfil pure and holy ideals and prove a joy and comfort to my dearest ones. I must just say one short word to dearest Aunt and Florence – they have been so kind to me and to you all and especially to darling Mother. Though one so dear is now resting in the Paradise of God, someday there will be a glorious reunion and forever happiness and joy will reign. I know the cross has been very heavy, but you have bravely borne it.*

*If it be the will of my dear Lord to call me to his Holy presence, may you find comfort in knowing that I possess a joyful heart, knowing that I have done my best to fight the battle of life. I feel so happy and I possess a deep spirit of peace – I simply cling to the Cross and whatsoever He wills – must be. If I make the journey beyond – to that brighter home – I pray that He will grant you His Holy spirit and help you to bear the sorrow. Such spiritual comfort is far above any which this world can afford.*

*I am indeed proud to think that I am here doing my bit for my dear old Country, my King and my beloved home. It is a glorious* thing to fight for one's country and in a cause for freedom. May God grant us victory which will lead to a glorious peace and to the further extension of His Kingdom on Earth. What a happy day for all – when the world will utter forth the thanksgivings of a just and righteous peace. I hope and pray that that glorious day is not far distant, may it be soon.

It is time to conclude, so my dearest ones I will say farewell in Christ Jesus. I pray that as a family here on earth, may we be reunited in the realms above. If I meet you not again on earth I shall wait in glory at the golden gates of Eternity. There, beside my dear Lord you will be welcomed by the Prince of Peace and together we shall enter that House of many mansions, where for ever as a family we shall fall down and worship before the Throne of God and the Lamb. May these words welcome you as you enter the realms of eternity "Well done good and faithful servants enter thou into the joys of my Lord". What a day of rejoicing when all loved ones will be reunited – thus transplanted to rise and shine in Heaven. May Heaven's richest blessings be showered down upon you all and may happiness and joy ever reign within the walls of our dear home. My dearest love to you all my dearest ones. Do not lament – but say "It is Thy will O Lord". Remember some day we shall meet again and nothing can then separate us – we shall be for ever with the Lord.

My dearest Father and Mother good bye, my dearest Barbara and Mary and Edward farewell – Mother darling cheer up the home – dearest Father will be a great source of comfort. I will close thanking and praising God for His many and rich blessings which he has abundantly bestowed upon me. I shall always go into action trusting wholly in my creator. He will cover my head in the day of battle. I am so happy and I do not fear the battle – my dear Lord is waiting for me – if he calls me to his eternal presence, I breathe "O Lamb of God I come".

"Finally, dear ones farewell, be perfect, be of good comfort, be of one mind. Live in peace and the God of love and peace shall be with you". I commit you all unto the divine keeping of God, may his manifold blessings be showered down upon you all and may the Holy spirit of God strengthen you all.

My dearest love to you all – Farewell in Christ Jesus.

I remain,
Ever your beloved Son,
Arthur G. Wilson
Lt. R.F.C.

*1st January 1918*

>Up 2½ hours – Williams wounded – another cheery evening, Darnley sings "The Floral Dance." Went to find my old Regt. 5th W Yorks, by motor cycle side car – after long search find them near Vlamertinghe. Have lunch with Col. Oddy and Hqrs Staff.

*5th January 1918*

>Still dud so flying party go to St Omer for day and we lunch at Vincents and eat many oysters. Bertie* says Gardner has got his Sqdn. – so we have a tremendous evening and dinner of rejoicing. After Gardner's departure next day Gilly takes me to tea with Leitch again – re-examine many forms of bacteria under microscope.
>
>Hunter stands on his head for 5 minutes although BALD! C.O. goes on leave. More snow followed by rain. The Lekkebokke Beke overflows. Appalling mud.
>
>Horses are being allowed for RFC – hurrah!

*16th January 1918*

>Fly on shoot with McClurg – training hard for Rugger Cup on 19th against No. 9 Sqdn.

*19th January 1918*

>First round of Wing Rugger Cup on Aerodrome – match played against No. 9 Sqdn. Immense gathering including the Chinese. We play at top of our form especially Isett and John Vic and Borman opens scoring with drop goal. Wilmott and I score tries with both conversions by Peter Holm. Half time 14 pts to 0. Second half still on top of our form. Gilly presents me with 2 more tries, one conversion – then Firth scores after long run. We win 1 drop goal, 3 goals, 3 tries to 1 try, 28 pts to 3. A Mark I celebration declared and the Binge Boys celebrate – a tremendous night – chaos long before port is circulated. Very few in for breakfast. The two horses arrive, one a large grey.

---

* The young men of 7 Squadron were quite something. To my knowledge Bertie Sutton stayed on in the RAF and became a much respected Air Marshall and was knighted; Leonard Isett became Air Vice Marshall Sir Leonard Isett, Chief of New Zealand Air Staff; Maurice Harland became Bishop of Durham 1955-1966; Ian Johnson-Gilbert, "Gilly", became Sir Ian Johnson-Gilbert and was Lord Provost of Edinburgh, among other things. They became friends for life.

## 21st January 1918

*Went for a ride – mounted grey – disgraceful scene as horse bolts and makes for Proven. Notice on board "Horses must go through village at the walk." Belgium Police attempt to stop me – horse gallops through village on cobblestones and jumps clean over motor bike and side-car and finally halted at the big level crossing gates. I take horse through flooded area and tire him out and finally return quietly to Sqdn and have my leg severely pulled. But I find the horse is blind in one eye.*

Aerial Reconnaissance photograph of Front Line – possibly of Yser Canal near Ypres. Note the total destruction, shell holes and opposing (?) trench systems.

## 23rd January 1918

*Up with Gilly over Allsopp's Farm, exciting 10 minutes with Hun machine-gun duel. Machine hit and left tail control shot away. Great difficulty in flying back, I wireless for ambulance to stand by. Gilly does very well but we crash heavily on landing. We didn't catch fire and I am sawn out of wreckage in half an hour – although both escape serious injury apart from local bruising. We are sent up immediately on another 3 hour patrol and return aching. C.O. and Flight Commanders gazing on wreckage.*

Proven 1918. RE8 Machine. "Gilly" Johnson Gilbert 4th from left; Bertie Sutton 6th from right; Rex Facey 4th from right. (Peter on leave.)

*24th January 1918*

*Up with Wattie on "verticals". Hun very busy.*

*25th January 1918*

*Burns Nicht. Gilly prepares banquet and ready for sticky night. Haggis arrives from Edinburgh and we have a most lively evening. Gilly bolts after dinner and I follow him over hop field and he finally arrives at Machine Gun post near Sqdn. Office. He mounts and fires M Gun and Sentry and myself lie flat in mud. Fortunately he had a stoppage and I jump the sand bags and collar him, then apply an arm-lock and lead him along duck boards to his hut and put him to bed. Facey declaring, "I don't like haggis but I do whisky."*

*28th January 1918*

*Went on verticals with Gilbert. Prosser and Durham in other machine. Our escort fails to turn up at rendezvous nevertheless we cross enemy lines to Fiver Wood and take a lot of photos over counter battery area. Heavily attacked by Archie and enemy aircraft – Prosser furious with Gilly for pushing far over Hunland.*

*Jones and Brown decide to ride horses – Brown decides to ride the brown. After a short time Jones returns in an ambulance with terrible abrasions of face and hands and doesn't like my first aid treatment with Iodine etc.*

*Chinese decorate hut and catch sparrows by a most subtle trick. Bertie returns from leave. We have very cheery evening in Mess with Jones giving us delightful treat on piano!*

*31st January 1918*

*Austrian prisoners decorate the mess and one (an artist) produces a clever cartoon entitled "HAVA NOTHER". He paints new RAF Badge on canvass and the Binge boys register the arms as their coat of arms.*

*2nd February 1918*

*Visit "CWS" Central Wireless Station. Meet the signallers who take down my signals from the air and then visit several of the Batteries I use when doing destructive shoots. I discover several graves of my old Regt. near front line, mostly 1915.*

### 3rd February 1918

*I go to Dunkirk shopping for men and buy fresh fish from comic very fat French fisher girl who has 2 big mobile teeth. Food much cheaper in this Belgian Zone and I save a lot of money and am able to charge less for mess bills. 3/- (three shillings) per day for all meals and free drinks at dinner. I soon accumulate a healthy bank balance with the "Banque de France".*

### 5th February 1918

*Went for most exciting "Contact Patrol" with Gilly over Gravel Farm at 300 feet. Get excellent view of German Trenches. Very heavy German Machine Gun Fire. I well remember this area of the front line from the summer of 1915.*

### 6-10th February 1918

*Went to stay with RFA Battery near Poelcappelle for 4 days. See battery in action with 6" Hows. The Huns reply with heavy counter battery shelling. Most unpleasant; reminds me of my days on the Somme in 1916. We are entertained by mice who transport paper in tunnels when torches are shone on them. The 6" Battery appears to me to be very near the front line. The whole region is saturated by deep very sticky mud and we can only walk on duck boards. Here we are in the Passchendaele zone with total destruction of all dwellings and not a single tree left standing. Tremendous artillery duel going on night and day and casualties from shell fire to Battery Personnel. I make extensive examination of the area with the Battery Commander and can see how the advancing infantry have no chance if wounded – they can only seek shelter in the huge shell holes which are half full of water. It is almost impossible for the Stretcher Bearers to collect the severely wounded. I return to my Sqdn. at Proven on the night of 9th as I am going on leave tomorrow with Isett.*

## 12th-26th February 1918

Leave. Stayed night at Hotel Flandre, Calais – Good crossing. Caught night express at Kings Cross for York.

Grand to be home again with the family and my brother, Edward, gets leave at same time from his ship. Have an excellent day's hunting with the York & Ainsty Foxhounds – given an excellent mount – young 4 year old hunter, very fresh – plenty of Military out and we have superb run over grass. Meet at famous Askham Bogs and soon find fox and then pack run over the cream of the Y and A country. I take a toss at one big hedge and my Father says, "Come and take my mount, that young horse is too much for you." So I change my mount and ride his aged hunter. One Senior Officer who saw my embarrassment says, "Young man, I think flying suits you better than hunting." However, I join in the hunt again and have a super ride on my father's mount. The fox goes to ground and we have a long ride home together after a most enjoyable day's hunting.

I have a splendid leave and enjoyed the days in our dear home – my brother helped me in the garden which was full of colour from the crocuses and snowdrops. Made several trips to York to visit the Hunts and other friends and bought my two sisters a silk blouse each at Leek and Thorps.

Returned to London night of 26th and went to "Pamela" at the Palace. Lily Elsie excellent. Arrived back at Squadron on March 1st. Play No. 10 Sqdn. at Rugger – splendid match before our Rugger Final. We play a pointless draw – the first time I have ever played in a drawn match at Rugger. Went to No. 9 Sqdn. with Gilly to lecture on 1st Battle of Ypres. John Vic orders stout as drink for training for Final on Monday

## 4th March 1918 – Rugger Final against No. 21 Sqdn.

Huge crowd and all No. 9 Sqdn. turn up to support us. They fire lots of Verey lights and noise from klaxon horns tremendous. The game commenced at a tremendous rate and No. 21 nearly score.

Our forwards then take control, Isett breaks away supported by John Vic (HAC). Isett sells a perfect dummy and scores a super try. Peter Wilson kicks goal. Klaxon horns then deafening.

Then Geoff Borman (South African) scores a second try which I failed to convert. Gilbert superb in tackling and saves certain try. Ding dong struggle most of second half then just on time A.M.

*Lane makes a long run down line to score in the corner.*

*Our forwards splendid and although much lighter than 21 Sqdn. we get most of the ball. The whistle goes for time and W/Cdr Barratt\* presents the cup. The noise is so terrific he can't make his speech heard and all he can say is "Well, Hall, here's the cup."*

*Then all retire to the Mess and Morgan, our super Mess Sergt. provides champagne and the cup is filled and circulated, then go into dinner and Sgt. Morgan and Staff put on a splendid show – 40 completely blotto by dinner and several carried to their beds during the celebration banquet. I assist many guests to their cars and the rumpus carries on until midnight – when finally I retire after a most historic day.*

### 5th March 1918

*Went with my pilot, Gilly, to Hazebruck also Borman to see them off on leave, then go to Hotel de la Gare to lunch with Walter Thompson and friend. A highly scented French belle attached herself to our table and I get most annoyed when she asks many questions. I strongly suspect her as a spy and she gives Walter a scented silk handkerchief and finally the hussy annexes my chocolate box which I had bought for our hut.*

### 6th March 1918

*I am on Dawn and Dusk patrol with Wattie most exciting and to finish the day another Mark I is ordered, a sort of private celebration for our Rugger victory. This is a final dinner to Wilmott who is going on HE (Home Establishment). Jones superb at the piano – all the Sqdn. sang recital – Padre Leonard a splendid sporting fellow – accepts the Sqdn. songs. To the surprise of all John Vic passes away for the very first time and asks to be put to bed. He is terribly upset at this undignified decline in his reputation.*

### 9th March 1918

*Go with Facey on Counter Battery Photos for first time – very exciting.*

---

\* I believe the Wing Commander was "Ugly" Barratt, who became a very distinguished Air Marshall. The winning team is featured on the back of the jacket sleeve.

### 10th March 1918

*Work hard on my garden. Seeds from Banbury. Bertie looks on and is very sarcastic. Wattie helps me with the digging. Spot the puppy bites a hole in my tunic pocket – he comes on flight and sits with me in back of plane. He is most amazed when I fire the machine gun – can't understand the falling cartridge cases as they hit the floor.*

### 12th March 1918

*Our Scout Sqdn. has record battles with the Hun Sqdns, they bag 15 Huns and two balloons in three days. Quigley bags one EA (German plane) and one balloon.*

*I do very well with mess a/cs and increase our Bank Balance with Banque de France in St Omer. I strike oil in the Belge area and get two cases of whisky in one of their canteens – only pay 3/- per bottle i.e. for 24 bottles 72/-.*

### 14th March 1918

*Boxing at No. 9. Saunders meets Goodwin and is beaten on points after 15 rounds of 3 minutes. A splendid sporting fight. Bandsman Rice, English Runner-up takes on Padre Leonard, our Chaplain, who puts on a capital show. Seventy in for dinner, Wattie and Buckley found late in evening in corner of mess lying on floor with their minds still on the Boxing Events. Wattie murmurs, "Hit 'em on the jaw" and promptly gets in a smashing blow to Buckley's chin – Buckley having no guard accepts the blow and reciprocates by giving Wattie a real smasher – also has no guard – we put them to bed and there are still faint murmurings on the night air, "Hit 'em on the jaw."*

### 15th March 1918

*Went to Hazebruck and lunch at Hotel de la Gare with Wattie and Durham. We are told that Mlle de la Chocolat departed for Marseilles on Sunday wanted by French Police. Facey and I take a walk in the town and pass several private houses obviously "Maison Rouge" and are most annoyed by the persistent approach of several wee girls all 6 – 7 who bombard us with the saying, "you Jig-a-Jig with my sister" – this quite astounds us and they simply would not leave us – we were relieved to get back to the tender.*

*16th March 1918*

>Up early with Facey and we leave in dark on bombing of Hun gun emplacements – we chase wild duck over the flooded areas.* Hapgood, our Intelligence Officer, is great help to me on my flight reports.
>
>When playing footer match had sudden alarm and we had to take to the air in footer togs – action reconnaissance area over Front Line.

*18th March 1918*

>Went on Obliques with Burgess and had super new large camera fitted – went on long flight to south to Merville Estacres – a Race Horse Farm. I saw old trenches of 1915 and spotted some old billets – many fires all over area mostly farms and stacks.

*21st March 1918*

>Went to visit Gunners and join Sqdn. Boxing for match with Gunners. I had stiff fight and was heavily plastered by a much fitter opponent but lasted three 3-minute rounds.
>
>Report of SAD loss in Channel when U-boat sank a ship load of whisky off Dunkirk.

*24th March 1918*

>Went on reconnaissance with Castleman and drop four bombs on Hun Toc Emma. McClurg made Flt Cmdr. – passed over Gilly and Wattie. Gilly, Castleman and Burgess going on HE tomorrow.

*25th March 1918*

>Following McClurg's appointment as Flt. Cmdr. of B Flight, there is much indignation in the whole Sqdn. and Gilly, Burgess, Castleman and Isett put on Home Establishment. Bad luck on Wattie being in Flight with Junior Officer being I/C Flight. Embarrassment could have been avoided if new promotion

---

* This shows how low they flew.

had come from another Sqdn. Terrific celebration in Mess tonight to celebrate going home of Binge Boys. A most noisy affair during whole of dinner – many "shot away". Gilly cracks the drum and takes endless alcohol and rushes out of mess – across fields to Leitch's Pack Hut – I follow and discover him bogged in deep ditch – most difficult to get him "rescued" and I get in frightful mess with mud – water over all my uniform. Have to cling on to him all way back to Sqdn. and manage to get him into bed. Celebrations still going on until midnight and most of Sqdn. "Flat out". Facey and Buckler shot away and both put to bed singing.

**26th March 1918**

Up on early reconnaissance with Maurice Harland, who was at St Peter's School, York, with me. We got lost in terrific ball of cloud and come out well over Hun lines over Straden. We are heavily archied and I am very windy as I am only in pyjamas under Flying Kit. Keep a sharp look out for Hun Scouts and I tell Maurice to fly W back into cloud and make for the Belgian area via the Houlthurst Forest. Most exciting trip, we fly back at 1000 ft and I soon spot Ostende and coastal towns and then cross Belgian zone and head for Yser canal and our own zone. Finally, we find our way to our aerodrome at Proven. After breakfast we see Gilly, Isett and other "Binge Boys" off on H.E. After train had left we found out that Gilly had left his precious "Duller Virginian" cigs in tender. We race off and finally catch up train and Gilly and Co spot us racing up road. We manage to get on to track and hand up cigs safely to Gilly as train rushes by.

**30th March 1918**

New Pilot killed in crash. Hun offensive in South – another new pilot loses himself as soon as he is airborne and lands in some distant aerodrome. He is posted back to Training Sqdn. near St Omer. On landing with Harland we crash. I am immediately requested to fly with my Flt. Cmdr. and take urgent photos of Poelcappelle area – successful and one photo shows Hun plane intact in trench area. After return I go on shopping trip to Hazebruck and town is heavily shelled so I proceed to St Omer. Reports of massive Hun attack down south.

*4th April 1918*

McCudden's brother killed – was once a motor cyclist in this Sqdn. I prepare for a special Mark I tonight as 29 Sqdn. our 'Scout Escorts' our guests. Radwell O/C 9 Sqdn. also guest. After excellent dinner, round of Sqdn. games with Cock Fighting and Glass Breaking display. Bertie and Huffy Dixon (c/o of 29 Sqdn) have remarkable glass breaking display. Singing of all Sqdn. songs with Jones super at the Piano.

*6th April 1918*

Went on special flight south to General Farm – extensive area of countryside blazing with fires. Could not contact any of our troops to establish lines of defence. Did not see any Hun machines or any of own. A small RE2E machine spotted on ground on Belge aerodrome. We send transport over and salvage machine which is in good condition. Quickly overhauled and flight tested – successful. Went up for flight in "Querk" over Belgian area and pass over Berguis most enjoyable.

*7th April 1918*

Up again with McClurg on "Counter Attack patrol" to W. of Ypres. Call up CWS (Central Wireless Stn) on Klaxon Horn. Hunter appeared and I arrange with Padre to motor to CWS at 6.30 a.m. after breakfast. Padre arranges to give Holy Communion to Wireless Operators. I cross Bridge 4 over Yser Canal – Haven't been here since 1915 when I was with 5th W. Yorks. Regt. Pass Essex Farm – all ruins.

*9th April 1918*

I join tender for Boulogne which is taking Howard and Barnes on leave. When at leave boat General Trenchard joins us in conversation and tells us RFC only unit allowed leave at present. He was delighted to hear Bertie Sutton was our CO. He told us Bertie used to be his Staff Capt.

On our return from Boulogne we pick up Harland in St Omer at 2 a.m. Very cold drive – driver falls asleep and we nearly crash into a tree.

Sudden early morning news of dramatic Hun attack down on

*Armentières Front. Much excitement in Sqdn. Sent on special reconnaissance down south as I knew the area well from 1915.*

### 10th April 1918

*Up at 4 a.m. with Harland and I know village of our objective. Very dull morning, rain and fog. I direct Maurice and see many farms burning – spot Glenny in his machine and suddenly see him nose dive – I fear he is hit. We fly low over well-known area and get heavily shot at by Hun machine gunners. I manage to make contact with Worcesters by my lamp and klaxon. Then we were flying at 200-300 feet. Most important contact with Worcesters – amazing sight to witness French evacuation of Armentières. We return to Proven and just before landing see a landing RE8 blow up as bombs explode. King and Hughes killed.*

*Habgood gives me excellent help with reports – ours the <u>only</u> machine to return from the initial six sent out to check German advance.\**

*Up again immediately with McClurg as we proceed South to Bomb Merville. Fly over hordes of Huns on roads and they blaze away at us as we fly over. We bomb our old billet of W Yorks of 1915 and flying low I fire 400 rounds at masses of Hun troops. Whole countryside ablaze from Merville to Armentières. We land to find many machines missing but to our joy Glenny turns up wearing a comic bowler hat. Inman and Gersen still missing and Lloyd Rey wounded and landed at St Omer. The French Staff arrive to take over Proven Aerodrome and I'm told we move to Droglandt tomorrow. Very busy packing up Mess. Morgan works admirably.*

### 13th April 1918

*Orders for move to Droglandt is confirmed. Machines leave carrying dogs, kit, very many cases of whisky and goat and all our possessions. I follow with men, kit and Headquarters. Utter chaos on roads. Civilians wheeling their possessions and infants in prams and small carts.*

*Cpl. Morgan quickly establishes mess and prepares an excellent dinner for Headquarters Staff. I'm very busy arranging new mess*

---

\* It was for his vital work under heavy fire during the retreat, reporting where British and German units were, that he was awarded his MC.

*comforts. Facey, Wattie and Harland journey to local estaminet and refresh rather heavily in champagne. On way back to aerodrome Facey falls in ditch, gets very wet and covered in mud. Wattie brings him into our hut and as he has no bed yet I cover him with blanket in his valise. Up early with Wattie for Contact Patrol over Ypres Salient – up nearly four hours but didn't see a single Hun – all trenches empty only just had sufficient petrol to reach aerodrome. Up immediately again with McClurg on French Front over Mont de Cars and Hemmel.*

### 15th April 1918

*We soon located battle from fires everywhere and identified French troops from 500 ft along Mont de Cars. Watch French Infantry attack German Trenches. Whole battle front amazing sight and lines of French 75s in action firing at point blank range at Huns. French Gunners in bare chests loading 75s – terribly fast and causing tremendous havoc in German lines. Saw French Infantry capture German Trenches. We flew backwards and forwards along battle front at under 500'. It was clear the French had succeeded in halting the main German attack and at this point, with the terrific support from the scores of French 75s, were inflicting immense casualties on the Huns. I watched this mighty battle for two hours and finally left for our return flight to Droglandt. On arriving back found Wright DCM and Coombes missing somewhere near Merville. Now snowing and roads in a frightful mess. All in favour of the wretched Hun. Retired to my hut early as I was very exhausted.*

### 18th April 1918

*Next day I went to Proven shopping\* and found the village was being shelled by the Hun. I called at our old aerodrome and looked at my veg. garden to see the early seeds were growing well. Up early on 19th and went on Counter Attack Patrol in the Ypres area. On return found Col. Barratt had arrived in a Silver Nieuport to discuss the Sqdn. moving to St Marie Cappelle as Hun advances.*

*We found No. 9 Sqdn. had moved to rest at Calais. I motored*

---

\* "Shopping" – remember Peter was Messing Officer, so partly responsible for provisions.

over with Padre Leonard and found them resting in a most desirable billet. Did some shopping and then return to Droglandt. Huns bomb us every night.

### 26th April 1918

We had a big dinner party and entertained lots of French Air Aces including George Guynemer, who introduced himself to each of the Sqdn. as follows. He stood erect in front of each of us and repeated his slogan, "Et moi, Guynemer, Chevalier Legion d'Honneur, Medaille Militaire, Croix de Guerre quatre palmes" to each of us, saluting each member before his oration!*

By the end of the evening almost all our French guests had "passed out" and at midnight we saw them to their cars.

### 28th April 1918

Fletcher and I were detailed to visit St Marie Capelle aerodrome. We were NOT impressed, as no place for mess, no huts for sleeping quarters, only big hangars with few huts as stores. We met Col. Barratt in St Omer and gave him our report. He was most unsympathetic and told us it would do and we could sleep in hangars and take our meals there. So we returned to Droglandt and reported to Bertie. Facey and Harland and others returned from local Estaminet after lots and lots of champagne and in hut when all in bed, Maurice kept repeating, "I can't eradicate this machine from its spinning proclivities. The machine would roll and turn."!

### 30th April 1918

Our Sqdn. Commander Sqdn. Ldr. B E Sutton DSO MC calls on me early in my hut with most exciting news. He tells me, "Peter you have been awarded the MC and here is a copy of the thrilling signal." It was a copy of Army Orders by General Sir Herbert Plumer, Commanding the 2nd Army.

"Military Secretary's Branch, IMMEDIATE AWARDS Under authority delegated by His Majesty the King, the Field Marshal Commanding-in-Chief has made the following awards for

---

* My father's writing was tricky to read particularly regarding place names and surnames. Lyn Macdonald informed me that it could be Guynemer. If not Nungesser.

*gallantry and devotion to duty in action.*

*"The Military Cross to Second Lieut. A G Wilson, West Yorkshire Regiment, attd. Royal Air Force."*

*There were 12 names awarded the MC for gallantry during the recent German push. Imagine my thrill at this exciting news. The CO orders a Mark 1 for tonight, so I go off shopping to Dunkirk. Leete comes to help me buy wines, fish and other special foods. Eighty for dinner including some French Pilots. A terrific night in mess and Padre grants me a dispensation for Binge. I should mention here that I had been almost TT since August 1914 only permitting myself a small port when toasting the King's Health.*

---

COPY OF TELEGRAM FROM GENERAL SIR DOUGLAS HAIG C/I/CHIEF B.E.F.

TO OFFICER COMMANDING 7 SQUADRON R.A.F. 30 APL.1918.

UNDER AUTHORITY GRANTED BY H. M. THE KING COMMANDER IN CHIEF
AWARDS MILITARY CROSS .- LIEUT. A. G. WILSON WEST YORKS. REGT.
FROM 2ND. WING. R. A. F.

TIME 07:30AM.

---

COPY OF LONDON GAZETTE.    AWARD OF MILITARY CROSS.   30

LIEUT. A. G. WILSON, 5TH. WEST YORKS. REGT. ATTCH. R. F. C.
"FOR CONSPICUOUS GALLANTRY AND DEVOTION TO DUTY . HE FLEW UNDER
MOST DIFFICULT WEATHER CONDITIONS AND OBTAINED UNDER HEAVY FIRE,
VALUABLE INFORMATION WHICH HE EMBODIED IN A SERIES OF EXCELLENT
REPORTS. ON ONE OCCASION, WHEN A SMOKE SCREEN WAS PUT UP BY THE
ENEMY, HE FLEW ROUND AND MADE A CLOSE RECONNAISSANCE FROM BETWEEN
500 TO 1000 FEET UNDER HEAVY ANTIAIRCRAFT AND MACHINE- GUN FIRE."

---

*Wattie comes into dinner plastered with ribbon – a leg pull on Guynemer, the French Ace – he causes a sensation with the French Officers. Facey brings 20 double whiskies to me and orders me to drink all. I am Mess President and kept control of my alcoholic intake and went through dinner successfully – the noise is colossal. The French get heavy treatment at "Stiff Man." By 9 p.m. feel "shot away" and we stagger off to join No. 10 Mess. The wing MO lifts me on to the top of the piano and I make many speeches and finally I crash through the top of piano into the works. Jones plays the piano sitting on the floor. We carry many guests to their cars and the French Officers drive into ditch. The Cecil Aldrin pictures appear very mobile towards 11 pm – I am made a "Binge Boy" and I reassure Bertie Sutton and the Pig Glenny (the other member of No. 7 Sqdn. who was awarded a bar to his MC) that I am OK by pointing to many constellations in the Heavens! I then attempt to get into bed – but the damn bed would "roll and trip."*

*Here I must quote a written report of Wilbur Fletcher: "Peter appears a little off the rails here with the assistance of Dafforn (and much assistance was necessary) I put Peter to bed and three of us found it necessary to sit on Peter for some time before he would stay put."*

### 1st May 1918

*I wake early with amazing thirst and Barber our super batman brings me an early cup of tea. I surprise everyone by eating a good breakfast. My wounds suddenly become very irritable and break out in several places. MO puts me on Water Cart but fit to FLY.*

### 3rd May 1918

*Gauntlett wounded in foot. Flying with Wattie over Ypres Salient on Contact Patrol and when flying back over Wattan I think I spotted my old W Yorks. Colonel sitting in deck chair 200′ below. I ask Wattie to fly round and round as I write message and drop it by streamer almost on top of Colonel. He jumps up after reading my message and confirms OK. I drop 2nd message inviting several officers to dinner. When back at Droglandt manage to contact Adjutant of W Yorks and confirm my invitation. But was told the terrible news that the 5th W Yorks had been annihilated at front – Poelcapelle. They went into action with 640 and had all Officers killed and only came out with 21 troops.*

*I send tender to collect Officers of 5th W Yorks and 5 came to dinner including my old Company Commander, Captain Ken Mackay. We had a grand evening and we arrange several flights for them.*

*6th May 1918*

*Up nearly five hours with Wattie over Ypres Salient – take oblique photos – petrol exhausted after landing on aerodrome.*

*9th May 1918*

*Ascension Day. Padre arranges a service with Holy Communion. Bertie offers me "Home Establishment" – I ask to stay in Sqdn. until June. Went with Wattie and Leete shopping to Berques and Calais. We fill up with petrol at no. 9 Sqdn. They play tennis and "fare sumptuously" every day. On way home some Yankee drunks stop the tender. We nearly have a rough house. Wattie with red face and wild hair causes a retreat.*

*10th May 1918*

*Balance at Bank – Mess funds in healthy state. Mess bills now only 35 Fr. a week. Free drinks at dinner and cigars. Hun fighter plays havoc in our observation Balloon line. Take off with Bertie to try and deal with Hun Pilot but he is much faster than our RE8 and we fail to make contact. This Hun shot down six balloons in flames. But on his return next day our fighters cut him off and shot him down in flames.*

*Went with Coomb-Taylor in big Armstrong Whitworth in flight to visit Hun Prisoner Camp and take tea with Commandant.*

*11th May 1918*

*Thick fog on way home, we fly at 100' and nearly bump into tall chimney. I wireless to Wing Headquarters to warn them of fog.*

*12th May 1918*

*Went on special photo-reconnaissance. Verticals at 12000 ft. with Scout Fighter Escort. Photo Hun Counter battery area most exciting. Sky full of planes, our escort were superb and gave us super protection.*

*7 Squadron Officers, Droglandt May 1918.*

Bertie Sutton centre seated row. Peter on ground fourth from left. Note the different uniforms of the volunteers from many regiments who composed the RFC in those days.

### 13th May 1918

> Went with John Vic to Boulogne and pay lots of Francs into our account. We now have 5000 Fr Credit. We lunch at Officers Club and then shop. When back at Sqdn. told that Facey and self are for LEAVE on 15th. We are bombed at night and two Hun bombs explode in next field!.

### 14th May 1918

> Darnley after his marriage has new habit of flying far over Hunland – this annoys his Observer Leete who insists on sitting on cockpit floor. This cures him and Darnley promises to keep within reasonable distance of our own line. Trip to Winezelle for dinner with Bertie to dine at "The Widows". He appears in his famous goatskin. During dinner his goatskin is stolen from his Crossley Car. He is furious and seems uncommonly upset. Hock and Scotch fail to bring comfort.

*15th May 1918*

>Bertie still most worried over loss of goat skin. He suspects "The Widow" or French officers have pinched it. Busy clearing up Mess Books as we prepare for leave. Wattie, Buckler and Harland leave with us and we drop them at Winezelle, Hun planes follow us to St Omer – busy bombing us but bad misses. We stay at Hotel du Commerce for night. A very annoying French demoiselle keeps chasing me around hotel. Facey laughs and refuses to come to my help.

*16th May 1918*

>Next morning long hot ride in train to Boulogne and find that there is no leave boat until late in day with Destroyer escort. Very calm cruising in evening and on arriving on leave train we find masses of females to greet us with refreshment at Victoria. Taxi to Kings Cross where I catch last train north to York. Great welcome at home – arrive breakfast time by taxi from York. Delighted to find Mother and Father well and Barbara does wonders with succession of banquets. Garden looking fine and Shaw, helps me trim the apples and pear trees and put greenhouses in order. Vines showing good growth for the coming fruit season. Had glorious fortnight at home with lovely weather. Had several visits to York to the Hunts and they give me great welcome and bountiful hospitality.*

*23rd May 1918*

>Final day of leave so prepare for return journey to Kings Cross. Gilly met me at Kings Cross and we rendezvous at "The Long Bar" the Trocadero. Join up with Facey, Wattie, O'Callaghan, Durham and others. After dinner at Troc we take a Box for "Yes Uncle". Dinner causes me much embarrassment as I feel I must stay on the Water Cart. Noise at our table at the Troc causes much anxiety for the head waiter. The whole party very tight as we leave for the Theatre – great difficulty in getting all into a taxi. We arrive very late the Commissionaire reluctant to allow us into our box. The Party soon leave the box for the bar and speedily return with lots of alcohol including Gilly with two bottles of whisky. Facey and Wattie bring lots of soda. "Thunder and Turf", what a feeling to be

---

* I suspect that a Hunt daughter may have been a girl friend!

*painfully sober. Appalling noise from drunken hearties and Durham dashes into Box to tell us of approaching APM (Military Police). I hastily lock the door and the rumpus in the box seems to disturb the leader of the orchestra. I seem to be the only one with "wind up" and picture myself reduced to the ranks. There is a loud knocking on the door and I hear loud voice, "Open the door at once, I am APM London Command, if you don't open the door I will have it broken." I reply that I will see the party in the box behaves. Meanwhile all attention is transferred from the play to our Box. Leslie Henson and Julia James are very fed up. The APM returns and demands our names and to open the door. We still refuse and suddenly the act ends and the lights come on and everyone gazes our way. Gilly amuses the audience by dispensing more whisky and Facey sits with his legs dangling over edge of box. The lights go low and Act 2 commences and the hearties now remain quiet. I quickly open the door and walk down the corridor and find the APM has departed. Returning to the box I find Julia James is singing a song which pleases Rex Facey who amuses the audience by his exquisite facial expressions as the heroine sings. Then Gilly enters the scene as Leslie Henson has an angry scene with Julia James. Gilly shouts out load and clear, "leave the Bloody Bitch." Chaos prevails and we force Gilly to the floor and he promises to be quiet. Leslie Henson gets very fed up and in his song he introduces a clear rebuke. "The boys in the box from the Umpteenth Brigade have had nothing stronger than iced lemonade."*

*The audience was delighted and finally the play ended and I managed to get the party evacuated safely on to the pavement.*

*Gilly tramps me around London until 4 am and we finally arrive at the Grosvenor Hotel where I meet up with Facey who looks very much like "the morning after." We catch the Boat Train and sleep all the way to Dover. We had a good crossing and take train to St Omer where Buckler meets us and we finally arrive back at the Sqdn. in time for dinner.*

## 25th May 1918

*"Spot" our fox terrier is very low with severe distemper and looks as if he is "going out". Up on special "Obliques" of Trench area. Take three boxes of photographic plates from 300 feet – Hun busy firing his MGs at us. We make a successful trip along Yser Canal.*

## 28th May 1918

John Vic to be posted to Group so we make a final dinner to celebrate and for the first time I see him down and out. Up at 5.30 a.m. working on tennis court and we receive a surprise visit from Hun. We dash to plane to use machine gun. Hun departs and we do not have time to go into action. Spot improving. Barnes gets wounded with splinters in knee when flying with Facey.

## June 1918

Up on dawn patrol with Facey. Huns put bullet through my camera tube. We finish patrol and I wireless Corps Hqrs. As Fletcher "Takes off" he unfortunately crashes straight into line of 5 RE8s and plays havoc with the rigging. Poor Harrison observer looks very worried. We go to Czerney with Fletcher and Darnley to collect two more RE8s to replace yesterday's disaster but when flying the machines back to Droglandt they meet a storm and get lost – both machines crashing – one in midst of a battery and the second in a cabbage field.

Busy flying all June. CAP patrols. Photography and shoots with 6 Huns. Excellent results. Take photos of shots and visit gunner with photos to show them results of their shoots – most satisfactory. Meet Sqdn. Ldr. Mannock VC, DSO, MC. He lunches with us. Most delightful chap he has already shot down 54 Huns. He is killed the next week. This is really what he wanted,[*] so he told me, as he had seen many of his victims shot down in flames. He has memorial in Canterbury Cathedral.

## 13th June 1918

Lecture 49th Division on role of RAF with Infantry and attack. Guest of No. 10 Sqdn. and have to make a speech. I feel it most unnecessary.

## 15th June 1918

On Counter Attack Patrol with Allanson over Ypres Front. Up at 2.30 a.m. with Facey. We take off in darkness and fly over Ypres and drop special flares on Hun working parties. Alarming sight from back seat of RE8.

---

[*] I understand that this syndrome affected several aces on both sides.

### 16th June 1918

My friend at No. 10 Sqdn. Coomb-Taylor, killed in crash. Was his guest at No. 10 Sqdn. only last night. Now have to get Rex Facey packed up but he still appears doped with last night's final dinner. We take him to St Omer to catch train and he has a long heated argument with French Station master as he wants to board ambulance train but is "turned down".

### 18th June 1918

As we are all enjoying lunch an Orderly arrives with special message from Corps. Headquarters. Bertie reads it and taking a pen writes on the form and looks at me grinning all over his face. He hands the form to me to read and it says, "Arrange for lecture to the American Corps. School." Bertie's reply written on form states, "Lt. Wilson will lecture American School at Merckegheim."

I am very surprised, windy and irritated by this sudden act.

### 19-20th June 1918

Very busy all day preparing lectures and arrange to leave early as Merckegheim is a long journey right in the Belgian zone. "Subject of lecture – artillery co-operation with Aircraft." Harper accompanies me and we arrive at No. 10 American Corps School. I am amazed at huge audience in large hall. Many senior officers present and large display of flowers. Hosts of Yanks produce note books and I proceed with my lecture for about 40 mins. Then long spell of discussion and questions for further half hour. I am entertained to dinner with US Staff with excellent food and much wine. Finally my driver arrives with Harper who is very cheery and we leave for Droglandt at 10.30 pm Long drive back arrive 2 am.

### 21st June 1918

Went to Dunkerque shopping – have to dash back as I have to lecture NCOs of 49th Div. on Contact Patrols from the air.

### 22nd June 1918

Mess meeting. Have now cleared all Mess Bills including a large a/c at Fortnum and Mason and we have a balance with Banque de

*France of over 8000 Fr. Hand over mess accounts to Buckler. Receive many thanks from members of Mess. After lunch go with Bertie and Glenny to 24th Brigade RFA sports in car. Bertie tells me he has applied for me to go on "Home Establishment" by end of June.*

### 23rd June 1918

*We have Holy Communion Service in Hut and Padre departs. I welcome pilot in Aerodrome who has come to visit Bertie. He is dressed as NCO pilot and I take him as this but what a surprise for me when he opens his tunic and I see he has DSO and Bar, MC and 2 Bars. I am really stung.*

### 24th June 1918

*Final days shopping. Went to Dunkerque and take Cpl Morgan and Barnes. We have visit from John Vic and he surprises everyone "Passing Out" at dinner. He almost weeps as he remarks, "Sorry, Chaps, but those devils in my new wing can't drink. I never thought I would let you down like this." Later coma and mild snoring.*

### 25th June 1918

*Tennis after breakfast with Leete, Happy and Jones. Many in bed with flu – CO tells me I am for HE on 28th.*

### 27th June 1918

*Final flight with Rex Facey – but we have engine trouble so I bid farewell to Ypres Salient area – so well known to me 1915-1918. Prepare for final Mark I ordered by Bertie to wish me well. We have terrific party and I have to make final speech but I go to bed under my own steam. Feel very sad I am leaving Sqdn. for Home Establishment.*

### 28th June 1918

*Up early, hand over Mess to Buckler. Au Revoir to Bertie and all the chaps. Aerial escort to St Omer and went to Boulogne. Had good crossing and reported to "Bolo House" (RAF slang for Air Ministry). Report to Miss Vaucour who gives me a month's leave. Now for some Brown Trout. Leave King's Cross for York. Arrive home – high summer found all family well.*

## With the RFC in England: Instructor and Trainee Pilot

### July 1918

*Package of Old Chelsea china I bought in Poperinge arrives safely – all china intact – this is a lovely set. Pater now anxious to have hay cut and Jock Brittain gets busy with reaper and weather remains fine. Due to go to London on Monday for Med. Board. "Passed fit" but wounds still rather inflamed.*

*Went with Herbert Mount-Somerly to the Children's Home at Mitcham, given lunch, and infants, mostly orphans, appear very cheery and well. One little girl about 6 comes up to me and says, "Thank you, Mr Airman, for keeping me safe from the Germans."*

*Returned North to continue leave. Pater busy with hay making – I join in and greatly enjoy exercise – good crop and all hay safely in stack.*

*When in London buy Mary a new tennis racquet and she does great work on tennis court. I greatly enjoy many games with her. I then tackle "thinning out" 100 bunches of Black Hamburg Grapes. Very fine crop in big greenhouses. Barbara does splendidly with lawn cutting and flower borders.*

*I am greatly enjoying rest and total change from the hectic days of flying with 7 Sqdn. I find quiet services in Parish Church very comforting and service of Holy Communion well attended.*

*I discover three wasps nests in orchard and dealt with them with cyanide of potassium but put my foot in hole in hedge and got savaged by hordes of irate wasps. Get 10 stings in one leg. Dealt with this large nest.*

*My brother Edward[\*] shoots three rabbits in paddock with .410 single barrel gun. Go to York with Tim Mason and buy fishing tackle and flies in preparation for our fishing trip to Helmsley.*

---

[*] Edward was considerably younger, born 1901, but I understand he was in the Merchant Navy well before the end of the war, still very much a teenager. With the ferocious German U-boat campaign in the Atlantic, this must have been a great worry for his parents.

***9th July 1918***

*Left early for Helmsley and arrive after lovely peaceful drive through Vale of York. Lovely to see this glorious scenery and peaceful villages. Arrive at 4 pm and start evening fishing. Fish rising well and I manage to land brace of grand trout.*

***10-11th July 1918***

*Heavy thunder storm upsets our fishing for day. River rises very much and brings out local farmer with a small spinning rod and he has a remarkable catch of at least a dozen trout. I get two brace of trout by swimming worms. Edward arrives with super fly rod lent by Uncle Alf and we enjoy more fishing together.*

***12-14th July 1918***

*River quickly settles after storm and trout rather dour. Grenville's Glory the best fly – but caught most fish fishing with worm in stickles. We have super meal at our Farm House. Marvellous York ham and most restful night's sleep after day on river. This lovely little river comes down from heather moor and Tim gets five lovely fish today. We have final day on river and between us get 17 fish including 1 grayling. Greatly enjoyed our holiday in this delightful region of the York Dales. Enjoyable drive home from Helmsley. All country most delightful. Family enjoy dish of trout.*

***17th July 1918***

*Going to Knaresborough today – to stay as guest of Dr and Mrs Robinson and met many friends. Had enjoyable chat with Mr and Mrs Watson at Becketts Bank and had chat with Robinson and staff. Managed to collect some superb fresh farm butter from farmer. Back home on 19th.*

***20th-24th July 1918***

*Going to Filey to see Mary who is staying there on holiday. Lovely day. Went with Tim Mason to walk down to Filey Brig a delightful bit of coast. Fish for mackerel off Brig – rough sea. Had great fun fishing for mackerel and they "fight like mad". We take 10 grand* fish back to Haxby. Mary greatly enjoying Filey with friends and weather lovely, enjoying bathing.

Have to go to London tomorrow night. Take sleeper and meet Leete on train and share sleeper. Have Medical Board at Hampstead and both passed fit and detailed for duty at Reading – to go on Staff for lecturing cadets in RAF front line flying and tactics. Return home to finish leave. Busy hay making.

## 27-28th July 1918

Due at Reading on July 27th. Report Headquarters Erlagh Road, and given billet with Capt. Carmody. This is a doctor's house and he has wife and son (wee boy, Patrick aged 6). Capt. Carmody is Chief Med. Officer to the RAF School in Reading Headquarters. I am very happy here and go off early each day for 9 a.m. lecture at Erlagh Road on Observation and Artillery Co-operation with aircraft. All cadets about 20/21 years old and very keen on their course. Twenty in class.

I use blackboard and prepare lectures a.m. and p.m. First month goes smoothly but at end of first fortnight I notice a frivolous atmosphere in class as a barrel-organ plays every afternoon a verity of hymns at about same time. I suddenly discover cause of humour when I quickly turn round from the blackboard and spot two or three cadets throwing coins through the window down on to pavement.

I swiftly go to the window and spot the organ grinder picking up the coins. I rebuke him fiercely and order him away. That is the end of the "joke". I lecture the pupils on their lack of respect for me and we proceed on the subject matter with a smooth run for the rest of the course which was successful. I continued with my instructional course all August, September and October and was happy and very comfortable at the MO's house.

One Sunday morning Pat took me to morning service at St Mary's Church and that morning Capt. and Mrs Carmody were giving a cocktail party for about 20 officers and their wives. On arriving at the house, young Pat became wildly excited as he spotted a "Double-dog" locked in nature in the middle of the lawn. He didn't wait a second but rushed into the middle of the drawing room – shouting in a most excited manner. "Do come and look on the lawn, there is a 'double dog' out there."

Imagine the sudden excitement in that crowded drawing room as this wee boy, all excitement, dashed around and demanded the *assembly to come and view this great spectacle outside on the lawn. The wee boy was NOT to be denied but hauled the guests to come and see his wonder "double-dog". I did my best to drive the "dog" outside the front gate, but the humour exploded in the drawing room for several minutes.*

*It was interesting that on the RAF Reading Course, several of my old friends from No. 7 Squadron were on the staff with me and we shared some lovely games on the excellent Sunning Golf Links.*

*It is interesting that at this stage the Allies were having great success in the field of Battle. The Allies had captured 130,000 prisoners and 3,000 guns and made spectacular gains of territory. Great victory in Palestine, 45,000 prisoners.*

## 28th July 1918

*Bulgars ask for peace.*

## 12-30th September 1918

*Apply for week's leave to go to Cefu to stay with Uncle Alf as Mother just gone there. Leave granted – long train journey to St Asaph. Uncle met me at St Asaph, found Mother much improved. The river looks fine in spate and I notice dozens of salmon leaping the falls and watch two wily poachers get two lovely salmon as they leap the side of falls. Uncle Alfred fixes me up with super light fly rod and I have grand evening on fly – net six brace of fish – mostly on Greenarth Glory. My friends, Allanson and Anderson, both killed in France in 7 Squadron.*

*Yank Push most successful – 15,000 prisoners.*

## October 1918

*Great advance at Ypres and Houlthurst Forest. Thousands of prisoners and guns.*

## 7th – 28th October 1918

*As Dr Carmody is ill, I decide to take him to Haxby for a week's leave and he puts in for leave for me. We both go to Haxby in fine grand weather. We went to look round the Minster and other York ancient gems. Doc gets my old violin going and plays well. We go* shooting with Mr Sharp in Sutton-on-Forest. Had a grand day of mixed bag pheasant, partridge and rabbits (30).

Great Battle before Roulers, so well known to me from the air. Lille taken and Ostende, great German losses.

Flu breaks out in RAF school in Reading. Hundreds become victims. My classes very depleted and hundreds unable to attend classes and parades – two deaths so far.

**31st October 1918**

Turkey surrenders in full. Austria asks for Armistice.

**7th-8th November 1918**

Rumour that Germany is asking for peace. Edward arrives home on leave.

I get delivery of my 'thanks offering' to the Vicar of Haxby and the Church a "Burse and Veil" beautifully made by the Wareham Guild. It is finally decided by the Vicar that he would prefer me to give it to my school, St Peter's School, York, founded 627 a.d. – this is carried out and the School accepts the gift with much gratitude.

**10th November 1918**

At home from Bentham and there is great excitement that the Armistice is about to be declared. Holy Communion at 8. so glad to be home for this service.

We are invited to take evening meal at the Hall with Mr Hood, with my Father and Mr Sharp.

**11th November 1918**

Due to return South in morning. At York by 10 a.m. Hear Armistice has been signed; the Minster Bells ring out in wonderful peal. Catch train for Kings Cross. Met by Rex Facey. There is very much excitement. Station packed with Troops and excited civilians.

All London streets packed. Flags out everywhere. Rex and self join in crowds of excited folk. We walk down The Mall to join crowds at Buckingham Palace – never seen so much excitement. Thousands round the railings at Buckingham Palace.

King and Queen receive tremendous reception from the Balcony – they put in several appearances and it is dark when we return to the Strand to find traffic congestion and excited crowds everywhere.

Trafalgar Square incredible sight – crowds jump in the water sections and climb lions. Buses and taxis crowded with passengers and make very slow progress down Strand towards Piccadilly. We manage to get into Restaurant for dinner and join in with party of eight – very funny nobody knew each other. Three girls join in with us for celebration dinner. By 8 pm many very cheery folk, both sexes and our waiter is excellent. The restaurant put on a splendid dinner and we enjoy good wines and the dinner goes on for a couple of hours. Outside in the Strand the whole street is crowded and buses simply cannot move. Rex and I collect two of the very attractive girls from dinner and join in with the rejoicing crowds who ramble aimlessly up and down the Strand and round Trafalgar Square.

Many in the crowds were heavily intoxicated but no sordid scenes. Several friendly types offered us drink from bottles of wine. Some hearties had produced some fireworks in Trafalgar Square. We decided that by 12 we had had enough and said au revoir to the two charming girls who seemed sad to say farewell. Rex took me to his home in Harrington Gardens for the night and we finally retired at 2 a.m.

### 12th November 1918

My leave is up on Thursday 14th. Mrs Facey makes me most welcome and Rex and I decide to continue with the celebrations by journeying into the city.

### 13th November 1918

The city is now crowded with thousands of happy citizens. On our return to Piccadilly we find crowds of excited folk everywhere. Eros is crowded with climbers and I fear for the security of this pleasing monument. We join in with dancing round a captured German Gun in Piccadilly. This continues to be cause of much excitement and Police look on with controlled interest.

Rex and I go into the Long Bar at "The Troc" for a drink and meet several old 7 Squadron comrades and after "nourishment" we make up a party to get a table at the Monaco and I succeed in *persuading the Head Waiter to give us a table for 6.*

*I fear some of our party are very noisy as they had refuelled heavily at the Long Bar. This dinner went on for at least a couple of hours and Leete collects a heap of rather hard bread rolls and bombards a table of "Jews" and there is much indignation and irritation. The Head Waiter approaches me to say we must leave the restaurant at once unless we promise to behave ourselves. I am able to restrain the 'rebellious young airmen' and we finally leave the Monaco after an excellent evening and we manage to collect a taxi to take us down crowded Piccadilly. Four of us sit on the top of the taxi and we make an excited journey right down the route to Hyde Park Corner. Crowds still everywhere and some 'hearties' are having fireworks in Hyde Park. Rex and I finally arrive at Harrington Gardens at 1 a.m.*

*I say good bye to Mrs Facey and thank her for her bountiful hospitality and much kindness. I return to the city for special Thanksgiving service in St Paul's with King and Queen present. Wonderful service – superb music and much pomp and ceremony with the Royal Family and the Lord and Lady Mayoress. Had splendid view of the King and Queen from the Mansion House. Had an excellent "Fish lunch" with Mount Somerly at "Station Fish Restaurant" in the City. Rejoicing still going on everywhere. I make my way to Paddington and decide to stay the night at the Great Western Hotel and leave for Reading early on the morning of the 14th November.*

### 14th November 1918

*Arrive by early train at Reading and all well at my billet. I spend morning marking exam papers and arrange for my new class, all Sergeants. Course on co-operation with Aircraft.*

### 16th November 1918

*Decide to go to London for weekend. Saw Royal Family again at Buckingham Palace and large procession of discharged soldiers with Prince of Wales in their parade. Went to Savoy Theatre and saw "Nothing but the Truth" – most amusing. Play had great reception. Late in evening demonstration in Piccadilly and Trafalgar Square. More Firework Displays in Hyde Park.*

*17th November 1918*

This Sunday, "Day of Thanksgiving throughout the Empire" – I go with Mount-Somerly to service at St John, Red Lion Square ( a most lovely church). An impressive and beautiful service. Jack Betts joins us for lunch at the "Chanticleer".

Am invited to tea with Sir Wm. and Lady Smith, Sheriff of London. He is busy preparing his Election Address for the Scottish University Election. (Later did not get in).

*18th-20th November 1918*

Carry on with my course with class of intelligent keen sergeants. Report that the German High Seas Fleet to be handed over at Scapa Flow on 21st November. H.M. The King to be present. Sudden notice that I am to commence PILOTS course at Reading School on 21st.

Very excited that I can commence Pilots Course. Met several of No. 7 Squadron on the course. All most interesting. Studying instruments and aero-engines. All most thrilling. Working on "Bristol Fighter". Three Observers arrive who had been in Holland three and a half years.

A General Election is launched. Letter from home. William and Merville cousins from New Zealand forces been to Haxby for leave – both very well.

*26th November 1918*

Great preparation in French capital for celebrations. HM the King and Prince of Wales leave for Paris. Now most of Pilot's course spent on rigging – all day, very tiring. Exams tomorrow. Papers and Practical.

Did well in Exam, 85%.

*28th November 1918*

Dad's birthday (63) – he is very well and very keen on getting more days in the hunting field. York & Ainsty Packs all ready for coming season.

### 1st December 1918

*Church at St Mary's. Very fine sermon. Very wet day. Wounds troublesome.*

### 2nd-31st December 1918

*Now on Engines. All day at Redlands. Great fun running Camel and DH5. Course now very concentrated. Passed "fit" in Medical.*

*Having evening lectures now.*

*Pilot's course continues. Engines at Redlands and Instruments at London Road. Now fully settled on Pilot's Course. Most absorbing and enjoyable. Manage to get some enjoyable games of Golf with Leete.*

*Had weekend leave and went to Chesham to Uncle Charles. Found all well and enjoyed driving to Tring and attractive country ride. He seems to run two successful cinemas.*

*Course continues over Christmas, so no leave. We continue on engines and change to rigging after Christmas.*

*Election continues well for Coalition. Mr J G Batchen in by 10,000 at York. Labour do well. Asquith and old gang "kicked out."*

*Very busy. Write 25 letters and do all Christmas shopping and complete all Christmas work well on time and get all parcels off.*

*Making good progress on course and continue into New Year.*

### January 1919

*Adjutant sends for me and tells me I am to discontinue with my Pilot's Course and that I am to be posted to RAF Worthy Down, Winchester.*

*Say farewell to Dr Carmody, Mrs Carmody and my friend, wee Pat and au revoir to Leete and my friends on Pilot's Course.*

*Arrive at RAF Worthy Down, four miles from Winchester.*

*Very cheery mess and delighted to find "The Pig" Capt. Glenny is in charge one flight of Bristol Fighters. The Mess Sergeant (a first class type) runs the mess perfectly and I find is "Butler" to a Peer of the Realm.*

*I am made Mess President, obviously a move by "The Pig" as he brings up my history as Mess President of VII Squadron, Proven. I find there is quite a good shoot at Worthy Down and the shoot (8 guns) meets on Saturdays, so I can anticipate four more* days this season. First two shoots very enjoyable. Mixed bag, pheasants, partridges, hares – long walks and we shoot small woods near aerodrome. Later we finish season with "Cocks" only and have most enjoyable day in woods. Also get several hares. I have several very enjoyable flights with "The Pig" in Bristol Fighter over Southampton, Isle of Wight and Portsmouth. On one flight over Portsmouth we get fired on by anti-aircraft – we were "too low" and "too near" secret area.

I make contact with Captain of sport at Winchester College and arrange for Soccer Match with the School 1st XI. Excellent game which School win. This game much enjoyed and much appreciated by Squadron XI. I greatly enjoy services at Winchester Cathedral and enjoy its superb structure.

## February 1918

Very happy and enjoyable days with the Squadron and spring brings in glorious days. I join in all Squadron duties and always enjoy the flights over this very attractive part of England. I stay at Squadron for weekends and many married officers offer me generous hospitality.

I hear from my old Squadron (7 RFC) which is now situated on the Rhine near Cologne, that they are the advanced Squadron and are heavily engaged on duty Patrols and morning flights over occupied territory. Squadron Leader R E Saul is new CO and Bertie Sutton is posted to England. Squadron was at Spich before moving to Mulheim.

Granted leave late January from Worthy Down. Went direct to Haxby and got busy pruning fruit trees with Shaw. My father greatly enjoying his hunting on his two hunters and David assists as groom. He arranges for me to have a day's hunting (January 28th) with the York & Ainsty. I am given an excellent mount from Mr Foster, a fiery 4 year old who has not had much hunting this season. I join up with my father in York in the Mount and we ride together to the meet at Askham Bogs. This is probably the best meet of the Y and A season. Many cavalry officers at meet and happily it is a fine day. Hounds soon found fox in the Askham Bogs and the pack in hot pursuit very early. A grand sight with the hounds in full cry over the famous Askham Stretches. My mount gets most excited and I need very strong control – but he jumps well – my father seems anxious that I do not have perfect control but the fox *goes to earth and we have a short rest and manage sandwiches for lunch. Another draw in a good cover produces another fox and we are in the famous Ainsty country. Super fun follows and it is a grand sight to see the cavalry leading the lively run and I was much amused to see my Father well up with the leaders. At this stage my mount loses control, or rather, I lose control of his galloping and he bolts and jumps several tough fences – but all the riders are in full cry and the thundering of the hoofs stimulate my mount. He just won't stop. He finally comes to a halt and I slip out of the saddle. At this stage my Father rides up and orders me to mount his hunter – a 12 year old and a perfect mount. He assists me in mounting and he mounts my lively four year old. We rejoin the hunt – which is in full cry and soon find ourselves in the excitement of the chase. One Military rider – I suppose a Colonel – riding beside me says, "Young man, I think flying suits you better than hunting." I smile in return but feel rather browbeaten and away we continue for a glorious run – over this cream of the Y and A Hunt. The Huntsman leads on his pack but the fox manages to escape and finally with the field well spaced out the hunt finally ends and my Father leads the long way home back to York which is about 8 miles and the large Field slowly disperses in all directions. All the military returning to Fulford Barracks where the cavalry are stationed "The Royal Scots Grays". My father re-mounts his own horse when we arrive back at Mr Foster's stables and I am most grateful for the generous mount I had so greatly enjoyed. Now, my Father had to ride back four miles to our home at Haxby. I found my way home by catching a train from York to Haxby. I was gloriously tired when I arrived back home and my father arrived back just before me. How we enjoyed a super dinner my dear sister Barbara provided for us after a scalding hot bath. I would say here that it was rather tough luck on me that I had a lively four year old hunter for my mount – but I loved every moment and think my father was very wise to swap his mount with me after my fall. I revelled in every moment of that final run with a succession of grand fences and a lovely finish to the day.*

*We had snow falls during the rest of my leave but I did enjoy my gardening with Shaw. We finished all the pruning of the apples, pears, raspberries and currants. I went up to Bentham to spend a few days with Leete and had a most enjoyable holiday. Was most interested in the family jewellery business, Moor Reed and Sons, in Newcastle. Had enjoyable golf with Hugh at Gosforth links. Hugh v. good golfer.*

*28th February 1919*

*On returning home built some excellent fences for fruit trees with Shaw.*

*Had a wire from the Lord Chamberlain to attend my MC Investiture at Buckingham Palace. Invitation for my Mother and Father also – we went up to London and also took Uncle Walter from Chesham. A wonderful sight in the Palace Ballroom where King George V decorated over 30 service personnel.*

*In the evening I took mother and father to see* The Brig Boys *– Violet Lorraine and George Robey. It was most amusing to see how Dad was very anxious to catch an early train to York so that he would be sure to get in a day's hunting!*

Peter at Buckingham Palace with his parents to attend the Investiture.

*March 1919*

Return to Worthy Down and greatly enjoy flying in Bristol Fighters and aerial photography up to 15,000 ft with vertical photos. Keep fit with squash and enjoy lively games with "The Pig" (Glenny). Have many visits to Winchester Cathedral and enjoy many services. Isaac Walton's grave in Winchester Cathedral. The Mess Sergeant makes most delicious mayonnaise and we are fortunate in being able to get a fresh salmon. We have a WAAF officer who is in charge of messing and she arranges all the main meals. Her special Mess nights are superb and commendable.

March is very enjoyable at Worthy Down and after flying duties I greatly enjoy Squash Racquets on an excellent court.

## Germany: Army of Occupation

*April 1919*

In early April the Adjutant gives me a private message that I am shortly to be posted to "The British Army of the Rhine" back to 7 Squadron at Mulheim. I have had a very happy time at Worthy Down.

*Peter in Bristol Fighter at Mulheim. Note the uniforms are now RAF.*

> My posting comes through and I get 48 hours leave and then report at Air Ministry and given tickets to proceed to Cologne. I arrive at 7 Squadron which has an excellent mess in the "Town Civil Building". Delighted to meet many old friends including Barnes of 'B' Flight. We travel 7 miles to our aerodrome which is at Mulheim and we have three Flights of Bristol Fighters. We make very early flights – 5 a.m. over the Rhinelands. This is to impress the large German population of the vigilance of the RAF. After early flight over Rhine-Koln and Bonn and Dusseldorf, we return to mess for breakfast and later return to the aerodrome and the further duties of the day.
>
> I play with Squadron Rugger XV and enjoy matches with Army teams who seem very keen and fit.

I greatly enjoyed life with No. 9 Squadron as No. 7 Squadron had returned to the UK. We continued with the early morning flights in Bristol Fighters at 5 a.m. Squadron Leader R. Saul was our CO and he was keen on all forms of sport, being a superb tennis player and champion of the Rhine Army. During the early morning flights we flew over large areas surrounding the Rhine and down as far as Coblenz. We returned to the mess in Mulheim for breakfast and afterwards a bus conducted us back to the aerodrome for daily duties. We visited aerodromes up the Rhine basin and our chief visit was to Coblenz where we collected quantities of sugar for our mess. Flying over the Rhine was most attractive as we flew over Bonn and the Drachenfels.

One Saturday the Squadron had an entertaining trip on the Rhine: we all went on a luxurious river steamer and spent the whole day on board. We were provided with excellent meals and drinks and the scenery was wonderful. We were very near Cologne which had an excellent shopping centre and the hotels and restaurants were also good. The cathedral at Cologne is a magnificent building with two massive towers. There appeared to be hawks nesting in the structure who preyed upon the pigeons which abounded.

The great joy was the Opera House where there was a most efficient opera company. The RAF had a permanent box on the first balcony and when attending a performance, a restaurant provided a superb dinner, with a long interval permitting ample time to enjoy it. On Sunday evenings there was usually a special performance of one of Wagner's Operas. This was a wonderful affair which attracted very special artists from all over Europe. I usually attended four operas a week and always attended Mess night which was on Friday evenings in the Squadron.

In May and June I greatly enjoyed trout fishing as there are some most attractive tributaries of the Rhine and both dry and wet fly fishing was possible.

All June, July and August we played exciting cricket matches around the Rhinelands. Many of the officers attended special classes at Bonn University. I attended Chemistry and Language classes which were most beneficial. All travel by train was entirely free and one could get on and off trains without difficulty.

Close by there were delightful walks and one could get some good rock climbing. Weekends at all the attractive resorts were most enjoyable and the German staff gave us a great welcome. It was interesting to visit Trier and the Porthnigra up the Moselle and I enjoyed many weekends at Bad Ems, Wiesbaden and all the Rhine towns. As we were in the advanced area of the Rhine Army we had horses and could get in long rides in the huge forests.

During my stay in 9 Squadron I was engaged in a very special "aerial photography," as the Commander-in-Chief wanted a special mosaic of the whole of the Rhine region from the Swiss border to Holland. It was necessary to fly at 22,000 to 23,000 feet and as we did not have oxygen it was a great strain and terribly cold. The flights lasted three hours and I usually took three dozen photos (vertical). One could only make one exposure every 90-100 seconds as there was a big overlap if exposures were made less than 90 seconds. Sometimes it was so cold we got frostbite and we had to cover our faces in scarves.

In the summer of 1919 the Sheriff of London and Lady Smith made an official visit to the Rhine Army and requested from the Officer Commanding the Rhine Army that 'Flt. Lt. A G Wilson, RAF, should be attached." So I was appointed for a week for this exciting adventure. Our last episode was a visit to Wiesbaden and we had super hotel rooms at the Hotel Rose and a box for Wagner's opera *Die Walkure*. This was a most enjoyable weekend and we had reserved train accommodation for the long journey back to Cologne. We also visited the London Regiments and were given splendid receptions.

As soon as September dawned I was aware of the bountiful flights of partridges in all the local fields around the aerodromes and especially in the huge asparagus fields along the Rhine banks. It was my luck that I was the only officer with a double barrelled gun, so I had most super shooting of partridges and hares. I also had a large supply of 12 bore cartridges. Almost every day in late September and all October I went shooting and often had 10-12 brace hanging in my hut. I provided the married officers with game for two months. Even the General Officer Commanding the Rhine Army asked me if I would lend him my gun for some special days partridge driving.

*September 1919*

Knowing that after I finished my spell in the Rhine Army I hoped to go to Oxford to start my long medical training, I was able to buy half a skeleton, a superb Leitz Microscope and two anatomy books *spaltholz* and *Sabotta*. The rate of the Mark was most favourable for this purchase. All the summer and autumn I was able to enjoy swimming in the special Rhine baths. These bathing places were very cleverly moored to the main river as the river flowed very swiftly through the whole of the swimming pool. With a Gunner friend of mine we visited Bonn and inspected the "Beethoven Hall" and he received permission to play the famous organ; while he was playing, it was amusing to watch the faces of the many English troops as they gazed up at the organ loft. All through the late Autumn I revelled in many attendances at the Cologne Opera House, and the arrival of the "Goose Season" provided us with superb meals of roast goose and a long season of *Pate de Foie Gras*. Our box at the Opera was filled every night and Squadron Leader Saul joined us frequently as the Opera Company provided a superb list of operas with Wagner Opera specially presented every Sunday evening. Squadron Leader R E Saul, and the Padre, joined me in fishing excursions and we collected many prolific baskets of trout.

*November 1919*

I had a letter from my old Pilot of 7 Squadron, Rex Facey, who was at Brasenose College Oxford reading Medicine, and he told me that he had seen the Bursar of the College about my coming to BNC for the commencement of the Lent Term 1920. I was delighted about this and I was given a special appointment with the Principal and Fellows of the College. I applied for leave to go to Oxford for these interviews and I had a very pleasant meeting with the Principal and Fellows. I explained that I had been serving in the Army and RAF for six years and had not had any academic activities. At the end of this interview, Dr Heberden, the Principal, said that the College would welcome me for my medical training in January 1920. So I returned to my Squadron at Cologne for a final month of flying duties which I greatly enjoyed as the weather remained fine.

*Extract from diary*

*11th December 1919*

> *I was given a "Final Celebration Dinner" by the Mess – most enjoyable and these were my final days of service before being discharged.*

**15th December 1919**

*Returned to the UK and reported at Bolo House. Had dinner with Bertie at his Club. Called in on Sir Wm. and Lady Smith at their home. Was given invitation to attend special celebration welcome for the* Prince of Wales *at the Guildhall.*

**18th December 1919**

*This was a wonderful occasion and attended by the Lord Mayor and the Sheriffs – Great welcome for the Prince of Wales. He spoke very well – the Guildhall looked marvellous with the large array of important guests, and celebration most successful.*

**19th December 1919**

*Called on Cox's Bankers and banked my Gratuity paid for whole of War Service. Did some useful shopping in London before catching train for York and finally arrived home in time for Christmas.*

*Had most happy Christmas with the family. Went to Harrogate for three days as guest of Mr Peacock and his family. Had most happy stay at the Cairn Hotel. Enjoyable dinners each night, three in succession.*

**31st December 1919**

*Left to arrive home for New Year's Eve.*

# Chapter Six

## OXFORD 1920'S

I spent the early part of the New Year at home before going up to Brasenose College, Oxford. It was quite an experience to be in mufti after wearing uniform for six years. I made the journey to Oxford by train and had a large quantity of luggage.

After a long train journey I finally arrived at Oxford and found the station yard full of undergraduates. I managed to hire a hansom carriage to transport me to BNC (it was lovely to hear the clattering of the horses' hooves) and I arrived safely. I reported at the Porters' Lodge and was told that I had a room just to the right of the Tower and that Ernest Panting was to be my Scout. It was a great thrill to meet my old pilot, Rex Facey, of VII Squadron RFC who had rooms quite near me. I met several members of the College in the Junior Common Room (JCR) before Dinner in Hall. The undergraduates seemed to be divided into two classes. All the seniors had been in the war and were in their final year. I was, of course, over a year late in arriving at College and was mostly associated with Freshmen who were in their second term at College having come up in the October term, 1919, mostly straight from school.

The College Hall was most attractive with the walls adorned with superb paintings – many dating from 1509, including delightful paintings of the Bp. of Lincoln and Sir Richard Sutton Kt. Founder of the College. There were several superb paintings of 16th and 17th century benefactors of the college. At the High Table sat the Principal, Dr Heberden, and all the Fellows. All the Seniors (War members) sat at the main side tables and all the Freshmen sat at the middle tables.

The Bible Clerk Pedder, who took the check at the 8 a.m. daily morning service, told me that I was excused morning chapel as I had been in the war. All Freshmen must attend the daily morning service. I retired early to get on with my unpacking. The view from my window was most thrilling, with the spires of All Souls College and the glorious University Church standing out in the moonlight. I was reminded of the grim tragedy of Tudor days when Queen Mary had Archbishop Cranmer tried and condemned to death and burnt at the Stake in the Broad. He made that wonderful defence in St Mary's Church and was marched out to face his terrible burning; he actually passed to his burning immediately below my window and had several Spanish RC Monks trying to get him to renounce

---

* Written when Peter was 93 years old.

his faith and rejoin the "Mary Regime". I had a peaceful first night in College and Ernest Panting called me at 7 a.m. and I took breakfast in Hall.

I called early on my "Moral Tutor," Mr Michael Holroyd. He gave me a warm welcome and told me my curriculum and that I should attend lectures and labs in the subjects Chemistry and Physics. The Lecturer in Chemistry was a delightful fellow who told me, "all this will be strange to you after over six years of war and academic stagnation."

*Oxford High Street looking towards Carfax, 1920.*

I found the Physics Labs very strange and beyond my present standard of intellect. Here again I met delightful Tutors who arranged to give me private tuition which was a great comfort to me. At the end of my first morning in the Labs I met some BNC students. I walked back to College with a most charming pupil, Derek Dunlop, who was in digs with another friend from the Edinburgh Academy, Arthur Blair, reading languages. He asked me if Arthur Blair and himself could lunch with me every day in my room. I was delighted to do this, so Ernest Panting prepared our College lunch consisting of Commons (Bread) and delicious College Cheese, with Butter from BNC farms. Rex Facey also joined us and we had a very happy party which continued uninterrupted until the end of the summer term.

### *Lent Term 1920*

I had an early meeting with "Sonners", Dr Stallybrass, who was Vice-Principal. He gave me a warm welcome and told me he was very glad I was going to play Rugger with the College 1st XV which contained three Rugger blues. The BNC Rugger Field was first class and I started training straight away and we played two matches a week. We had a super XV and won nearly all our matches. It was grand to play with such superb players, especially Evans (England), Neser, a South African Rhodes Scholar reading law, and Alan Roe, a Rugger Blue from Australia. The Captain of Boats asked me to join the Rowing Section and requested me to come down to the River to the BNC barge for rowing practice. I did this and enjoyed it but after a few weeks I found this enterprise took up most afternoons, and I simply could not miss the valuable labs experience.

I became alarmed that I seemed so tired I could not carry out my evening studies after dinner in Hall; I often fell asleep with NO valuable studies carried out. On one occasion my Scout came into my room at 7 a.m. and found me fully dressed and fast asleep on the floor under my table, like being back in the trenches.

I found that reading in the College Library was no better, so I returned to my room and made a hot drink which helped a bit. I was told to present myself for a weekly Physics Tutorial with Mr Stocker, a grand old Yorkshire don, and I told him of my difficulty in the Labs; he gave me special tuition and the hour with him was a great help and comfort. By the end of my first term he had put me on a steady path to grasping the fundamentals of this not attractive subject, but it was one of the essential Prelims I had to do.

It was a great joy to me that I made contact with Maurice Harland who was at St Peters School, York, with me in pre-war days. He was one of my Pilots in VII Squadron at Proven and Droglandt in Flanders (1917), and was now reading History at Exeter College. It was quite remarkable that Rex Facey and Maurice Harland were both in "B" Flight 7 Squadron with me and that they should both be at Oxford. I loved the peaceful weekends and my great delight was to attend Evensong at the glorious St Mary's Church. I used to sit near the special carved pillar where

Archbishop Cranmer made his famous sermon to his accusers which led to his "burning" in "The Broad" during Queen Mary's Reign AD 1556. It was the custom for undergraduates to attend the Principal's lodgings for tea on a Sunday during term. Dr Heberden was a bachelor so his sister, Miss Heberden, was hostess – this was a social event greatly enjoyed.

Half-way through Term the "Rugger Cuppers" were in full swing and the Inter-Collegiate battles were most exciting. Our first match was against Univ. who had Jerry Crole, the Scottish International as their Captain. The match was on their ground and we were only just beaten by 5-0 – a most exciting "ding-dong" battle. Our 1st XV played eight matches and won six (v. Oriel, Magdalen, Queens, John's, Exeter and Christchurch) and lost two (to University and Balliol). We had two schools matches (lost to Bedford, 0-12 and v. Cheltenham won 23-8). I converted three tries.

*March 1920*

In the mid-month I went several times to St John's College to inspect the superb Rock Gardens which contained many glorious rock plants in bloom and several I had never seen or known before. On one visit I met "The Bidder", a don who was in charge of the Rock Gardens. He was interested that being a Commoner at Brasenose College I visited the gardens so frequently. I told him that after six years of war I was delighted and thrilled with the peace and beauty of the lovely St John's Gardens.

Just outside Balliol College, in the "Broad" there was a special memorial Cross erected to the memory of the "Martyrs" who were burnt during Mary's Reign. I heard that there had been an abuse of this Sacred Monument and an undergraduate had placed a "Jerry" upside down on the top of the Cross. It was enamel and next day the Police tried to shoot it down but they only got loud tin reports from their bullets. Now, following this vandalism, a Senior Don of Balliol requested the presence of one of his undergraduates whose Grandfather had been known to carry out the same exploit and had been sent down from his College, Balliol. Now the interview, I am told, was most unfair. The Don, knowing the history of his grandfather, questioned the young undergraduate who was a Commoner at Balliol

"Did you climb the Martyrs' Memorial and place a Jerry on the Cross?"

The young undergraduate replied, "As you have asked me direct I must give you the correct answer which I think is most unfair. Yes, Sir, I did climb the Martyrs' Memorial and place the Jerry on the Cross."

*Oxford Students.*
*Peter in front, Rex Facey left. Could it be the "luncheon four"?*

The Don then said, "I must now inform you that tomorrow you will be sent down from Oxford and from your College, Balliol."

Next morning there was a sensational gathering outside Balliol. The guilty undergraduate was placed in a Funeral Hearse, pulled by black horses and cramped in a coffin surrounded by champagne bottles. The excitement was intense and crowds of onlookers viewed the slow procession as it travelled down the High Street and thenceforward to the GWR Railway Station. I joined the undergraduate assembly and followed the hearse. I'm certain there were 100 undergraduates in sympathy with the unfortunate victim. When we were all in the Station Yard, the Procter and the Bullers[*] closed the gates and then tackled the job of questioning every undergraduate. Coming to me they said, "Are you a member of this University?" I said "yes". "Your Name and College please" – this I supplied and after much excitement the parade terminated. Later in the day a message was delivered to me and several other members of the College, that on the morrow we should attend the Proctor's Office clad in official cap and gown, at 10.00 a.m. I was fined £1.00 and severely reprimanded. I think the behaviour of the Balliol Don, in his interview with the culprit, was disgraceful and ungentlemanly. He knew perfectly well that this young undergraduate

---

[*] Bullers was the name given to University Law Officers.

was the grandson of the previous culprit and bullied the present victim to admit his guilt!

Each Saturday evening after Hall, the College Debating Society met in the Junior Common Room, and we had lively meetings and full debates which often went on to the midnight hour.

The Governing Body had met the wishes of Brasenose Men by placing a war memorial in the lodge. It was plain in character – the outer frame having as its only ornament a few small Tudor roses – and was surmounted by a handsome coloured representation of the College Arms.

Beneath the main slab of stone were these words:

> This accord is here set that those who pass may be put in mind of Field Marshal Earl Haig and all the other Brasenose men who devoted themselves at home or abroad to the Service of their country in the time of peril.

I continued to get help in Physics from my Tutors and spent long hours in the labs. I greatly enjoyed the rich friendship with Derek Dunlop, Arthur Blair and Rex Facey and our luncheon together was a real joy.

In sport mid-term found much activity on the river and I greatly enjoyed "The Torpids". On the final night, the 1st Togger bumped Trinity before reaching the Gut. I raced along the tow path and saw this exciting event.

I was most interested in the various College Clubs and joined the Ingoldsby Essay Club founded in 1879. After a lapse of five years the Club was revived on December 3rd 1919. We had four papers this Hilary Term and one read by John Buchan, on "The Grand Captains", was particularly entertaining with his own experiences of war.

I had now settled into better concentration and was most happy with life in the college and in the Labs. I had made many new friends and I collected some Physics and Chemistry books to take home for study during the Easter Vac.

It was grand to enjoy the peace of my home and I worked on my books every morning and spent the afternoon in the garden with Shaw who prepared all the seed beds and greenhouses. I visited the Hunts in York and met Violet and Reggie and we had long walks. My father was still greatly enjoying his hunting and, with his two horses, was able to hunt three days a week with the York & Ainsty and Lord Middleton's Hunt.

*Summer Term 1920**

I returned for my second term. Oxford in the summer was most delightful and all the College gardens were very colourful. Lectures in Physics and Chemistry were attended every day and I spent long hours in the Physics Labs. I also enjoyed many visits to the Ashmolean and the Pitt Rivers museums which contained an abundance of treasures. Derick Dunlop, Arthur Blair and Rex Facey joined me for lunch every day in my rooms and I purchased half a super Stilton Cheese in the market.

*Eights Week*

All the college barges looked gay with their flags flying for Eight weeks. I paraded on the towpath which was crowded and the river crammed with punts and tea parties.

On May 1st a most thrilling event was staged, when large crowds assembled on Magdalen Bridge and near the College at 5 a.m. The ancient custom of the choir singing hymns from the top of the main tower was unforgettable and had gone on for centuries. After the bells struck 5 a.m. there was a silence, then, suddenly, the choir commenced their chanting of hymns which, coming from the top of the College Tower, sounded most glorious; as if some celestial choir was rendering eternal praises. For fully quarter of an hour the glorious singing continued and was greatly enjoyed by the huge crowds. I was most impressed by this ancient custom and my early rising was well rewarded.

I managed to escape from the afternoon labs to enjoy some games of tennis on the College courts and also enjoyed watching the University playing cricket in The Parks.

The Principal, Dr C B Heberden now resigned. Five years before when he had wished to resign, the Fellows made an urgent request that he should continue to remain Principal until the shock of war had passed. For 31 years he had guided the fortunes of the College, and the honour of being Principal of Brasenose now passed to Mr C H Sampson who had been Senior Tutor for many years.

I continued to have tutorials with Mr Stocker once a week as my

---

* At about this time his brother Edward escorted Alfred Wilson's daughter Gladys to New Zealand where she married her Hull cousin Merville. Edward remained in New Zealand until 1924 when he returned home for his sister Mary's marriage to Eric Monkman. On the boat he fell in love with May Thorne, a talented New Zealander whom he courted over the next few years.

Physics was still very rusty. I met Dr Gardener and his charming wife Violet who was a great friend of Bertie Sutton, my Squadron Leader of 7 Squadron RFC. I spent many happy hours in the lovely gardens of St Johns College where their rockeries were adorned by rich alpine plants. A great-great uncle of mine was a Classics Tutor of St Johns and enjoyed the living of Cheam in Surrey as a gift from the College. He spent the whole of the long Vac in Cheam and employed a Curate during the term times. (He was always referred to as "Uncle Bennett.")

I was very happy to discover that each Sunday a.m. Pusey House held a Sung Eucharist, which I greatly enjoyed. Dr Darwell Stone was Head of Pusey House and Mark Carpentier Garnier was Assistant Head. The Summer Term seemed to pass so quickly and the final week saw most of the "War Candidates" taking their final exams before "going down" – most took shortened courses for degrees. I noticed that a special Commemoration Ball was to be held in the College on June 21st and the tickets were 35/- each. Rex Facey said he would join me in a "party" and that an elderly "Chaperone" must accompany young partners! So we made up a party of eight and Chaperone, and the Ball was most enjoyable and ended at 5 a.m. when the whole assembly met in the Quad and were photographed. It was a gloriously fine night and Newman's Band played with much enthusiasm. Perhaps I should mention here that at the beginning of Term the Brasenose Ground was under water which was lapping against the steps of the Pavilion and swans were in undisputed possession.

I said *au revoir* to my many friends at the end of term and collected some study books for the long Summer Vac which covered the months of July, August and September.

I arrived home in late June 1920 when the weather was fine and the garden and greenhouses were in superb condition. In early July the strawberries and raspberries were abundant, but the asparagus was over. I arranged with my friend Tim Mason, to take a fishing holiday at Helmsley on the River Rye. We found a delightful farm house where we were made very welcome. As there had been no rain for some weeks the river was very low and the fish not keen to take the wet fly. So we had to resort to swimming the worm down the "stickles" – this was more successful and we had good sport. During our second week we had a heavy storm which put the river in spate. Our host, the farmer, was early on the swollen river with his short "spinning rod" and Devon spinner. He was successful and in a few hours had a superb basket of trout, some well over a pound. I think he had ten brace. Tim and I were compelled to fish the swollen river with "Swimming the worm" and we had a few very fine trout and enjoyed excellent sport. The river quickly returned to normal and we enjoyed a few days "fly-fishing" and were able to return home with several brace of trout.

I quickly returned to my text books and spent every morning studying and in the afternoons I joined Shaw in the garden. The Village Show was due and Shaw and I prepared a large list of entries. We got up at 5 a.m. the day of the show and our entries were first class. Tray of Fruit (six varieties) – then dishes of strawberries, raspberries, cherries, black, white and red currants, gooseberries and large list of vegetables. We took all our entries to the large Marquee and arranged them in their different classes. We had entered into the competition for the "Silver Cup" and much to our delight we had captured so many "First Class" prizes that we were awarded the "Silver Cup". My father was Secretary of the Haxby Horticultural Show and while the judging was going on there was a special Luncheon in the extra tent, where the local MP, for Thirsk and Malton Division was to make a special speech. An interesting feature of the show was that a heavy bullock was placed in a special pen and tickets to guess the "dead weight" of the bullock (1/- each) were sold, with the village policeman in attendance. This attracted many visitors and locals to try their luck, as the local butcher was to slaughter the bullock and record its weight in a sealed packet on Friday following the Wednesday Show.

It was a glorious day and the judging of the farm horses and foals and the classes of bullocks caused great interest. The judging lasted many hours and the final event was the "Horse Jumping" which was well supported with many entries. The prize money for the main entries was generous, as my Father collected a large sum of money from the Hunting Community each season to support the show. During late August and September I took my gun into the cornfields to attend the corn harvest as there were many rabbits, and I enjoyed excellent sport.

I made several visits to York Minster and I was most interested in the wonderful collection of Mediaeval Glass. The "Five Sisters" Window had been fully restored and was a joy to behold. I attended a special recital of Mendelssohn's *Elijah* rendered by the York Choral Society and Orchestra. This was held in the vast nave and was a great success.

I continued with my morning studies all through the long vacation and spent most of the time with my Physics programme. I was well prepared to return to Brasenose College for the commencement of the Autumn Term (early October).

My father was full of preparations for the coming hunting season. Early October saw the start of the "Cub Hunting" season and he was busy with his two hunters. I enjoyed several early morning rides.

*Autumn Term 1920*

I returned to Oxford a few days early as I had much preparation for a busy term's work. An addition to my programme was my entry to the School of Anatomy and Physiology. This meant I would spend most mornings in the dissection labs and attending lectures in Anatomy and Physiology. I also had to continue my studies of Physics and Chemistry. I was fortunate that during my last few weeks in the "Rhine Army" I managed to get some very helpful equipment for my Medical Training: half a skeleton, a superb Leitz microscope, and anatomy books. I was indeed very fortunate that I had all this useful and expensive equipment.

It was grand to be back again. It was noticeable that all the Freshmen were Public School Boys (aged 18+). In the College now, of all undergraduates, there were only two who had been in the war. There were six Rhodes Scholars from USA and South Africa in this new entry.

The Rugby Football Team had to face many losses, especially the war candidates, but we quickly got into training and of the first six matches the College won three and lost three. We beat St Johns (7-6), Queens (14-9) and Univ (3-0). We had a lively match against Cheltenham and lost (11-24), Jesus (3-16) Balliol (3-6).

As I had the Lent and Summer terms behind me, I had covered most of the necessary schedule of work. I greatly enjoyed my anatomy dissection in the labs. I commenced by dissecting the worm and had Derek Dunlop as a dissecting partner. Professor Arthur Thompson was the Anatomy Professor. His lectures were superb and his drawings of anatomical subjects were incredible, as he could use both right and left hands at the same time. Physics still provided me with problems: I failed the Physics Exam but was able to get much needed help from my Physics Tutor. I admit here that I had *no* affection for this subject. Life in College was a great joy.

One little episode occurred during term. *The Beggar's Opera* was performing at the local theatre and Arthur Blair made friends with several of the cast and invited them to luncheon in my room. I returned from the dissecting lab rather late and Ernest, my scout, met me on the stairs and told me that Mr Blair was entertaining a large party to lunch in my room. I entered my room and found at least a dozen enjoying lunch and to my horror I saw that the many guests had made a serious attack on my treasured Stilton Cheese. Three quarters had already disappeared! Arthur made a profound apology for this pillage. The guests had *not* partaken of the excellent College Cream Cheese from BNC farms! and the many guests were full of praise and thanks – I then commenced my own lunch and the cast of *The Beggar's Opera* left for a matinee, much to my relief!

Every Saturday during term the Oxford University Rugger XV played a match against the "Best Club XV". I went with Rex to these thrilling games. During this Michaelmas term we had four delightful papers in the Ingoldsby Essay Club and the Ingoldsby Dinner was held on October 29 after which Mr R W Jeffery read a paper on Brasenose Account Books.

I was fortunate in meeting Ripley Oddy of Oriel who was a nephew of my Colonel of the 5th West Yorkshire Regiment (1914-1916) and we played squash twice a week – this I greatly enjoyed. It was delightful that my CO of No. 7 Squadron RFC (1917-1919) Wing Commander B E Sutton DSO MC, visited me and Rex when he came to stay with Dr and Mrs Violet Gardener of Merton Street. Bertie was at University College with Dr Gardener when he entered there from Eton.

I found much interest in attending the Sutton Society Debates and three debates were held during term.

*October 1920*

The Sunday evening service at St Mary's Church was always well attended and on the Feast of All Saints 1920, the Preacher was the Bishop of London. Each "All Saints" weekend the Bp. of London was a guest of Radley College. After Matins in the School Chapel where he preached, he lunched with the Head Master and then set off on the long walk to Oxford via the tow Path. This took all the afternoon and the Bishop appeared for evensong at the University Church. On arriving at "The Ancient Pulpit" the Bishop commenced his sermon with the words, "this morning I preached in the School Chapel at Radley and walked to Oxford along the River Bank." I was told after the service that on previous "All Saints Services" he *always* commenced his sermon with these words!

This was a very happy, active term and I still attended Mr W N Stocker for my Physics Tutorials. I was told that he was still breaking records in "pedestrianism" and in one short week during the long vac, he walked 120 miles and had an accident when a motor car ran into him and broke his umbrella – happily, without injury to himself. On several Sunday afternoons there was a most enjoyable Organ Recital in Christ Church which gave me much pleasure. Dr and Mrs Gardener of Merton Street were most kind to me and Arthur Blair had special singing lessons with a Tutor every week at their home. Violet Gardener joined me in playing Golf, which was highly entertaining, and we managed one game each week on the Varsity Golf Course.

Our Dissection Seminars in the Anatomy Labs were most enjoyable and Professor Arthur Thompson continued with his excellent lectures and I found my Anatomy Illustrated Books most valuable. Our happy luncheon parties continued through term and Rex Facey, Derek Dunlop and Arthur Blair were excellent company. Gerald Panting was an excellent Scout and produced the College cream cheese and Brasenose ale.

Mr Jeffery, a History Don on our Staircase became a delightful friend and he told me about his country cottage at Thornton Dale in Yorkshire. His only daughter was a victim of Polio and needed a wheeled chair to get about.

The many "Old Peterites" of St Peter's School, York, at Oxford elected me as President of the OP Society and we held regular meetings and a very enjoyable Dinner Party. I missed, very much, many of the War Candidates who had gone down at the end of summer term, but quickly established new friendships with many of the "freshmen" who came up at the beginning of term, especially C H Knott, Tonbridge, R A Henniker-Gotley, Cheltenham, and H W Standring, Rugby.

We soon had a very useful Rugger XV and several of the Freshers joined us. It is interesting to note that a year ago, the BNC Ground was flooded, the water lapping against the steps of the Pavilion. T*his term* the ground was not in a very good state owing to want of rain. Fortunately rain came late in Term and during the vacation.

I returned to my home at Haxby, Yorkshire for the Christmas Vacation and was able to carry out useful studies in Anatomy and Physics. My Father greatly enjoyed his hunting with the local packs and no frosts interfered. Christmas at home was most enjoyable with several delightful parties in the village.

### *Lent Term 1921*

The Reverend Mark Carpenter-Garnier, Pusey House, asked me if I would "Serve" for him every Friday 8 a.m. at St Thomas Convent. I readily agreed and after the early service we were given breakfast of bacon and eggs. Although it was Friday, *I* was given *meat* but Mark C-G was given fish! Oxford became mellow and a spring-like atmosphere prevailed for the final week of term.

In the anatomy labs I finished my "Head and Neck" and had fun in reading the anatomy books especially *Veralius* and found my two German anatomy atlases *most* useful. I had a useful talk with Derek Dunlop on the prospect of going up to Edinburgh for the "special Anatomy Course" under Professor Ryland Whitaker at the historic Surgeons' Hall. This would save me a full "Oxford Term" as I was so late in coming up to BNC from the "Rhine Army" (1920). I arranged to do this for the whole of the Long Vacation and also persuaded Gerry McElligott of Hertford College to join me as I would try to arrange "digs" in Edinburgh. The Course in

Course in anatomy would commence Tuesday after Bank Holiday and last eight weeks.

I found that I had conquered my "sleeping habit" of falling asleep during the "after-dinner" sessions in my room by going to the College Library with my Text Books.

*Summer Term 1921*

I was heavily engaged with my dissections in the Anatomy Lab and I took "off" several sessions to spend some pleasant hours in the Parks watching the University 1st XI play in the three-day cricket matches with a selection of the County XIs. I greatly enjoyed my swimming sessions in "Parson's Pleasure" where the River Cherwell provided us with ample water. During one of our swimming sessions Gerry McElligott slipped on the wet grass and tore a knee cartilage and I had to take him to the Radcliffe Infirmary where he was dealt with by the Orthopaedic Surgeons.

On the River, the "Eights Week" was a sequence of misfortunes for our 1st VIII who had to face a descent of five places. I think the cause of this misfortune was due to the lack of coaches.

The cricket season revealed much talent in the College 1st XI who performed splendidly in the Cricket Cup. In the first round we beat St Johns, then in the 3rd round we beat Exeter when our Captain captured seven wickets for six runs. The most exciting match of the season was provided by the semi-final when we played New College, whom we disposed of for 191. We lost four wickets for 80 by the end of the first day. On top of this we found ourselves 50 runs in arrears with only two wickets to fall. Our Captain, with the valuable assistance from E A Rae, secured the necessary runs. In the final we faced Magdalen who won the toss and elected to put us in. After a disastrous start some fine batting by Stevens (83), Pritchard-Gordon (49) and W H Standring (61) enabled us to compile 359. Magdalen were dismissed for 96 being powerless against the bowling of Steven and Badger. In their second innings Magdalen scored 236 and some remarkable bowling by R A Henniker-Gotley, whose analysis was 5 for 80, won us the match.

Following our Cricket victory, a special dinner was held in Brasenose Hall – the jolliest "Bump Supper". The Principal made the speech of the evening – there were 30 speeches and of course some were rather short!

It was May 24th and the College heard the sad news that Dr Charles Buller Heberden, former Principal, had suddenly been taken ill and was removed to the Acland Home where he was operated on. He died on May 31st.

The coffin was brought to the Chapel on the night of June 1st, a most glorious night, with a sky of the deepest blue, and with the old tower of the College standing out clear with the lofty dome of the Radcliffe beyond. The College chapel was filled from end to end. The Chaplain read the prayers and the Principal, Dr Sampson, stood, as all the undergraduates quickly passed him on their way out when it was almost midnight. On June 2nd the funeral took place in the Chapel at 2.15 where the service was Choral and conducted by the Dean of Canterbury, the Reverend C A Whittuck. The lesson was read by Dr Sampson. The coffin was carried round the Quadrangle and then the procession from Balliol College joined up with the College procession, and proceeded to Holywell cemetery where he was laid to rest.

I had a great thrill when I was elected to "The Vampyres" Club, which had 21 sporting members, with Hector Watt as Secretary.

Mr C H Sampson settled in very well as our new Principal and the Sunday Tea Parties in the Principal's Lodgings were very popular. It was a great thrill for the College as G T S Stevens was appointed Captain of the Varsity Cricket XI for next season.

On Sunday, June 5 1921 an address was delivered in Chapel by Dr Sampson, the Principal. He delivered a most moving oration:

> "Every memoir of Dr Heberden speaks of his intense love of music, he used to organise Chamber Music concerts in the Hall of Balliol, where he was always the pianist. Next to his love of music was his love for open air and the beauty of natural scenery and his triumphs on the Matterhorn. During his seven years of Vice-Principalship he was striving for the headship of the River in "the Eights" which to his great joy we achieved in 1889.
>
> This is not the place to speak in detail of him as a Classical Scholar. No one ever had a finer instinct for the beauty of Greek and Latin literature and a deeper insight into the meaning. Gently, I must touch on his abundant generosity. Nothing that was good for the college was outside the scope of his generous sympathy. By his will an organ scholarship will be established and the foundation of the Harrow Scholarship. Here in Chapel we owe him the organ, the organ loft and all that pertains to it. My brothers, I have tried to describe him as I have known him for 38 years. Last Sunday evening I spoke to you those splendid words of St Paul which speak of the Charity that hopeth all things, believeth all things, endureth all things and I ask you today to read it quietly for yourselves. Keep it in your hearts."

This term I shared the hiring of a punt at Magdalen Bridge and Gerry McElligott was my partner. We did some long trips up the Cherwell but I found I could not concentrate on my various text books as there were so many distractions. The final weeks of the summer term passed by all too quickly and I finished the term by going to the Oriel Ball and was joined by Dick Symmonds and his sister. It was a most delightful event and a glorious night.

I told Professor Thompson that I was going up to the Surgeons Hall in Edinburgh to join Professor Ryland Whitaker's anatomy class and he was delighted.

*Sheena's autograph book*

## Summer Vacation 1921

I spent most of July at my home in Yorkshire and enjoyed some rabbit shooting in the harvest fields and helped harvest the hay crop. My father's hunters were put out to grass on the two paddocks and would be there until the Cub Hunting Season commenced in October.

I arrived in Edinburgh and was joined in my digs in Marchmount Crescent by Gerry McElligott and our friend Hamilton, a barrister and an old Etonian who was anxious to get a medical degree. Our Landlady said, "Gentlemen, you can have your bath on Mondays as it is my laundry day." She had a large lead bath which was an old Edinburgh antique. I met Colonel Alexander Blair, a Writer to the Signet, Arthur Blair's father. I also met my old No. 7 Squadron Pilot of the RFC and his wife Ian Anderson Johnson-Gilbert, who was a very active member of the Edinburgh City Council and on the staff of the Sun Assurance Coy.

We commenced the course of Anatomy at the Surgeons Hall where Professor Ryland Whitaker gave a warm welcome. He lectured brilliantly every morning and then we went into the dissecting rooms in late morning and every afternoon (Monday until Friday). It was very concentrated work.

The Professor was very keen that all medical students who were attending lectures and carrying out the strenuous dissection programme should be able to remember the complicated anatomical details. So he adopted an amusing "Gilbert and Sullivan" attitude, e.g. he would stand in front of the class, then recite the lyric relating to the part he was demonstrating, holding a skull in his hands. He would then make the whole class recite the lyric. Of course, during the two months course we had at least 20 rhymes to recite and we never forgot these important anatomical details. I was fortunate in being given the friendship of our distinguished professor, who presented me with his special anatomy book of the "Brain"!

After the hectic days of the week we welcomed Saturdays and all the Golfing students went to the historic "Braids" Golf Course, above Edinburgh. I had a regular partner who was a scratch golfer and a member of the Oxford Golf Team, Reg Bettington, an Australian Rhodes Scholar. I was lucky to have such a brilliant partner in my games and we also made two Saturday visits to Gleneagles Golf Course.

Arthur Blair very kindly invited me to meet his parents and dine with them at India Street. I was invited to join the family in Arthur's 21st birthday celebrations which were held, far north at their delightful cottage at Cruden Bay. During my visit to Cruden Bay I enjoyed several rounds of golf and I had two very long and entertaining walks with Colonel Alistair Blair, who gave me a wonderful history of the complicated "Ecclesiastical" details of the various churches of Scotland in the 19th and 20th centuries.

I visited the Edinburgh Art Gallery where there was a most superb collection of pictures, many lent from the ancestral homes of the Scottish Peerage.

Professor Whitaker carried on the special anatomy course into early October and I made splendid progress, easily saving a complete Oxford Term. The teaching had been wonderful from such a gifted man and the whole course of students completed the course with marked gratitude.

### *Autumn Term 1921*

Back at Oxford there was a large contingent of "Freshers", Scholars and Commoners. My friend, Ralph G Cummins from USA, had just taken his shortened course in Jurisprudence and asked me to be his best man in Dublin, where he was to marry Ethel Chance, daughter of Sir Arthur and Lady Chance. I agreed to do this but an urgent communication from Lady Chance requested me to cancel my visit as she suspected trouble with the IRA, who would object strongly if a member of the RAF landed in Dublin. Already several members of the RAF had been shot, including one of my personal friends.

I quickly settled into my rooms and our normal luncheon party went merrily along. Derek and I attended the Physiology Lectures of Sir Charles Sherrington who was President of the Royal Society. Sir Charles had a special collection of chimps who travelled with him to several continental countries. He gave the local medical students a special session with the apes and these sessions were most entertaining.

We swiftly got down to rugger training and soon had a very fine 1st XV with some excellent Freshmen.

The College Rugger XV had a most exciting match against Tonbridge School XV who beat us 10-19. They had an excellent pair of Half backs, Young and Francis (South Africa). Both got blues at Cambridge. Francis who came from South Africa was not allowed to come to Oxford, as his father said he would not succeed in obtaining his blue.

A new Fellow was elected to the College, Mr Maurice Platenauer. His father had been my Company Commander when I was in the 5th West Yorkshire Regiment. Maurice was a Shrewsbury boy and a New College Man.

Half-way through term I had an unknown visitor who called on me. He was the Secretary of the Richmond Rugger Team, and he asked me if I would play Full Back for Richmond against Cambridge University at Cambridge. I felt greatly embarrassed by this offer and told him I would need to ask the Vice Principal, Dr Stallybrass, if I could have permission to leave Oxford for the day to play for Richmond against Cambridge. I went immediately to the Vice Principal. He was amused at the offer and willingly gave me permission for the enterprise. The Richmond Secretary was delighted and he told me we would meet the team at Liverpool Street

Station on the Saturday morning. The whole Richmond Team and several supporters all crowded into the Luncheon Car and I was amazed at the enormous amount of beer the players consumed during lunch, i.e. only two hours before the match. After this huge lunch and beer we finally arrived at Fenners Rugger Ground and we had a most exciting match. It was a glorious afternoon and we led for most of the game. I kicked two goals but we were beaten in the final minutes – by six points! The rugger match was a thrilling combat and the Cambridge Scrum was superb. The Cambridge side contained two English internationals. The Richmond Rugger XV put a splendid fight and I had a very strenuous game at Full Back.

How fond these young men were of their beer and on the return journey they were able to consume a great deal of it. The Secretary presented me with a Richmond 1st XV Rugger Shirt. I finally arrived back at Oxford after a most entertaining day.

During this term I spent a lot of time in the Oxford College Chapels and lovely gardens. The Old Peterite Club was very active and held several entertaining meetings and the Head Master of St Peter's School came down to Oxford as our Guest at the Annual Dinner.

It is interesting to note that W B Cardew (Matr. 1877) saw one of D'Urfey's songs at the Rose Tavern, Covent Garden in a book on old inns of London.

> Three merry lads met at the "Rose"
> To speak in praises of the nose
> The flat, the sharp, the Roman Snout
> The hawk's nose circled round about
> The crook'd nose that stands awry
> The ruby nose of scarlet dye
> The Brazen Nose without a face
> That doth the learned College grace

I spent a very happy Christmas Vac at home at Haxby and did some useful reading.

### Lent Term 1922

The Rugger Committee appointed A D Grant and Derek Dunlop and myself to assist the Captain and Secretary in the early training of the rugger teams. We had about 50 keen rugger men to get into training and had three XVs and soon had a first class 1st XV.

It was a good term for rowing: I had some thrilling scrambles on the tow-path. I witnessed five bumps, and the 1st were in tremendous form. After these races the 1st entered for the Ladies Plate at Henley and for the first time in over seventy years they won this race. Dr Browne was responsible for the special coaching. The four gained a final success in the "Coxwainless Fours". The "College Four" beat Merton by five seconds. Then they beat Magdalen "A" by seven seconds and Trinity by four. What a wonderful year!

My work in the anatomy labs was most successful and I felt that one more "Summer Vac Anatomy Course" at Edinburgh under Professor Ryland Whitaker would be of immense value to me. Gerry McElligott agreed to join me in the adventure.

I attended the annual "May Morning special Service" conducted from Magdalen College Tower (5 a.m.) as usual. The morning was fine and a huge assembly of visitors turned up – the singing was superb and was greatly enjoyed. Dr and Mrs Violet Gardener of Merton Street were most generous with their hospitality all the term and we went on several picnics.

When playing in a rugger match against Worcester College I had a very severe blow on my nose and had to attend Dr J Robinson FRCS of Beaumont Street. He had to straighten the septum and I was a fortnight out of the game. During this match I converted one penalty from my own half.

My war friend Stanley Griffin MGC, 1916 Clipstone Camp, visited me at Oxford for the weekend and I took him to visit the Robinsons where he entertained them on the piano. He is a superb pianist and the Robinsons were most kind – he stayed at the Golden Cross Hotel.[*]

I noticed that Pusey House was holding a "Retreat" for three days run by Dr Carpentier-Garnier. I decided to go, and found it a great blessing and, spiritually, most uplifting.

I had a very quiet and restful Vac and continued with reading Physiology and Anatomy. Holy week was very peaceful and I greatly enjoyed the three-hour service which was beautifully taken.

### Summer Term 1922

When I arrived in College for the summer term the Old Quad looked most colourful, with the floral window boxes in front of every upper

---

[*] MGC = Machine Gun Corps. My father used to account how Stanley lay in No Man's Land for many hours with a gaping wound in his back. He was just able to flap an arm from time to time. This was eventually spotted and at nightfall a patrol brought him in, hardly alive. Another survivor.

window and there was a great thrill with the College holding four university cups. The Ladies Plate, The Soccer Cup, The Cricket Cup and "The Trophy of the Fours". It is interesting that only the stroke of the winner had his name carved on the ancient cup and it is remarkable that Percy Mellen had his name carved like his father 40 years ago (1887). The only instance of father and son being stroke of the coxless fours in their year at BNC.

After ten Bumps made by the two eights, Brasenose marked their success by the time-honoured Bump Supper on May 30th. This was a tremendous success and the Principal proposed the Toast of the "Two Eights". But there was a wonderful scene when ALL the members present insisted on Professor Stuart-Jones making a speech. He made an admirable oration. It was declared that this was the most remarkable "Bump Supper" held within the walls of Brasenose, for never before after any Eights Week were there ten victories to celebrate!

Dr Spooner, the Principal of New College, was well known for his "spoonerisms" but it is well to remember that our great Principal Radcliffe who died on 26th June 1648 was an early perpetrator of spoonerisms. On one occasion Dr Radcliffe solemnly announced "A proud man will buy a dagger" whereas he meant "a proud man will die a beggar."

During the term I was invited by a friend at St John's College to attend the Archers Club for Luncheon and afterwards to shoot at the targets on the huge lawn. There were 14 who attended the luncheon, seven St John's College members, who had superb green blazers with a Golden Arrow on, the breast pocket and the seven guests. The luncheon was a lavish affair with a set of beautiful ancient Silver Loving cups, which were circulated for the whole luncheon. I think there were five large loving cups in circulation the whole time, so one was popping up and down every three minutes. The cup contained a very fine vintage champagne. The luncheon went on for well over an hour and before the end several of the members appeared very lively and seemed to me to be rather dangerous gentlemen, when in action with bow and arrow. We all eventually arrived on the scene of action and the St John's College Captain asked me if I would shoot with his bow (there were four targets). I gave the bow a lengthy test before I was in action. Taking careful aim I made a mighty pull of the bow and off shot the arrow, and to the surprise and delight of the Archers I scored a Bull. This was a mighty surprise to me and the Captain was presented with a bottle of wine for this success. This result caused a rush of archers to me requesting me to use their bow – hoping for another Bull. The Bow which was handed to me was a good six inches longer than the first, and I gave it several mock releases of the cord before releasing the arrow on to No. 2 target. To my great horror the arrow went sailing through the air well over the top of the target, and straight to a garden seat which contained a sleeping Bishop, which was nearly 100 feet from the line of targets. Mercifully the arrow fell just short of the sleeping bishop and stuck in the lawn. This mighty error, which could have been dangerous, was due for just punishment and the owner of the bow was fined £1.00 by the club secretary – I was not allowed to pay for my error. The Archery went on for a full hour during an afternoon of sunshine. There were no further disasters and I enjoyed many exciting episodes with the targets, but no more bulls.

Very shortly after this happy event with St John's Archers I had a letter from the "Bidder" who was the Fellow in Charge of the Rockeries at St John's College. This was a great honour and surprise. I was invited to a special luncheon party which consisted of celebrated horticulturists, including Sir Frederick Keble and Lady Keble and the famous Miss Wilmott. This luncheon was a delightful event, with about 24 present. After this excellent lunch, the whole party repaired to the area in the College Gardens and the rockeries which were a sensation with masses of special rock plants. The colour was glorious, provided by several pockets of *Gentians*, especially *Gentian Verna*. I was partnered with Miss Wilmott who was most delighted with it; she taught me a lot about many of the flowering Alpines.

As the weather was fine and warm I went regularly to the various Thames Bathing Regions, especially Parsons' Pleasure. Swimming was most refreshing after several hours dissecting in the anatomy labs. I was fortunate in being able to attend "The Greek Plays" held in New College Gardens and these were sensational and thrilling. The OUDS had certainly presented the University with a superb entertainment.

My friend, Arthur Blair, took his BA degree at the end of June and went down. Greville Steven had been a most successful Captain of the University XI and C H Knott was also given his Cricket Blue.

I went to Thame to the Oxford County Show as the Apiary Section was demonstrating a new American Bee Hive, "The Buck Eye". I was most impressed and I bought one which was sent to my home at Haxby to add to our collection of four bee hives.

I went to tea with one of the BNC dons, Mr Wakeling on two Sundays during term and cut his lawns at their North Oxford home and invited two Norwegian girls to tea in College. Mrs Wakeling had several girl guests from Norway during the Summer Term.

Lady Ethel Sherrington (wife of Sir Charles)* arranged for me to go to Florence at the beginning of the long Vac to stay with a friend of hers, an Italian Countess. I was most fortunate in this superb opportunity to visit this ancient city.

There was much activity in Oxford for the concluding weeks of the summer term and many of my friends were taking their finals. I continued every Friday morning in "Serving" for the Reverend Mark Carpentier-Garnier of Pusey House at St Thomas's Convent and I was invited to go and stay a weekend at his family home in Hampshire. I played in a local cricket match and made one catch in the deep field. This was a most happy event and I greatly enjoyed every moment.

Derek and I had to look for digs for our final year at Oxford and we found excellent rooms with Annie Osborne in Long Wall just opposite the Magdalen Choir School, so every morning during breakfast we heard the choir boys singing.

I finished the difficult "head and neck" dissection and this cleared the decks for me to appear at The Surgeons Hall in Edinburgh at the end of July. At the end of term, at the Dons Inspection I was given a favourable report on my work. I said good-bye to Ernest Panting, my Scout, who had looked after me so well over the past two and a half years, and moved all my "possessions" to our new digs in Long Wall Street.

In my final week I called on the Sherringtons, the Gardeners and Dr and Mrs J Robinson of Beaumont Street, who had all been most kind to me with their hospitality during term. I must mention here that I was initiated into the Freemasons and was made a member of the Apollo Lodge – the University Lodge, which had the much respected, P Colville-Smith, as secretary. I greatly enjoyed the Lodge Meetings and we met once a fortnight. I finished term by attending the special Centenary Ball at Christ Church. This was a superb event and was a great success. Dick Simmonds was in my party and he came from Oriel and brought his sister. Quite a lot of my rugger friends were going down after their final schools, and I finally returned to my home at Haxby at the end of June.

### Summer Vacation 1922 – A visit to Florence

The plans for my visit to Florence reached me at home early in July and I decided to take a fortnight's holiday before going up to Edinburgh. I arranged to travel via Calais and then by train direct to Florence. I was

---

* Very many years later, I think over 40, my father and Paula were able to look after Lady S. "Sherry" who had developed an inoperable tumour, while Sir Charles went to Stockholm to collect his Nobel Peace Prize. Sir Charles was for some years President of the Royal Society.

given a warm welcome by the Countess who gave me excellent and helpful instructions relating to my visit. Happily, the weather was glorious and very hot and I soon made plans and found my way round this glorious city. My first day was spent visiting the Bargello and I was staggered by the incredible beauty of Michelangelo's "David" and the beauty of "David" by Verrocchio.

*Extracts from diary*

>The Gallery here is most beautiful and the various statues are a joy to behold and in this peaceful atmosphere one can enjoy the many glories. Michelangelo's "The Drunken Bacchus" is a most glorious demonstration of MA's great genius. Just before lunch I took a short walk to inspect the "Baptistry" which has the amazing huge doors – this wonderful work was carved out in the xii century and the East door is covered by 8 huge panels of "Scenes of the Old Testament" by Ghiberti. It is amazing to inspect this wonderful door which is staggering for its beauty. It is well known in Florence that Michelangelo declared "this door on the East side of the Baptistry to be worthy of Paradise." Then walked into the Duomo. I was most impressed by The Dome which towers 300 feet above the Choir. This is second only to the Dome of St Peter's in the world.
>
>Florence at this season is well supplied with superb fruit, luscious peaches, grapes, figs which are giving me much pleasure.
>
>Close to the apse of this celebrated Basilica is the Museo dell' Opera del Duomo – it contains some xivth (century) statues of the apostles. Donatello's fine St John the Evangelist is a superb example of this glorious work. My next visit was to the Palazzo Vecchio where I spent a long while enjoying the superb statue of Andrea Verrocchio's "Incredulity of St Thomas." The Christ is superbly carved and the garments are beautifully completed. Here I discovered in one of the arches Benvenuto Cellini's Perseus, surely one of the finest statues in Florence. The powerfully modelled body from the winged feet to the very end of the slender fingers holding up the Gorgon's head. On the way out there is the copy of Michelangelo's famous David and Hercules and Donatello's Judith. All heroes of the Bible and mythology.
>
>It was most kind of my hostess to invite me to dine with her each night and we greatly enjoyed our conversation on the manifold glories of Florence. She spoke beautiful English and gave me excellent advice on my visit to the Uffizi. Before going I made an early visit to the Ponte Vecchio. Most of the shops demonstrated

superb collections of choice jewellery. These shops were to be found from one end to the other and I spent well over an hour here. Happily it was early morning, and there were few visitors on the bridge.

Now for the excitement of the Uffizi Gallery. It was a glorious day and the light was most favourable. The Galleria degli Uffizi and the Palazzo Pitti form a visit that is unequalled in the world and I am leaving the visit to the Pitti Gallery until next week. Of course, there are dozens of galleries in the Uffizi and there are several very thrilling statues in the early galleries before one comes to the main pictures.

I am not going to inspect the hundreds of celebrated paintings but concentrate on the masterpieces of Botticelli, Leonardo Da Vinci, Raphael and Titian. The first thing I notice is that the statues are displayed along glazed galleries, bordering the rooms where the paintings are on show. I was staggered by the glorious paintings by Botticelli, especially the Birth of Venus and Primavera and The Madonna of the Magnificat.

When I had a quiet view of Leonardo da Vinci's Annunciation I was most impressed by the beauty of the Angel and the dignity of the Blessed Virgin. I simply could not leave this picture. I am amazed at the large number of Raphael's paintings and especially impressed by the beauty of the "Madonna with the Goldfinch". I found the gallery very sparsely populated, so I was able to spend several hours surrounded by the many glorious paintings and the light was good and beneficial for the pictures.

I am most impressed by the number of Raphael's exquisite paintings and I bought several reproductions. Here in the galaxy of glorious paintings I was thrilled to find many of Titian's works and I greatly enjoyed these hours and took a long break for lunch, before returning to the Uffizi to spend the rest of the afternoon in the main galleries. I was able to have a long re-look at some of the morning's paintings which gave me immense joy and when I left the gallery for my slow walk back to my apartment I had never had such a day of rich artistic refreshment. After dinner, my hostess was able to give me much delight in discussing many of the superb works which I had enjoyed in the Uffizi.

The weather was again fine and I decided to visit the Monastery San Marco. Here in the most famous Dominican foundation in the world, are many glorious paintings of Fra Angelico and on the first floor are two "Annunciations." Mary, in her utter humility and in the third cell another glorious

*Annunciation*, beautifully painted. It is clear that Fra Angelico intended the occupant of the cell to be aided in his daily meditations by the beauty of the Annunciation. The cell of St Antoninus conveys the thrill of the Easter Liturgy and the Christ is superbly painted. In the Chapter-House at the end of the Cloister is the picture of the Large Crucifixion – this is staggering and it is worthy of note that the Crosses are T-shaped. The details of the paintings of the many Holy Men and Holy Women are superbly painted. It is easy to see the kneeling St Francis of Assisi in this group – he is holding a crucifix. Near the Monastery San Marco is the Museum for Etruscan Art. Here are interesting Stele's which are beautifully executed. Many of the exhibits are actually older than the Rome works of art circa 1st century. The Etruscan region of Italy is N. of Rome and immediately South of Florence and almost all the objects of interest, pottery, etc. date from 500-300 B.C.

Visiting the Church of Santa Croce was a tremendous thrill. This historic Church is as old as The Duomo and is the largest Franciscan Church in the world. I was most impressed by the manifold glories of this ancient church where a fragment of "The True Cross" is kept in great reverence. This Church is divided into three aisles and is bare of <u>all</u> ornaments – there are several of Giotto's Frescoes. The most celebrated Fresco is that which portrays the life of St Francis of Assisi.

It is incredible how much there is to see in and around Florence and today being fine and warm I decided to walk to Fiesole and I know the best time is early in the morning before the sun is too high. The climb must be made on foot. San Dominico is the first stopping place and it is interesting that in the Chapter House there is a Fresco by Fra Angelico. The situation of the Monastery is superb, half-way between the City and Fiesole. I continued the climb and after 20 minutes I arrived at the Badia Fiesolana, Fiesole's original Cathedral which overlooks the Magnone Valley. The battlemented campanile can be seen against the sky in a sort of saddle where the town is clustered. A broad street leads off the main square and winds its way up to the highest point of the hill. On the summit the view over the city of Florence is staggering. A thousand feet below Florence spreads its riches and I rested here for half an hour to take in the manifold glories of the city. I had lunch outside and greatly enjoyed the fabulous view. The view of the little monastery of San Francisco is delightful. This has stood since 1352 on the Etruscan necropolis and around its walls there is a dazzling carpet of flowers. I then had the great thrill of enjoying the Roman

Theatre which was in a wonderful state of preservation. I spent the late afternoon in quietly walking the return journey back to Florence and the light of the afternoon sun greatly enhanced the glories of the widespread city of Florence.

It was a joy to meet my hostess and tell her of my thrilling day at Fiesole.

I was anxious to see several of the superb works of Michelangelo, so I went to the Church of San Lorenzo and here the Tomb of Giuliano de Medici in the New Sacristy was magnificent!

I moved on to visit the huge church of Santa Maria Novella and I could get a good view of its vast dimensions from the opposite side of the square in the small gardens. The interior is majestic, with Gothic arches, recalling the Duomo. There are wonderful frescoes, the work of Dominico Ghirlandaio; Filippino Lippi's "Raising of Drusiana" and by the same artist, the "Miracle of St Philip".

In the evening I invited my hostess to dine with me at a delightful restaurant – this was an immense pleasure and we greatly enjoyed this evening together. Next day, my hostess allowed me to purchase a most beautiful bronze statue of The Boy Extracting Thorn from his Foot – copy of the original is in the Vatican museum in Rome.

I was very keen to make another visit to the Uffizi so I could get a quiet and long look at my favourite pictures. I spent the whole morning there and then prepared for my return journey after my marvellous fortnight's visit to Florence. I was able to get my dear sister Barbara a most beautiful copy of Raphael's Madonna and the Goldfinch – from the Uffizi Gallery. I spent the final afternoon wandering round the many delightful streets and enjoyed visiting several shops. Next morning I said "au revoir" to my delightful hostess and went to the station early to catch the express train which made the return journey from Florence to Calais.

I arrived home at the end of July and found the family well. I did a month's work in the garden with Shaw. I prepared for my special visit to Edinburgh to attend the anatomy course under Professor Ryland Whitaker and took my anatomy books and half-skeleton with me. I joined Gerald McElligott and Pat Hamilton at our digs in Marchmont Crescent. Gerry was ex-Munster Regiment. Pat Hamilton was a Barrister at University College, and had been an Officer in the Indian Army; he was also present at the Amritzar Tragedy and massacre, when scores of Indians were shot.

We all arrived in our digs and presented ourselves for the mid-day meal. It was an incredibly hot weekend and when the meal – "Irish Stew"

– arrived at the table, Pat Hamilton gasped, quickly left, and went up the street to return with a 1 lb bag of greengages which he consumed instead of joining Mac and me with the Irish Stew. We had to make an excuse to our anxious landlady!

The Anatomy Course commenced on the Wednesday morning and about 50 students attended. Professor Whitaker gave us a warm welcome and his first lecture was on the Skull. It was very hot in the dissecting room and McElligott, Pat Hamilton and I tackled the Head and Neck. This difficult dissection took us nearly a month as we attended the lectures each morning and did our dissection in the afternoons. In the evenings at 5 p.m. three times a week, we attended Physiology Lectures which we found very interesting. Dr Whitaker's lectures on the Brain were a wonderful presentation.

On one Saturday I joined Reg Bettington (New College) who was a Cricket and Rugger Blue on a day's golf at Gleneagles – most entertaining. We returned to Edinburgh Station by train, arriving about 8 p.m.

August Sundays were most restful and I went to Churches and the Cathedral for various services, which I greatly enjoyed. During some of the hot evenings Reg Bettington and I went to play golf on the Edinburgh City Golf Course at the Braids which was 1/- per round and a most delightful sporting golf course.

The Anatomy Course with its lectures continued all through September and we made excellent progress with our programme. I was able to meet Derek Dunlop's mother and also Arthur Blair's family.

There was much excitement with the coming General Election. In Glasgow there was a dramatic sweeping victory for the Socialists. This victory greatly upset our friend, Pat Hamilton, who felt that if a Socialist Government was returned to power he would lose all his capital. He took a morning off and went to his Banker and Stock Broker and transferred all his sterling balances into Canadian dollars. This amounted to many thousands of pounds. He returned to the fold much relieved, and continued with Mac and me on our dissections for the remainder of September. The Socialists did not win the election, so Pat Hamilton arranged with his banker to transfer all his dollars back into pounds sterling and he greatly rejoiced to learn that he had done very well on the deal!

I found much interest in visiting the ancient Edinburgh Castle, the superb War Memorial and the Edinburgh Art Gallery which contained many glorious paintings.

Just before the course ended I arranged with the lab attendant to go to the local Maternity Hospital and purchase the body of a stillborn baby. I paid £2 for a splendid specimen, which they kept for me until the end of our anatomy course.

All the medical students from the many Oxford and Cambridge Colleges, were most grateful for the extensive course which Professor Whitaker had conducted during the two months vacation, when he did not take a vacation himself. I was signed up for 6 parts in my extension dissections and this meant that I had saved two whole Oxford terms, which coming late from the war meant a huge saving of time and much finance.

During the course I met my old pilot, Ian Johnson-Gilbert; I went to his home in Ravelston Dykes at weekends and also played several games of golf with him. He was employed as an Inspector with the Sun Insurance Coy. His father, a lawyer, and his mother made me very welcome at their home.

At the end of September, I went to the Maternity Hospital to collect my stillborn infant which was parcelled ready for the long train journey south. I caught an early express and got a seat in the end coach so I could be near my three cases. There were three other passengers: a married couple and a single male. When the train was well on its way to Newcastle, there was a surprise visit to our compartment by two plain-clothes detectives who said politely, "Who is the Mr A G Wilson, whose luggage is labelled to YORK?"

Naturally, I was most surprised. They declared that they were detectives and wished me to accompany them to the Guard's Van, where they demanded to inspect my luggage. They said there were some IRA travellers on the train who could be carrying explosives. I was very firm in telling my two detectives that I was a medical student and had certificates to confirm my vacation course at the Surgeons' Hall. I also had half a skeleton in one of my cases, dissecting tools and a stillborn baby. They looked upon me with much suspicion, but on opening one case and seeing the half skeleton and the two large anatomy books they seemed satisfied. They did not want to see the stillborn baby – and allowed me to return to my coach.

I stayed at home nearly a week and did quite a lot of work on the stillborn baby. My sister Barbara was most interested in the infant dissection. I then packed for Oxford for the commencement of the Michaelmas Term.

## Autumn Term 1922

On arrival I went to my digs with Annie Osborne in Long Wall Street and met Derek Dunlop who was already in residence. I told him I would go early in the morning to take the precious stillborn baby to the Anatomy

Dissecting Laboratory. There was very much excitement when the stillborn baby was put in the dissecting room. It had been injected with special preservative before it left Edinburgh.

Soon the term was going along merrily. Professor Arthur Thompson gave us lectures in the Anatomy Theatre. Several friends joined us in the dissection of the baby which lasted us until nearly the end of term. We had some exciting rugger matches and Derek was a most useful forward and was splendid in the line out. We greatly enjoyed several school matches. We had some most delightful "Ingoldsby meetings" and Derek was the President.

My physiology tutor gave me very hard work and I wrote a paper for him every week when he came up to College from London. This was also a useful preparation for my Physiology Finals in June. The College Bursar very kindly asked Dr Pearson, who was on the Staff of "Barts" in London to give me a Physiology Tutorial on Saturdays until the end of term. This would be a great help for me for my 1st MB exam in December.

Sonners, a bachelor, very kindly invited me with six others to dine with him in his rooms and he gave us roast woodcock and an excellent wine. Dr and Mrs Gardner had their baby son baptised in Univ. Chapel and I acted for Bertie Sutton as Godfather, as he was serving his country in India (RAF).

St Hugh's, the ladies college, made contact with the BNC Sutton Debating Society and asked if their Debating Society could hold a Joint Meeting. This was agreed and the subject for the debate was "That this House does not think the Book of Psalms contributes any merit to literature." The meeting was agreed to and Derek Dunlop led the BNC team at St Hugh's College. The meeting was a great success and when Derek arrived there was quite a "flutter" in the crowded debating hall, as the female students were highly stimulated by Derek's good looks. The debate went on for almost three hours and there were many delightful speeches by both male and female members. Derek spoke brilliantly on the manifold merits of the Psalms as a superb contribution to the gems of English literature. Several lady students were full of criticism of the Psalms and spoke against the motion. The final verdict was that "The Psalms made a commendable contribution to the merits of English Literature."

The term seemed to pass very quickly and it was good to see that so many of the Freshmen were brilliant in all areas of sport. I was able to enjoy some splendid games of Squash Racquets and Fives. This helped to keep me fit.

It was soon time to face our anatomy exam and we wrote the first papers in the Examination Schools. We spent the final day with anatomy vivas and I had to face my viva with Professor Parsons from London. I put in some final revision during lunch in my digs and concentrated on the lower limbs. I could hardly believe my luck when presenting myself to Professor Parsons and there before him he placed the anatomy specimen of the lower limbs – *perfect specimens*. He fairly put me through it, but his many questions were closely associated with my revision hour at luncheon. I felt I had done well. I joined about 30 other students in the anatomy laboratory, and there was much excitement as we awaited the vital paper to be pinned up with the names of the successful pupils. A great hush prevailed as the Janitor carried the paper to the demonstration board. Derek was near the front and we were able to wave to each other that we had been successful[*].

We were both highly delighted, and had a celebration drink in College. We were conscious of the fact that we had to face our two final terms in preparation for our Honours in June for our BA Natural Science Degree.

I collected several Physiology Books to take home for reading during the Christmas vacation and did some useful Christmas shopping.

I arrived home for the Christmas Vacation and found all the family well. Several families entertained us and I had happy visits to the Hunts in York. I put in some useful hours with my studies and concentrated on the many aspects of respiration.

### *Lent Term 1923*

I returned to Oxford for the Lent Term.

Most of the sporting activity in the College was associated with the river and training for Toggers was in full swing. We had a few Inter-Collegiate Rugger matches and some of the Freshers were very capable rugger players.

The programme in the Physiology Block was most active and Sir Charles Sherrington gave a series of lectures. I also put in several hours in the Zoology Dept. as there was an exam at the end of term. I became involved in a special research project which was organised by Professor Tannaca of Tokyo University. Sir Charles and Dr Gardner arranged that I should do special sessions in the Oxygen Decompression Chamber with Professor Tannaca, and that I should submit to psychological tests without the help of oxygen up to 23,000 feet. The Professor sitting next to me would be taking oxygen all the time. The tests would show how much the

---

[*] Derek Dunlop became Professor of Therapeutics at Edinburgh and was knighted. He was my Godfather

lack of oxygen would mean to sorting cards, maths and many physical tests. At the same time in the Pressure Tank the two British Himalaya Climbers (Mallory and Irvine), preparing for the Mount Everest Climb, were also doing physical tests with full climbing kit. They continued their tests up to 27,000 feet. My breathing became very laboured between 19,000 and 23,000 feet and I became very cyanosed. Looking through the observation windows were Sir Charles and Dr Gardner. There was also a Boy Scout (14) doing tests but he had to be withdrawn at 12,000 feet. There was a sailor who came out at 15,000 feet. I made several visits to the Pressure Tank to assist Professor Tannaca. Sir Charles, when observing me through the observation window on one occasion, thought I looked very cyanosed and ordered me out. I was actually chosen for this special experiment because I had flown as an Observer in the RFC in 1917-1918 and I had done long spells flying at 23,000 feet doing aerial photography of the Rhinelands.

I attended Lent services at Pusey House and at St Mary's Church and I found much delight in my visits to the Cowley Fathers' Church at Iffley.

The Shrove Tuesday Brasenose Ale Dinner in College was a very cheery evening and the Brasenose Ale verses were presented to all members. I made several enjoyable visits to the Pitt Rivers Museum.

I arrived home for the Easter Vac and was most pleased that I was able to enjoy the three-hour service in our Parish Church. It was delightful to see all the daffodils and spring flowers in bloom for a very colourful Easter.

I made several excursions to the farm fields, where plovers were nesting and had little difficulty in finding the plovers' nests. I only took one egg from each nest and greatly enjoyed them. My father was nearing the end of another hunting season and was now enjoying the popular point to point races which were held by the three local hunts. I joined Shaw in the garden for a planting session in the afternoons and I spent every morning with my text books. The Vac went by very quickly and I greatly enjoyed the company of my two sisters, Barbara and Mary.

*Summer Term 1923*

I returned to Oxford several days early and Derek joined me at our digs in Long Wall Street. We were heavily engaged in our revision and were ready for the hectic final term at Oxford.

Sir Charles Sherrington gave us a very concentrated series of lectures and presented his special demonstration of cerebral surgery on one of his chimpanzee apes. Now this was an annual event during the Trinity term – several visitors from abroad also attended.

Hunt, his lab assistant, brought in the delightful chimp and it was rapidly put under an anaesthetic. The lecture theatre was very crowded – with the lady students in front! Sir Charles, clad in white operating gown, was soon in action with his operating instruments and he made his initial incisions in the vault of the skull; then, using the trepanning instruments, he proceeded to remove the vault of the skull, exposing the cerebral cortex of the ape's brain. The chimp remained quite placid and showed no sign of distress. Hunt continued with the anaesthetic and Sir Charles offered his first question. At once, one of the lady students said, "Please sir, could you make the ape sneeze?"

Here Sir Charles used his electric needle and sought the special convolution of the brain which controlled the action of sneezing. At once, on touching the convolution with the electric needle the ape immediately raised its head slightly and then sneezed violently. There was much applause while Sir Charles waited for the second question from one of the distinguished visitors.

"Please, Sir, I would ask you to make the chimp move by the scratching of its face with one of its hands." Here Sir Charles made a special examination of the brain and then applied the electric needle to a selected convolution and almost at once the chimp moved an arm, and the fingers scratched its chin. Much applause! There was just time for a third question and Sir Charles was asked by an undergraduate to make the chimpanzee raise a leg. This again was most successful and Sir Charles then replaced the vault in position and sewed over the incised skin flap. Hunt then ceased to administer the anaesthetic and the chimp was wheeled back to its special bed. Then followed a series of questions and a lively discussion. The session ended with congratulations and thanks to Sir Charles for a unique demonstration of his skill and expert knowledge. I would mention that Sir Charles had six of these special chimps, some of which had accompanied him on excursions to the continent and the USA. The chimps were special friends and he visited them every day in the ape house in his laboratory. During this term, Hunt was disturbed by the rapid disappearance of his supply of bananas and blamed his lab boy. He was told by the boy, "Sir Charles, I most emphatically deny the charge that I have ever stolen a single banana." A fortnight later the boy was further blamed for stealing the bananas and threatened with dismissal from his job. Sir Charles said, "I didn't want to scold the boy, who was again most emphatic that he had not stolen a single banana." Sir Charles said, "Hunt, you and I will make an early visit to the lab on our bikes."

So, on Sunday morning at 8 a.m., they came to the lab and made a quiet entrance. But here, Sir Charles said, "Hunt, I am sure I heard the apes' door close, as I opened the entrance door." They went into the Ape

House and as usual the apes seemed delighted with the visit. They climbed about Sir Charles while he made a most extensive examination of their quarters. It was not until Sir Charles entered their loo that the apes suddenly became most disturbed. Sir Charles found their loo absolutely jammed with banana skins. Thus was revealed the source of the missing bananas.

Hunt cleared over 100 banana skins and the apes were punished for their unfaithful behaviour and all looked very sad and repentant. Sir Charles and Hunt left the Ape House and Sir Charles said, "Wait a while, Hunt, as I want to make a further visit unknown to the apes." After 20 minutes Sir Charles, wearing gym shoes, entered the lab and approached very quietly to the door of the ape house. He looked through the key hole in the door and what do you think he saw but an ape also looking through the key hole, from the apes' side of the house. Here Sir Charles said, "Two minds with but a single thought." Thus ended a great drama and very soon the apes were restored to favour and a happy life in their own home. But Hunt was quick to fix a bolt on their door to make things more secure.

It was about mid-term when a friend of mine in College told me of a special stunt which was about to be performed in the High Street. A farm tender would drive down the Broad slowly and when in the middle of the crowded street, opposite the Clarendon Hotel, would release two large sacks containing over 200 rats. He said that I should take a small party of friends to the Kardomah Cafe and make certain to arrange for my party to take an upstairs window table. I invited Lady Sherrington and Mrs Jim Robinson to join me at 11 a.m., and duly arrived and had no trouble in booking the window table. At about 11.15 I spotted the farm tender approaching our view point. We suddenly saw the opening scene of "the Drama" as the sacks poured forth the legions of rats onto the road near our kerb. On went the empty tender far up the High, to a realm of safety from any suspicion. Immediately, there was a high panic in the street, dozens of women screaming and men climbing lamp posts; crowds tried to crash into our Cafe and nearby shops. The rats all scrambled about the pavements and shop entrances and for about 20 minutes there was wild panic abroad. There was chaos in the main street and it was an amazing spectacle for us to see from our vantage site and several dogs joined in the fun, with much barking.

The whole episode lasted almost half an hour before order was restored and the last rats had disappeared. My party quietly dispersed and both the ladies and several of my friends had greatly enjoyed the fun. I heard later that the farm tender and the culprits got away with it, and were never questioned and returned to Islip.

During term I had three very enjoyable evenings with the Apollo

Masons Lodge with Sir P Colville Smith, from Mason Headquarters in London, who attended as our Secretary. Herbert Mount-Somerly came as my guest from his Lodge in London. We had very happy afternoons for the Summer VIIIs and Mrs Robinson, Miss Allen and several lady students were part of our party. The weather was glorious all the time and Rex Facey and Derek helped with the picnic teas.

Dr and Mrs Robinson invited Barbara and Mary to stay with them in Beaumont Street and they came to see me frequently. They lunched with Derek and me in Long Wall Street. They visited many colleges and the Ashmolean and Bodleian. I greatly enjoyed their visit.

Derek and I now commenced a most concentrated revision course and spent many hours in the labs. As we approached zero hour, Derek and I decided to leave Oxford for a week's special revision. So we took a villa above the Varsity Golf Course. In this delightful countryside we greatly refreshed ourselves and did some most valuable revision, returning to Oxford the day before the vital exams commenced. We had four papers to face and many laboratory exams. I found Dr Pearson had given me many useful tutorials and several of his selection of questions appeared in the critical exam papers.

In the meantime I had written to the secretary of St Thomas's Hospital requesting that they accept me and Gerry McElligott for admission as Medical Students. It was a great comfort that they accepted our application. Mac and I went off to St Thomas's before we knew the final result of our exams. Derek had decided to take all his hospital training in Edinburgh, so we made a final thank you to Annie Osborne for her great kindness to us. The many vivas in our practical exams were most exciting. I found my superb microscope served me very well and I seemed to do well in all practical exams. McElligott and I made a last effort of glory by going to the Commem Ball at Magdalen which, on a glorious warm, fine night, was most enjoyable. The final days of our happy years at BNC were almost ended. I said farewell to Professor and Mrs Sampson and to Sonners and many friends, and to my moral tutor Michael Holroyd. I made a final walk around college and All Souls in the evening light. I heard the bell toll "the 101" ringing out from Christ Church. I listened to the ancient grace of *"Oculi omnium spectant in Te, Deus"* and ate my final meal in Hall.

# Chapter Seven

## ST THOMAS'S HOSPITAL

**July 1923**

The Honours School in Natural Science at Oxford was still carrying out Vivas when I left college with my luggage for the Great Western Railway Station. I said farewell to many friends in College and arranged to fulfil my duties as Best Man to Rex Facey who was to marry Margaret Spiking at St Mary Abbot's Church, Kensington in early July, when the Varsity Cricket match was on at Lord's.

Gerry McElligott travelled up with me to Paddington and we reported to the Dean at St Thomas's Hospital and were given an address for our "Digs" by Hopkins. We were given Mrs Yelland at Fentiman Road near The Oval and were joined by Paul Bell, a friend of Gerry McElligott, who had been with him at Stoneyhurst College in Lancashire. He was reading for his Bar Exams. We were opposite Vauxhall Gardens and this was most convenient for me to take my early morning run round the extensive gardens.

The first few mornings were most enjoyable but I was soon joined by about a dozen factory girls from Braund's Factory. They all surrounded me with much laughter, but being Cockneys they had a great sense of humour and raced beside me. They could run fast and continued with their fun for about a month. I could not alter my time for the run as I had to take my cold bath – then breakfast and catch a train for St Thomas's.

Our first days in hospital were in the Casualty Department under the strict discipline of Sister Casualty. My friend at Oxford, Victor Sherborne, very kindly went to the Examination Schools to inspect the Finals Report and then telephoned Mac at St Thomas's. Much to my delight I had been awarded Second Class Honours. My other friends had been awarded Third Class Honours: Harold Tracey, Derek, Noel Chilton, Bill Hudson, etc.

We were very much occupied in Casualty as many severe cases turned up. Sister Casualty gave us some very difficult cases of dear old Cockney women with huge varicose ulcers. We had to prepare the special Unners Paste dressings and there was always a frightful mess on the Casualty floor which we had to clear up. If casualties turned up with seriously damaged limbs we had to arrange X-rays and then assist the Casualty Officer with applying plaster, dressings etc. Frequently Casualty was crowded with victims who had severe cuts and lacerations of arms, and I always enjoyed stitching these up. We had to attend several Surgical Lectures which were admirably delivered by Mr Philip Mitcham, FRCS, in the Lecture Theatre. Mac and I greatly enjoyed our duties in Casualty and we were fortunate in finding a very convenient Snack bar where we were given superb sandwiches and had time for half an hour's stroll on the Thames Embankment before afternoon duties. We worked all afternoon but there didn't seem to be so many casualties in as the morning. Two afternoons a week I attended Dr Hudson's excellent "Eye Out Patients" and he gave me a warm welcome and gladly demonstrated many eye problems of great interest. Mac and I were impressed by the very high standard of nursing from the splendid selection of Sisters and Nurses. We were shown Florence Nightingale's coach which she used during her arduous duties in the Crimean War.

### *August 1923*

We had now settled in very well with Mrs Yelland in Fentiman Road, Vauxhall, and Philip Bell, reading Law, was an admirable companion. Mac and I joined Sir Cuthbert Wallace's Surgical Team in the North Theatre and we had some thrilling sessions with major surgical operations; Mr Maybury was second in command. We continued throughout the late summer carrying out our duties as Dressers to Sir Cuthbert Wallace each day. Although it was mid-August, the schedule of operations was still working at full strength even though the holiday season reduced the number of Operating Surgeons.

### *September 1923*

As soon as September dawned I prepared for the Rugger season and went on training sessions at the Hospital Rugger Ground at Chiswick. I was thrilled to be picked as the 1st XV Scrum Half. We had a most interesting selection of Rugger matches with distant games at Bath, US *Portsmouth* and Plymouth. The 1st and 2nd XVs carried out most diligent training sessions at Chiswick and we did very well, winning most of our away matches, especially US Portsmouth, but we were narrowly beaten by Bath and Plymouth. I was much disturbed to find the Bath Forwards "handled the ball in the scrum" and when I called the Ref's notice to this foul play he merely remarked that they always played that way.

During the late autumn we continued to divide our duties between Casualty and the North Operating Theatre and Sir Cuthbert was most kind in his help to us with many surgical operations.

## October 1923

In October I joined the United London Hospital Guild of St Luke, and was selected as United Hospital's representative. The Matron of St Thomas's, Miss Lloyd Still, was very pleased to hear of this. We had useful meetings and services of the Guild of St Luke and I was impressed to see the interest that the Guild had in Medicine and the Hospital. When we were attending the busy Out-Patients Department, an amusing episode occurred. One of the attending Nurses had shingled her hair (this was not allowed) and Sister Casualty was not slow to spot the culprit. She promptly sent the nurse to "Limbo" Lydia Ward and reported her to Matron. Home Sister was told to address the 80 nurses and to say that Matron had decided to hold a vote at lunch time. Each nurse was supplied with a voting paper and pencil; if in favour of shingling they were to put a tick on the slip; if *not* in favour of shingling they were to leave the paper blank. Just before lunch Home Sister had stamped "Florence Nightingale's Lamp" on the Voting Papers. *All* the voting papers were completed and the sacred Casket was taken to Matron's office where the votes were counted.

Now what do you think of this result? For shingling, three votes only! Seventy-six Blank Papers. Therefore No Shingling.

Bravo for the Nightingale tradition!

Mac and I joined in many Surgical Sessions with Sir Cuthbert Wallace and Mr Maybury. We often had very severe cases, especially with the manifold realm of "Malignancy", where we were greatly interested to have our first intimate association with major surgery. The male cases were domiciled in Albert Ward and we were made responsible for the Surgical Cases from the North Theatre. We attended the patients in their beds in Albert Ward and did the dressings of their wounds with some of the Nursing Sisters. Sir Cuthbert, who had been on a special surgical team on the Western Front in 1917-1918 had many long chats with me about the Somme.

During all the long Autumn Session we attended the morning Surgical Lectures which were carried out by Mr Philip Mitcham and Sir Percy Sargent. I also had private lessons, twice a week, with Mr R H O B Robinson and I found these most helpful in the early months of our Surgical activities. I was now playing rugger regularly with the Hospital 1st XV and we had a match every Saturday afternoon.

On Sunday mornings from my digs in Fentiman Road, Vauxhall, I used to go to a Choral Eucharist service in the beautiful Church of St John the Divine, Kennington, beautifully sung by the choir. This Church had a clerical staff of five. One Canon Down had been at this Church for over 50 years. The Vicar was the Reverend Horne-Brown who was later created a Bishop for a Church in South Africa. All the members of this Staff had taken an Arts Degree from a College in Oxford and several of them had taken a Clerical Degree from Cuddesden, a Theological College close to Oxford. This lovely Church was situated in South London and had packed congregations each Sunday.

I had a peaceful walk back to my digs for Sunday lunch and, on the way, I often met a "Cockney Man" who had a decorated brass Push Cart which was packed with an ample supply of specially prepared Cats' meat (probably horseflesh) cooked and ready for sale. On entering Fentiman Road he rang a very special bell and scores of cats with tails erect, crowded round the travelling cart. Before it had gone a quarter of the length of the road – scores of women advanced and purchased the week's supply of meat. The Cats' Meat Man made four long stops in Fentiman Road and was sold out quickly.

The Post Mortem section of the Pathology Lab was a busy unit. In the morning a Post Mortem was carried out and details were carefully recorded for the Consultant of the Patient who had died the day before. When it was my turn, I carefully recorded the necessary details and did some very interesting investigations. I found the PM Lab man most helpful with the difficult cases and he dealt with all the "wrights" cases which were recorded in a special book. I had a most interesting case of a patient who was admitted to hospital and died within a few hours. The Medical Registrar told me that I must report this case to the Lambeth Coroner, the famous Dr Ingelsby Oddy (his brother, Colonel Oddy – a Yorkshire solicitor – from Pately Bridge, was my Commanding Officer in the 5th West Yorkshire Regiment on the Somme). I turned up at his Coroner's Court and he gave me a warm welcome when he knew that his brother had been my Colonel. The whole Coroner's investigation was most helpful for the general knowledge in a full hospital technique. I did not have any other Coroner's Cases during my five years at St Thomas's Hospital.

All our first winter Gerry McElligott and I worked energetically in the Operating Theatre. I was able to pay frequent visits to Dr. Hudson's Eye Out-Patients where I was able to inspect several rare and difficult cases.

On the football front I had a very heavy season with rugger matches every weekend. I greatly enjoyed the Plymouth Match but I found the long train journeys very exhausting. One very pleasant avenue of entertainment was the "Old Vic". Our landlady's daughter was in the Box Office there and she managed to get us excellent tickets for all the Shakespeare Plays. I greatly enjoyed *King John* as I sat with crowds of small Cockney children. When Hubert was having an interview with the young Prince holding the red-hot iron in readiness for the terrible act of burning out his eyes, the masses of young Cockney children screamed out "Look out, the Prince is about to burn out your eyes!" Most dramatic!

## 1925

In March the Hospital Rugger Cup was in full swing and the XV did very well and made its way to the Final. Our opponents in the Final were Guys Hospital and I was reserve for the Hospital XV. The match was played at Richmond and the crowds were immense with the stands packed with masses of Guys and Thomas's Consultants. St Thomas's won.

Gerry McElligott and Philip Bell were still very happy with Mrs Yelland and we had a spell with his very dear dog, a Kerry Blue. From the Hospital, Gerry and I made frequent visits to the most thrilling spectacle of the Mounting of the Guard at Wellington Barracks. Both of us greatly enjoyed this supreme performance of the troops, as we were both very keen soldiers who had been through the whole of the First War.

Philip Mitchener prevailed on me to join his special OTC who paraded every week for ambulance duties. I told him that I would only join as a Private as I did not want to be a Sergeant. Incidentally, I was the only "ex-war" member. Philip Mitchener was a Major-General in the Medical Branch of the Army. The St Thomas special Medical Branch went to attend Training Camp down at Folkestone and did a most thorough Field Ambulance Exercise, even giving anaesthetics to special volunteers. We greatly enjoyed this fortnight's special camp.

One morning when we were in the middle of an operation with Sir Cuthbert Wallace, the quiet privacy of the Operating Theatre was rudely interrupted as Sir Arthur Standley, the Dean of St Thomas's, entered and addressed Sir Cuthbert. Surprisingly, he introduced "the Emperor of Abyssinia" to Sir Cuthbert as he had made a very special and generous gift of Nursery Rhymes made by Doultons, in very colourful large pictures to the two Infant Wards in memory of his Mother, the Dowager Queen. The Nursery Rhymes were most beautifully painted and were fully illustrated on the porcelain. The sum of this magnificent gift was in the region of £30,000! This rare episode of an interruption of an operation lasted fully ten minutes and I thought Sir Cuthbert was superb. The anaesthetist continued quietly with his administration of the anaesthetic. The Ras. Tafarri departed and Sir Cuthbert returned to his surgical operation and chatted away about the generosity of the Emperor. I made several visits to the Ward when Doultons had finished installing the superb panels, and I was greatly impressed by the work of their pottery factory, just up the Lambeth Road, less than a mile from the Hospital.*

## Extracts from diary

### 1925-26

> *We now commenced the Course of Pathology Lectures by Sir Leonard Dudgeon. He delivers his lectures splendidly and makes the subject a very enjoyable one for students. Dr Robinson joins with Sir Cuthbert's team. We have many long sessions with operations in abdominal surgery – most cases cancer of stomach and lower bowel.*
>
> *Mr Maybury is partner with Sir Cuthbert Wallace on all major surgery and is most kind to Mac and me. I attend most useful sessions in the Pharmacology Lab. and this prepares me for my Oxford Exam which I pass just before Christmas.*
>
> *Mac and I commence our "Midder" in the Maternity Block and greatly enjoy attending the mothers during confinements. Sister Mary is most helpful to us and we enjoy the attention to the newly born. We take the new born babes to their mothers for their breast feeds. Four of the students who included Mac and me agree to take the four babies to four different mothers for their mid-day meal. All is quiet and the babes greatly enjoy their meals and the mothers say they have never fed better! After the meal when Sister and the Senior Nurses are at lunch we take the babes back to the Nursery and they all quickly settle in their cots and our plot was never discovered. We, of course, took the babies for their future meals for at least the next fortnight and the mothers never suspected us of "foul play". But I think they were a bit suspicious of the four male maternity clerks.*

At lunch-time we crossed the main road with the LCC trams and entered our splendid Pub which provided us with a lunch of delicious beef sandwiches. This pub was only a few yards from the hospital, and had a most delightful chef; he was famous in that he held the World Championship for opening oysters. We called him "Hermes". After eating our excellent sandwiches and our coffee we repaired to the Lodge of the Hospital to collect our Maternity Bag if Mac and I were attending a

---

* As a result of this episode, Peter went several times to the Porto-bello market and acquired some beautiful Doulton "seconds".

Lambeth mother in the afternoon.

Mac and I continued our special maternity work in Mary Ward and were busy all late December, and there was a delightful atmosphere in Mary Ward. Sister Mary and her Nurses arranged superb decorations for Christmas.

In the Rugger team we were very busy and played several enjoyable matches especially against the Metropolitan Police at Chiswick, and several matches away against the United Services at Portsmouth and the Royal Military College Sandhurst and also against Rosslyn Park. In my spare time I was enjoying visiting the National Portrait Gallery. I found many portraits most beautifully painted and one could assess the character of the subject from a diligent study of the painting.

I also made special visits to the Lord Duveen Gallery at the British Museum to make an intimate study of Pericles and his wonderful work on the Parthenon which was finished in 432 BC. Many of the sculptures were exposed to stone robbers, lime burners and religious iconoclasts and but for the intervention of Lord Elgin in 1800 it is probable that many of them would have perished and been damaged beyond recognition.

I wish to record a very special maternity case from Paradise Street, which is only 200 yards from St Thomas's Hospital. It was near Christmas when I received a call to attend a "Primip"[*] case late in the afternoon. It was dark when I left St Thomas's with the maternity equipment and Mac came with me. As I left the hospital I took a look across the river to the Houses of Parliament and noticed that the Beacon Light was transmitting its beams, revealing that Parliament was in session. We duly arrived at Paradise Street and were led by the Gamp to the downstairs (basement) room which had a bright fire blazing. The floor was covered in deep straw and the young expectant mother was lying on it. She was about 19 and was heavily in labour and the Gamp was urging her on. Mac and I felt that the time of the birth would be at least four or five hours. I was to perform the process of birth and Mac would assist me. The young girl was full of courage and did her best to use her pains but they were far from intense. The Gamp did her best to urge the patient, as did her Mother who was a splendid type. Now, this picture of "Maternity in Action" on the straw bed and only candles for illumination reminded me strongly of the Manger Cradle of Bethlehem, especially with the very young mother. Mac and I both did our best to comfort the young mother and we supported the Gamp, for three or four hours. By 9 p.m. the mother was extremely tired and cried several times as the pains were growing more intense. The Gamp was not very sympathetic and rather scolded her when the pains

---

[*] First baby.

appeared regularly. At 10 p.m. Mac and I went to a hot dog and pie stall near the entrance to Lambeth Palace and hoped that the young mother would get a short rest from her labour pains. We were only away about half an hour and returned to find the pains were now more intense and the Gamp had two large kettles of boiling water.

Mac commenced using the gas and oxygen and I could see the presentation was a "Head", which was a comfort. The Gamp seemed to lose her temper and slapped the mother on the buttocks. She then addressed Mac and me with the words "Doctors, it's like this, you can't get rats out of mice!" It described the picture of this case perfectly. This young girl was a small specimen of a mother.

Very soon the pains were in the final phase and the baby's head visible. I was able to complete the birth by delivering the body of the baby and soon had the afterbirth delivered. The young mother was given her baby son which had been bathed by its grandmother. I was greatly moved by this picture of a primitive birth struggle resembling the Manger Cradle of Bethlehem. I told the mother of the girl that in the morning I would arrange for the young mother and baby to be admitted to Mary Ward. It was nearly midnight when we reported back to Mary Ward and told the Night Sister of our unique experience and that the ambulance should collect the mother and baby from Paradise Street for admission, as the straw floor and bed were not suitable for the young mother and child.

Mac and I continued with our maternity duties in Mary Ward and brought several babies into the world and greatly enjoyed the experience. It was mid-winter and I was playing in many rugger matches up and down the west country. During a match with Sandhurst I sustained a fractured rib following a most robust tackle.

In early October, the Hospital Entertainment Committee arranged for a heavy programme to be prepared for the special Christmas Show which was presented in the Wards and for entertainment of the Staff and their families. Dr Cooke was President of this very active show and early on he collected Mac and me for special parts, which kept us heavily engaged in its preparation. There were ten of us in the cast and two were excellent singers, especially Archer. Mac and I took part in an ancient performance of Moorish activity. I was dressed in female garb which greatly amused the nursing staff. In a special Hospital sketch I was dressed as a Nightingale Sister which roused Sister City (Miss Pridham) to great excitement, even causing Matron (Miss Lloyd Still) to give her a rebuke. Our Christmas show was given a very special write up in the London Evening papers, with photos of the cast. The cast gave performances in several of the Wards which were a great success and extended over ten days. We were also most generously entertained by the Senior Members of the staff and their wives in Harley Street and Wimpole Street.

I now had to prepare to journey to Oxford to take my Pathology exam which lasted over three days and I greatly enjoyed this academic exercise. I was able to make valuable use of my excellent Leitz microscope during the several practical exams in the varsity laboratories. I found I was well prepared for this exam and enjoyed the papers and my vivas and was highly delighted to find I was on the Pass List. We also expected to take several of our final Medical Exams this autumn and I had to face Midder Finals and the Conjoint Board. I spent many hours in the Library preparing, and Sister Mary gave me several tutorials which were most helpful. For Midder Finals I wrote two papers and had two vivas. I felt I had not done very well. I did not succeed.

In Rugger, the hospital XV did very well. I played every Saturday until late March. When we played Guy's, most of their side were South Africans and they held conversations in Afrikaans. I met three of my Oxford friends in the Guys XV. I now spent long hours revising the details of operations as I had to face Conjoint Surgical Exam in the summer.

In March Mac and I joined Mr Wyatt in his special Surgery sessions on several cases of hysterectomy and of Caesarean Section. It was not until the middle ages that the first operation was performed with a live patient. The first recorded instance was about the year 1500 when a Swiss pig-gelder performed it on his *own* wife. Owing to the present low mortality of Caesarean Section the indications for the operation have been consistently extended in recent years. The chief exponent in this country is Munro Kerr. All our cases did very well and mother and child made excellent progress. Sister Mary acted splendidly in the Theatre giving us instructions. We continued with our Maternity Ward duties for several weeks into the summer.

Early July found me engaged in the Midder and Surgery Finals of the Conjoint Board. Both the activities were grim. The Conjoint Surgery Viva was very difficult but I had better luck in the Midder Viva and passed this hurdle. I was ploughed in the Surgery and referred to the October exams. I then took a short summer vacation at home.

It was July and I greatly enjoyed the superb crop of summer fruits, especially the raspberries. I took out my gun and joined in the early harvest and shot many rabbits on Jack Brittain's Farm. I returned to St Thomas's Hospital to continue my approach to the Conjoint Surgery. I was greatly helped by my tutor, Mr R H O B Robinson who gave me many useful hours with the surgical pots. He suggested that I read extensive Surgical Chapters and felt I was not really ready for the Final Surgery Exam until April. Mac became engaged to an Editor of the *Evening Standard* and married her in early December. He passed his Final Surgery and then decided to move to Italy to commence practice at Santa Margharita, Rapallo. He left London in early December.

I was so happy and contented with Mrs Yelland in Fentiman Road that I decided to remain with her and found useful preparation for my exam in the quiet evenings. I still took part in rugger matches and took all the conversion kicks and penalties. In five seasons I made 100 successful conversions.

I made an intense final preparation for the Surgery Final of the Conjoint and decided to sit the papers at the April exam. I had good papers in the Surgery Final and had helpful Vivas and all the Pots given to me for examination were easily identified.

# Chapter Eight

## MARRIAGE, HONEYMOON AND A PRACTICE AT RADLETT

I was delighted to find that I passed all my Surgery Finals and obtained my MRCS LRCP and had a thrilling return to St Thomas's Hospital. Fred Neilson and Mr Howarth offered me a job in their Surgical Out Patients. I worked very hard all the summer and learned a lot and enjoyed doing minor nasal operations – greatly helped by Fred Neilson. Here I would mention that I met a nurse who was on the staff and was a daughter of Mr and Mrs Claud Allan of Kilmahew Castle, Cardross west of Glasgow[*]. In October I was invited to stay at her home and was greatly excited to join in the Clyde Yachting races when Mr Allan won three flags.

Sheena Allan was the second daughter, aged 20, who had virtually run away from home to become a nurse. The Allans had a splendid steam yacht, the *Oriana* with its own captain and crew, and we had several long sea journeys to the Western Isles. The footman from Kilmahew came to sea with us and the chef prepared all the meals. Eight guests were able to sleep on the yacht. She performed splendidly in the NW Sea Passage. I bathed every day in the ocean, diving in from the lower deck. I greatly enjoyed the race from the Clyde up to Tarbert Loch Fyne, but the very rough seas made me sea-sick!

Towards the end of my happy visit, just before Sheena returned to her nursing duties at St Thomas's Hospital, I asked my host and his lady wife if I might become engaged to their daughter. Sheena knew that I would become a General Practitioner and agreed to our engagement. I returned to my House Appointment at St Thomas's Hospital and Sheena continued with her strenuous training, and Matron and her Staff were most kind and sympathetic. My appointment as House Surgeon continued and during this period I met Dr Jones who told me he had an excellent practice for me to join in Radlett, Hertfordshire. Dr Isaac Jones was a Consultant Physician with Professor Maclean, who was the Chief Med. Professor of St Thomas's Hospital and Chief MO to the Metropolitan Police. You can imagine I was greatly relieved with this comforting news and I made early enquiries with the Radlett doctors and they were most willing to accept me into this delightful practice. They were in no hurry for me to join, so I

---

[*] One day he walked into the hospital canteen and saw her sitting at a table. "I thought she was the most beautiful girl I had ever seen," he told Rosemary, my wife, many years later.

continued with my House Appointment at St Thomas's Hospital.

My own family were delighted with my engagement and I took Sheena up to Haxby to meet them. This was a most successful event. We had not fixed a likely date of the wedding but felt it would be some time next late summer.

On my appointment as House Surgeon to Mr Howarth, I took up residence in St Thomas's Hospital as I had to take all night admissions, which often needed acute surgery. I greatly enjoyed this appointment and was able to see Sheena quite a lot and take her to meet many friends. She was also able to watch me play in rugger matches.

The months passed by quickly and I was engaged in a great deal of Nasal Surgery and Mastoid treatment. At the end of Summer I felt it was time to commence dealings with my likely purchase of the Radlett Surgery, so Dr Jones took me to meet my new Partners. I decided this purchase would be most favourable and as there was a splendid home which went with it, I had no hesitation in making my offer. I gave due notice to St Thomas's Hospital and to Mr Howarth and Mr Neilson, and decided to complete the purchase in early summer of 1927.

Dr Isaac Jones was delighted that I was to take up residence in Radlett as his sister lived in the village and would be a great help to me. He would also be able to assist me in my consultant work. I found that the practice had very extensive midwifery engagements which gave me much pleasure. Sheena was delighted with my decision and she was able to finish her nursing training at St Thomas's Hospital. I had a final dinner with my friends and then moved down to Radlett the next day.

The financial arrangements for the purchase of the practice and house were most satisfactory. I was also able to purchase a very nice Austin saloon car for me to use in the practice, but I found it necessary to ask my father for some temporary help in the rather heavy financial commitments. I took a week off to arrange the necessary alterations of the house and engaged a housekeeper to take charge of the domestic arrangements. I made an early visit to the Hertfordshire County Headquarters to make arrangements for commencing the Medical Practice and was able to open my first surgery with great promise and success.

I received an encouraging letter from Mac who had made a successful commencement of his practice in Rapallo. He made all his visits by horse and carriage, even visiting Portofino patients.

I was delighted to find that there was a good parish church in Radlett and the Rector was the brother of the Principal at Hertford College, Oxford, Professor Crettwall (history). I had often met Professor Crettwall as Mac had been a member of Hertford College and I had even dined there as his guest.

The early days of the Practice went very well and I became a member of the Staff at Bushey Heath Hospital and did a special session of tonsillectomy, with Dr Millward giving the anaesthetics once every fortnight. Dr Millward had had several years doing very strenuous medical duties at the Hong Kong hospitals.

I had a visit one evening from six St Thomas's Hospital House Surgeons and we spent a delightful evening, after I had dined my visitors, at the Railway Inn in Radlett.

I went early to the Nursing Home and Convent at London Colney where several St Thomas's Sisters were resident, after doing maternity duties in South Africa. They also trained junior nurses for hospital duties. This convent also had a special section for senile nursing sisters, some a very great age. The medical side of the Practice was running very smoothly and I had quite a busy time with night duties. The local District Nurses were, very helpful, as there were several gravely ill patients with malignant diseases. I decided to carry out Surgeries at my home, the Red House, twice a day except Wednesdays. I had several visits from the Medical Consultant, Dr Isaac Jones, who was delighted that the practice was running smoothly. I carried out maternity duties and most of the cases were admitted to the maternity home at Watford. I carried out all my own cases and several "multips"* were pleased to be confined in their own homes. I had several visits from Sheena and she was pleased with the house and the practice. I decided to open up a Surgery in Shenley four days a week and that soon became very active. I found it necessary to visit patients quite regularly in Shenley and Mimms. I was greatly comforted in that I could take exercise on good local squash courts and had several partners. I was admitted as a member of the Porters Park Golf Club but rather disappointed that I could only play *once* a fortnight. I found I could only take a half-day once a week, and this continued all the first year in Radlett.

Sundays seemed to be peaceful as I only took serious calls, and I managed regular attendance at Church Services. I found the partnership with Dr Simmers very successful and took full duties for his day off and he did likewise for me. I found that I took early responsibility for medical duties for several important estates including Lord Aldenham, whose Head Gardener was the famous Edwin Beckett; Mr Walter Raphael and his gardeners and staff; Mr Pierpoint Morgan's staff at Aldenham House, and Mr Arthur Sansom at Letchmore Heath.

The Hon. Vicary Gibbs, Lord Aldenham's younger brother, was responsible for the running of the Aldenham Home and extensive gardens

---

* "Multips" second and subsequent babies.

with 110 gardeners. This large employment of the young gardeners was like a good public school as they were accommodated in two large residences and looked after by four domestics who prepared all their meals and did their laundry. All the young pupil gardeners had full horticultural training and at the end of their two-year course were ready to leave to take up full Gardener duties with the "Aldenham Certificate" at Gardens all over Britain, especially in country mansions. I myself had quite a friendship with the Hon. Vicary Gibbs and learnt a lot of useful gardening hints from Edwin Beckett, his Head Gardener. Edwin Beckett entered the competition for the Sherwood Cup at the Chelsea Show; he won it against all the big professional gardeners of Suttons, Carters and the big English and Scottish gardens.

I had now settled into the extensive running of a general practice. My morning and evening surgeries were well attended and I held my morning surgery from 9 a.m. until 10.30 and the evening surgery from 6 p.m., finishing about 8 p.m. I joined the RAFVR in the village which was very entertaining, especially in the winter months as we had fortnightly meetings. I was elected President.

I found St Thomas's Hospital very useful for my acute Medical and Surgical Cases and received valuable help from the consultants. It was most helpful to me that urgent cases could be admitted to the Hospital without any difficulty. I also used the Peace Memorial Hospital at Watford and the St Albans hospital for admissions. The National Orthopaedic hospital at Stanmore would deal with all my fracture and accident cases.

Sir Maurice Cassidy, Chief Medical Officer of the Metropolitan Police in London, made me a Divisional Police surgeon of the Elstree Region of the Metropolitan Police. This appointment led to much night duty, dealing with drunkenness and car crashes, amongst other things. The winter months made medical practice very strenuous especially as there was much snow and long periods of frost.

There were heavy motoring duties in the practice and I changed my car once every year by paying £50 and I had immediate delivery of a splendid new Austin.

Sheena had finished her nursing duties at St Thomas's Hospital and returned home to Kilmahew to prepare for her wedding. I went up to Kilmahew for a holiday and I had the thrill of making up numbers for the Clyde Fortnight in Claud Allan's lovely yacht. I was in two first flags racing in his yacht on the Clyde.

After my visit to Kilmahew it was decided that we should be married in September at the Village Church (Presbyterian) in Cardross. I arranged with Dr Simmers that I would take a month's holiday for my honeymoon in Italy. I had special help from Mr Claud Allan, Sheena's father, and I told him that my father and mother and my older sister, Barbara, would come up to Cardross for the wedding. Mr Derek Dunlop would come from Edinburgh, where he was heavily engaged in medical duties, to be my Best Man.

Sheena was accompanied by four bridesmaids: May Allan, her older sister; Jenny Mitchell, a cousin; Mona Mitchell, another cousin; and a school friend.

*Peter marries Sheena Allan at Kilmahew, September 1927.*
*Attendants from left to right: Jenny Mitchell, Mona Mitchell, Janet Mitchell (the child – she was killed by Flying Bomb in the Guard's Chapel), Mona Tennant (front), May Allan (Sheena's sister).*

The church was packed with guests and after the wedding ceremony all the guests made their way to Kilmahew for the reception. This was a very successful event and the floral decorations were superbly arranged by the head gardener and his staff.

The drawing room at Kilmahew was packed with a multitude of friends who gave Sheena and me a very warm reception, and toasted us in champagne. Derek Dunlop made a fine speech and I responded. He also made a speech to toast the Bridesmaids. The weather for this happy event was perfect, with glorious sunshine throughout the day. I was delighted to see many friends had made the long journey from the South of England

and my parents spent a comfortable night in the local hotel and there was a special dance in the evening. Aitken, who was Claud Allan's coachman before the war, motored Sheena and me to Glasgow Central Station where we took a train to Preston and stayed the night in the main hotel. We took an early express to Euston and we had the pleasure of being met by Mr Isaac Jones. He escorted us to Victoria where we caught the Pullman to Folkestone and had a comfortable crossing in the evening and took our reserved coach in the *Wagon Lit en route* for Italy.

Our destination was the Hotel at Portofino Vetta, which is situated high up on the Portofino mountain. We took a taxi from Rapallo Station and were very tired when we arrived at our destination. We changed for dinner and greatly enjoyed our evening meal. We retired early after the long and exhausting train journey.

In the morning we saw we had a superb view over the Gulf of Genoa and Rapallo, the Italian Naval Base at Spezia, and the coastline leading South. We made plans to enjoy walks from our Hotel to the colourful port of Portofino and Santa Margherita. We decided to take our first walk after lunch to Portofino and found this most enjoyable. We rested near the harbour and after tea made our long return walk to our hotel.

On our second day I decided to take a swim in the sea from the rocks on the coastline – this was the Mediterranean and I was told there were many sharks in the waters. The sea was very deep from the main rocks and would give ample room for sharks to attack and there were consistent waves all the time. I dived into the sea and had an easy passage along the coastline parallel to the shore. I didn't expect Sheena to bathe from here and I only spent a short time swimming in the coastal avenue of deep water. After this swim I dressed and walked with Sheena back to the attractive little port and harbour of Portofino Vetta. We had a good look round and selected a hotel for lunch. We had a wonderful lunch and after a rest in the Hotel garden, we decided to spend the mid- and late afternoon walking by the long winding cliff back to our hotel.

The hotel was most comfortable and we greatly enjoyed our dinner and tasty white wine. We decided on the morrow to walk down the steep cliffs to the coastal road and then proceed to travel to the Port of Santa Margherita. We arrived quite early, having walked five miles, and greatly enjoyed looking around the many attractive shops. Sheena found some delightful lace mats – beautifully made by local ladies. We found them inexpensive and Sheena made an extensive purchase of a full set of mats for a dinner service. We found Santa Margherita most attractive and had lunch in a local restaurant. We walked along the coast road until we entered Rapallo where we noted several very large and splendid hotels. There were many shops and we took a long and easy investigation and found much interest. Later, we rested and took tea in a local restaurant. As we had had a tiring day, I decided to take a taxi from Rapallo back to our hotel.

After a week we moved on to Rome where I had booked a comfortable hotel for a fortnight. Aunt Janie Allan* treated us to an excellent guide who spoke English and who had arranged for us to visit many places of ancient history.

We had a useful chat and decided to make a morning visit to San Pietro, as I knew the Cathedral contained the superb Pietà by Michelangelo, which I had longed to see owing to its great beauty.

We had a most marvellous stay in Rome and were delighted with the wonderful array of ancient art. On our last afternoon we enjoyed viewing the delightful streets and shops. We finished our final viewing by visiting the glorious church of St John Lateran and I recited the collect to St Peter as a special Thanksgiving.

> O Almighty God, who by thy Son Jesus Christ didst give to thy Apostle, Saint Peter, many excellent gifts and commandest him earnestly to feed thy flock, Make we beseech thee all Bishops and Pastors diligently to preach thy Holy Word and the people obediently to follow the same that they may receive the crown of everlasting glory, though Jesus Christ our Lord. Amen.

Back at my practice in Radlett, Sheena was very busy arranging the house and the waiting room for the surgeries. I arranged for Tonsillectomy sessions at Bushey Cottage Hospital, with Dr J K Milward giving the anaesthetics. We had a monthly meeting of the Staff on Sunday mornings. It was delightful work.

Sheena's mother and father paid us a visit in the late autumn. They made some excellent suggestions about our home in order to include a nursery. It was clear that Ada Allan's knowledge extended beyond yachts in relation to "accommodation."

The quarterly visit to St Anne's Home was due and I was anxious to see all details of the running was up to date. This home was the special accommodation for the St Thomas's maternity nurses from Central Africa, who were on home attachment. They also trained nurses for this work in Central Africa. The Matron was a first class nursing sister and kept her hand on every phalanx of nursing. When I visited her in her Office I was delighted to see some beautiful specimens of South African San Paulina

---

* A marvellous spinster and a suffragette, who could drive a coach and four (in those days extremely unusual). She became a much loved matriach and lived to be 100 years old.

Purple and White. The plants had been brought from Central Africa by some of the sisters. I often made two or three visits a week to attend to sick and debilitated sisters.

I attended a special infant dental clinic once a fortnight in the Radlett Masonic Hall and at the end of the clinic it was most amusing to see the mothers and masses of children, all holding blood-stained towels over their mouths. The mass of car travellers wondered why all these children were attending to their blood-stained faces near the Bus Terminus!

The late autumn held a very attractive list of orchestral concerts at the various London concert halls and Sheena and I greatly enjoyed them. We were all delighted with Sheena's pregnancy, the baby being due on August 13th. Granny Allan booked Nurse Wilson to come for her Maternity appointment and Dr Simmers was to be on duty for the confinement.

When I was returning from an early maternity call from Watford I was intrigued by a scene on the Aldenham village green. The blacksmiths, Ted and Edward Inwood, the factor of the Aldenham estate and several farm workmen were trying to floor Taurus, a huge white bull, as he badly needed his hoofs trimming. It was about 5.30 a.m. and I left my car and approached the dramatic assembly wearing my bowler hat. Many wives from the cottages surrounding the village green were most interested in seeing this event. They were amused seeing me carrying my maternity bag and several shouted "Hope it's a boy, doctor." Much laughter. The team of very strong men simply could not make any impression on the bull. Two farm employees attempted to fix a huge farm hurdle in between the bull's legs and topple him. Nil result. I said to the factor, "If you will give me permission, I will give the bull a special dose of anaesthetic and this will floor him in two minutes."

The factor said, "Is there any risk in giving this valuable bull an anaesthetic? He is worth £2,000." I said, "Just let Ted Inwood hold the bull's head and I will administer the Ether." The bull gave me a very dirty look. But cheers came from the many spectators. I had only used a quarter of the bottle of anaesthetic when the huge bull rolled from side to side and then crashed to the village green. Now the bull was static and the two farm workers sat on his torso. I had done a very swift job and the factor was grateful. We soon had the Brothers Inwood, with their special tool, hacking away at the huge overgrown hooves. Taurus was due to go on a special northern tour for stud duties. He was First Prize Bull at the Royal Show and his bookings for the northern tour were very lucrative.

I soon packed up my maternity set and left the operation still going. I received a loud cheer from the mothers of the farm cottages as I returned to my car. I arrived home at 7 a.m., had a quick bath, early breakfast and was ready for the morning surgery at 9 a.m. I called on the Bros. Inwood in the afternoon. They told me what a success the bull episode had been and the bull was on his feet again just after 7 a.m. and would be ready for his extensive "Northern Tour" by the weekend!

Dr Simmers would be going on his month's holiday at the end of the week and he was off to the North of Scotland to join his family. I was, of course, going to combine his surgeries with mine and this meant longer hours. I had a most enjoyable time carrying out these extra duties.

It was late August when I called on Vincent Vickers at Edge Green House. He quickly told me to sit quietly at the end of the large drawing room while he entertained and fed a host of wild birds. As soon as he opened the drawing room door, hosts of wild birds, some of which I had never seen before, flew into the drawing room and fed from Mr Vickers' hand and small bird bowls. This continued for at least half an hour and all the birds sat quietly perched on various bowls and continued to eat nuts and raisins. I thanked Mr Vickers for his great hospitality to the birds and me and quickly returned to my morning Surgery.

Later that week I saw a most remarkable sight of a "rat convoy", consisting of at least 60 rats (some of immense size), leaving a farm in Aldenham and migrating to a new domicile. I stopped my car and watched from 50 yards away. They took no notice of me as they wended their way along the narrow road. The whole column was about 25 yards long and moved quite rapidly led by the senior members of the rat colony, until the whole column disappeared into a deep ditch *en route* for their new domicile. I told the local Blacksmith, Robert Inwood of Aldenham and he was most interested. He had never seen a rat colony on the move.

A delightful family arrived for treatment. The Hon. Mrs Emmett had three young infant daughters and her husband, who had been in the Indian Army, was now doing business with the family coal field. He was a superb sportsman, an excellent shot, keen salmon fisher, keen polo player and a first class golfer. Mrs Emmett invited me to dinner with her mother, Lady Hastings, who resided in Eaton Square, London. The family had some very precious Cromwellian treasures including *Oliver Cromwell's Top Boots* which he used when riding at the head of the cavalry. I saw these top boots when I dined at Eaton Square. Captain Emmett made some excellent salmon flies for me.

With Dr Simmers away in the far north the morning and evening surgeries were crowded with a large number of small children suffering from catarrh and colds. I had several senile old women on my sick list and I visited them twice a week in their homes. The District Nurse also visited them and gave them a bath once a week. The weather was glorious; the herbaceous borders were full of colour and the main crop of roses was superb. In the fruit garden the main crop of raspberries was excellent and the Commice pears and Cox's Orange apples were superb. The two rows of sweet peas were magnificent with the main stems being tied up for the second time. Both vines were most abundant in their fruiting, the black Hamburg was excellent and ripe by late August.

**Notes by Michael Wilson**

There is a ten-year gap here (1928-1938) I think because my father, now 94, wanted to get to World War II before it was too late and perhaps because there was unhappiness in his personal life, which he preferred to skip. I have covered this period in the *Foreword*, but to complete the story a little more needs to be added.

My father confessed to my wife, Rosemary, that he had realised the marriage was a mistake on the first night of their honeymoon. My mother, for her part, also told Rosemary that she knew the marriage was not likely to be successful even before the wedding took place.

*Sheena with Michael and Fiona, 1934.*

I (Michael) was born in August 1928 and my sister, Fiona, followed in May 1931. There are some delightful snaps in the family album with both parents enjoying their children. Nevertheless it cannot have been a happy home because my mother left Radlett in 1932/3 and started a nursery school in Surrey, mainly for the children of ex-patriates. She was very able, as testimonials bear witness, especially one from Prince Leopold of Loewenstein, whose children she cared for.

My sister and I paid visits to Radlett. On one such, I recall going down with Scarlet Fever and being charmingly nursed by one Paula Colyer. Although they saw little of each other, except in a professional capacity until the 1960s (she was a trained nurse and lived in the Red House flat) Paula was to become my stepmother some twenty-five years later.

The Partnership took over the Red House for the expanding needs of surgeries and my father moved to Grove House, Park Road, where he was overjoyed to take over a wonderful garden, I think, from his friend Edwin Beckett, head gardener to the Aldenham Estate. The house itself became a beautiful home with ample space to reflect his many interests. He had superb taste in everything and over the years he skilfully and economically added to the few gems he had inherited. The vistas over his glorious garden enhanced the fine furniture within.

Fishing and shooting became his major hobbies at this time; initially mainly through invitations from the Allans but increasingly, as the Thirties progressed, from generous patients and friends in Radlett and the medical profession. Outstanding amongst these were Miles Brunton, Dick Bott (of Cresta Run fame), the Kearsleys and his farming friends, the Pearmans and the Halseys. His natural skills with rod and gun, combined with his enthusiasm and cheery, interesting company, ensured a steady flow of splendid invitations.

This is the story of his first salmon caught in June 1933, at Faskally, on the river Tummel as guest of Harry Allan.

> *My first visit to fish for salmon. Very happy at Fishers' Hotel, Pitlochry. Jean Allan and Major Lander also guests. After losing my first fish at the junction (Tummel and Garry), I hook a fish at 12 noon, 50 yards above Clunie Bridge. The battle starts in blazing sunshine. The fish bolts down stream line out to backing, ding dong over the rocks – no view of fish for first half hour. Fish rushes further down stream through arches of bridge, unable to follow. Send ghillie over the bridge to opposite bank. He casts minnow to hook up line and double reeling gradually lures fish back. After a final run fish is gaffed over steep rock. A clean fish, 22½ lbs. My first fish. Landed at 1/50 p.m.*

His cousin, Jane Paterson from Invergordon, recalls her Uncle Peter arriving at the Ord, "followed by an avalanche of suitcases, rods and guns – pandemonium accompanied by the joyous barking of the dogs". And Charles Allan remembers him "trembling with excitement long before the grouse were due to fly over."

By 1937 he was clearly a highly skilled fisherman and, as guest of his dear friend, Huddy, helped to break the record, intact since 1899, of nine fish in a day on the lower Brora (held jointly by Lord Londonderry and the famous Mr Haig Thomas).

> *On 7th we attempt record for lower water, 9 in a day, achieved three times since 1899. We land 6 before lunch. Then 2-5 p.m. blank. Then excitement rises as we land 3 from "The Ford" and Otter. I hook a big un in Ford but alas 15 lb kelt!!!\** *Finally I glance back to see John Campbell with rod bent at tail of the Rallan. I drop fish and run. John offers to hand me rod – but I take net and finally net fish 28½ lb. as darkness descends. Record broken. John romps home with 60 lbs on his bike.*

That week Peter landed 26 salmon, weighing 272 lbs, including a splendid 30 lbs fish from the Benjie pool on April 5th. Huddy, who loved to have his fish smoked by Mr Tulloch in Aberdeen, graciously allowed my father to have the fish mounted in a glass case. We have it still.

In 1937 tragic news came from New Zealand. My father's younger brother, Edward, had been crushed and killed by his tractor, leaving May to bring up four children, the youngest of whom was only a year old. It must have been a great struggle for her with little or no state help in those days, but somehow this "indomitable" little person managed, turning her hand to a variety of enterprises to make ends meet. I don't think her in-laws in England were able to help, being hard pressed themselves. Edward's parents by this time were dead and I gather Edward had been given his small share of the inheritance when he settled in New Zealand. I remember my father was frequently late in paying his share of my school fees, and was having a struggle to meet the mortgage payments on his lovely house in Radlett.

My mother and father continued to meet occasionally. We all met up for the Coronation of George VI and Queen Elizabeth in 1937. They exchanged friendly and chatty letters, mainly about us children. At the end of the decade, after some six years of separation, my mother's family approached my father and suggested a divorce, to free them both for

---

\* Kelts have to be returned to the river. They have spawned and are returning to the sea.

possible re-marriage. This was a tricky and dangerous proceeding in those days, especially for a doctor who exposed himself to the possibility of being struck off the Medical Register. (I have read there were some 8,000 divorces in 1939 as opposed to some 160,000 in 1990.) After some anxious moments, the divorce was granted. It was clear to all the family that during her lifetime my mother continued to have a very soft corner for my father and always asked about him when we returned from a visit.

# Chapter Nine

## TAKING UP ARMS AGAIN . . . with the RAF

*May 1939*

All May I had very busy surgeries in Shenley and London Colney while Dr Simmers was enjoying excellent sea trout fishing in Scotland. I attended several evening surgeries with the RAF at the Sick Quarters at Hendon and carried out "Medical Boards" on flying personnel in my capacity as an RAF Volunteer Reserve doctor. The men were RAF Air Crew and pilots who needed special examination for flying fitness.

A police officer called on me and requested me to go to the Police Station at Mill Hill to be fitted with a Gas Mask, which I took away with me and lodged at the Red House, Radlett. I arranged for the twins of Bertie Ishill to be fitted with a special carrier with twin gas masks. I made contact with the RAF Medical Section and was given the rank of Flight Lieutenant and attached to the Sick Quarters at Hendon Aerodrome. I attended for evening duties during late May and continued through June and July. There was great anxiety over likelihood of war with Germany. One or two families were arranging to move to the USA and Canada before the war which seemed inevitable. I received instructions as to what treatment I should offer to all likely emigrants who had arranged to travel to the USA. Three families arranged for sea passage during July 1939.

During June and July all surgeries in Radlett, Shenley and London Colney were crowded and the whole country was feeling the strain of impending war. Attending special evening classes at Hendon Aerodrome was very interesting and we were visited by several Senior Medical Officers of the RAF, who gave us most useful instructions. I realised that as soon as war was declared I should report at Hatfield Aerodrome as there was a Flying Training Unit there. Dr J K Milward was busy and Dr Simmers was quite alarmed at the strain that was already present in the practice. He knew that I held a Commission in the RAF Medical Service and that at the onset of war I would be swept into the RAF.

During July, we were making arrangements in our various practices for the attendance of surgeries so that there would be no panic among the patients. We made a very thorough inspection of our Maternity commitments and had useful contacts with the various district nurses and the maternity homes in Watford, Bushey Heath and St Albans. The

Matron and Staff at the Maternity Homes were all given special instructions so that they could conduct all maternity cases from the very outset of war.

I called on the Squadron Leader at Hatfield Aerodrome and told him that I would be joining his training staff to continue with the training of air crews and pilots.

I packed special war kit as it seemed most likely that war would be declared by the end of the month. Dr Jones called on us at the practice and remarked that the Government was ready to declare War on Germany. War was declared on Sept 3rd. I was ordered to report to Hatfield, and arranged for an overhaul of my car which I was to take on active service. I finally left my practice and Grove House, leaving Forbes Simmers and J K Milward in charge.

I arrived at Hatfield aerodrome and was immediately on duty with the Training Squadron and had early flights. I arranged for a series of First Aid and daily flights – especially with advanced pupils. After spending the first fortnight at the Hatfield Aerodrome, I received message from the RAF College at Cranwell to report there for duty as Medical Officer. I received a special message from Air Vice Marshall B E Sutton, OBE, DSO, MC. I was very surprised to receive this special posting to Cranwell and said *au revoir* to my early commitment at the Flying Training School, Hatfield. I set off on the Great North Road for Cranwell.

**Cranwell 1939-42**

I reached Cranwell and reported to the Adjutant who took me in to meet A V M Sutton, who was in Command of 21 Group. He was delighted to meet me again and said I had been given this special training appointment as I was the only doctor who had seen active service in the RFC, 1917-1918 as Observer. I was told that the two senior courses of RAF Pilot pupils were in their first month of training and resident in the RAF College. After having tea with Bertie I found my apartments in the College and was given an excellent batman and to my surprise I took over the rooms of Group Captain Jock Halley, who was a married officer and living out. That evening, the Suttons invited me to dine at 21 Group Headquarters. Bertie reminded me of the days at the Hoo, Eastbourne in 1920 and 1921 when I was up at BNC and was spending the long Vac at the Hoo, coaching their boys.

Cranwell was a very large station with two air fields and a large signal school under Group Captain Gould in East Camp. Large planes were used with the Signals pupils, doing flying duties and signalling. After finishing their training course they were posted as Signallers to active stations – mostly bomber.

On my first morning at College I took the 8 a.m. Sick Parade and afterwards called on the Station Hospital to visit sick students and flying staff. I prepared to attend Night Flying at the Night Flying Aerodrome and supervised the night meal for flying personnel. I was also interested in inspecting the flying of pilots and observers who were carrying out night flying duties in an active training programme. This night flying programme was not concluded until 5 a.m.

I spent some time with my batman arranging my quarters which were most comfortable and I was even provided with a gun room which contained my salmon rods. I soon found a squash court and arranged to play with a lively player from 21 Group. I found this an excellent relief in the evenings. I found many other avenues of interest on this very extensive active station and enjoyed investigating the Signal School in the East Quadrant of the Station. I carried out several examinations for flying fitness for pilots who had completed their training and were anxious to join battle squadrons.

There was a very large hangar which served as a Church for the station and on Sunday mornings there was a huge congregation of WAAF and male personnel, well over 1,000, attending. The Reverend Jagoe, the Air Chaplain, preached the sermon.

The first courses were almost over and the men ready for joining regular squadrons throughout the RAF. I gave several lectures to these special cadets, who were very keen to receive up to date lectures in Corps duties and active service. I received an invitation from the OC commanding to visit the RAF Hospital at Rauceby which is about four miles from Cranwell. I greatly enjoyed this as I met all the consultants of the various departments. I had met several of them in the London Hospitals, including Squadron Leader J Milner, who was a consultant in Eye Technique from Moorfield's Hospital. I was most interested in the physiotherapy department where they had an excellent staff who carried out special treatment on casualties from Cranwell.

Air Commodore John Jagoe called on me to ask if I would conduct the maternity case of the daughter of the Vicar of Cranwell, who was married to a fighter pilot from Waddington RAF Fighter Station. She would be resident at the Cranwell Village Vicarage. I had my maternity equipment with me so I went to the vicarage and met the Vicar of Cranwell and his pregnant daughter. She was very relieved and delighted I agreed to conduct her pregnancy. I also met her pilot husband. I said this action was secret as I was not allowed to conduct private confinements as a serving officer in the war and especially in my capacity as a Medical Officer to the RAF College. She was seven months pregnant so I took control of the final months.

I took an interest in the RAF families who were resident in the RAF cottages and arranged to carry out some urgent tonsillectomy operations, as normally the children had to go to Lincoln hospital. A V M Willock took me to lunch with the Countess of Londesborough at her residence, Blakeney, and I was asked if I would operate on her daughter for tonsillectomy. She was about ten years old and the case was acute so I agreed to admit her daughter to the Sick Quarters at Cranwell Hospital. Her tonsils were greatly enlarged and inflamed, but the operation was successful, and the grateful Countess gave me an excellent day's pheasant shooting in the best fields. Hares were not shot as they were for coursing. A V M Willock was one of the guns. All that autumn I had most excellent shooting at Rauceby as guest of Sir George Whichcote.*

**Extracts from diary**

> *Very busy courses for night flying and we give hot meals for pilots and air crews. Mostly Oxfords as night flying planes. Return to college at about 5 a.m. (use my own car). Excellent college library Peggy Sutton and Bertie give me most generous hospitality at their home at Headquarters.*
>
> *I meet F/Lt Lord a New Zealand staff pilot who helps with much swimming and PT for pupils. He won an Olympic medal for swimming for NZ. He helps as a pilot with my part in a special film on air training. I was filmed as I was recording his BP during a special examination for flying activities. Sick parades in the College at 8 a.m. I am dealing with the Flying Training Pupils Course which is now in full progress. I was able to check certain flying pupils' problems and went up in the air on several flights with them in Oxfords. From the first course I only rejected one pilot. There was an excellent section of WAAF personnel on the station many of whom serviced flying machines.*

---

* As a humble Flight Lieutenant he was always in very distinguished company, including a couple of Air Vice Marshalls (his pals), Group Captains, and Sir Neville Henderson (ex Ambassador to Berlin). The Canine Company was no less distinguished; one marvellous golden labrador "Solo" had won 53 first prizes and clearly enjoyed collecting my father's birds.

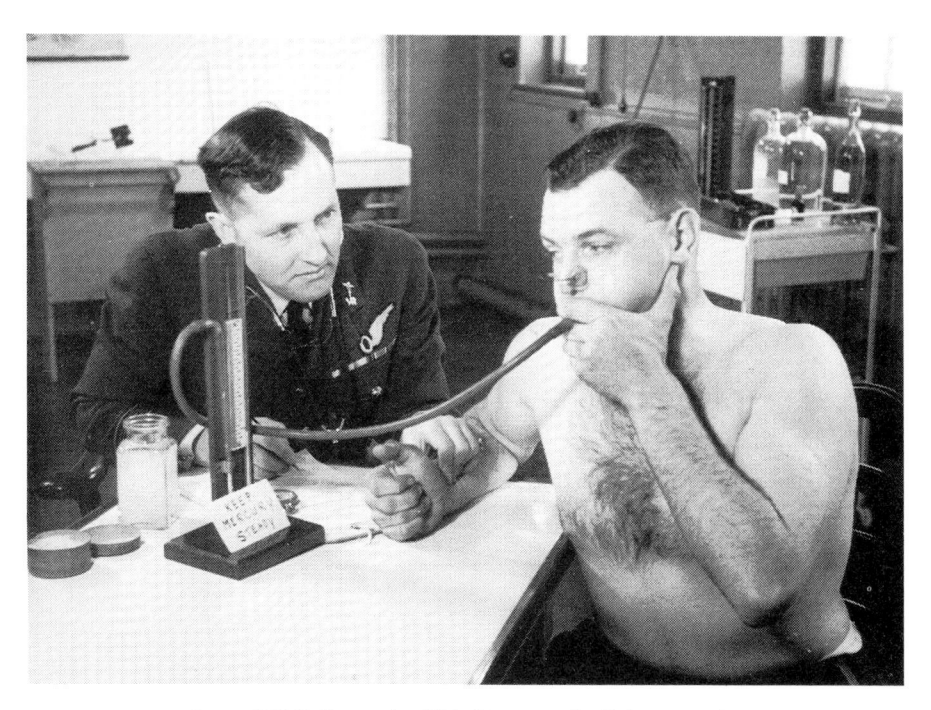

*Cranwell 1948. Doc testing Flight Lieutenant Lord's lung capacity. Lord – a splendid New Zealand Officer, was shot down and killed in 1944.*

### 15th January 1941

*We had a most interesting afternoon's sport hare shooting on the aerodrome. We had 100 RAF personnel acting as beaters. It was most amusing to see many hares mixed up with parked Oxford machines. AVM Willock, Captain Miller, Dr Satge among the guns. There was snow on the aerodrome and we shot the hares. A most entertaining afternoon. Very heavy frosts and cold nights. This gave the boy cadets an excellent opportunity to flood the corridor in order to produce long slides of ice leading to their wash basins. This caused many falls and I had to read the riot act. I have several patients with chest problems in hospital beds at the Cranwell Sick Quarters. Excellent RAF nursing sisters in charge of the in-patients, several cases of pneumonia – all did well.*

*Very cold, severe weather. Busy with sick parades. Gave several lectures to the flying course. Also attended night flying on frozen air fields for all January and February. It is interesting that Lawrence's* Seven Pillars of Wisdom *has been presented to the RAF College Library, 1st Edition. Lawrence of Arabia was stationed*

> at the RAF Station at Cranwell and took the name of Aircraftsman Shaw. He was most keen to demonstrate his technique of strict discipline. He was watched carrying out his duties as a Sentry on guard duty, by several senior officers, and his full movements when marching on his post and his superb rifle drill when coming from the slope to the Order Arms position was most commendable. Some officers observed him during the hours of darkness and in the total spell of duty as a sentry he was superb when, on his two hours of duty, he never let up but remained immaculate in every moment. It was a tragic end of his life he was killed in a motor cycle accident. I believe he was happy during his days at Cranwell.

Early one morning, when I was engaged in Sick Parade duties, I heard that Chief of Air staff Sir Achibald Sinclair, was visiting Cranwell. But there was a crisis. Two cadets had climbed the main flag staff during the night and placed a "jerry" on top of the mast! The Adjutant was at the foot of the huge mast and there were two air gunner sergeants with two .22 rifles who were shooting at the jerry to smash it (it was pottery). They had already fired several shots and hit the jerry but could not smash it. As soon as I finished sick parade I hastened to the scene of the crisis and addressed the sergeants on the technique of their musketry. They fired more shots which resounded with much noise but they said to me, "I can't smash the bloody jerry." All their shots were hitting the centre of the jerry which was obviously protected by the thick disc of timber and no bullets were going direct to the jerry. I said, "Let me have a go, Sergeant." He seemed relieved that I had asked him. I took a steady aim but did not aim at the centre of the jerry and my shot was immediately followed by the jerry crashing to the ground in several pieces. I had actually aimed my shot at the handle and had hit it full blast. The Adjutant was delighted, the two sergeants relieved and the smashed bits were speedily collected. I took the handle (which I still possess). A few minutes before the staff car arrived, all was clear and the airmen were in full parade in front of the college – at least 200 with rifles and officers with swords – all ready to give the Air Minister his full domestic welcome. The two Air Vice Marshals were ready to welcome the Minister and Jock Halley was also present. The troops performed splendidly and did many complicated marching movements. The Minister then made an extensive examination of the station.

    I greatly enjoyed many excellent games of tennis, mostly singles, with Jock Halley. He usually beat me after strenuous sets. I lectured on the various duties of the three flights of a Corps Squadron. "A" Flight who did destructive shoots on enemy targets, "B" Flight who did contact patrols on enemy trenches and photographs of enemy positions and enemy battery positions and "C" Flight who did destructive shoots on enemy batteries in counter battery positions. I had very special contact patrols during the first war when the Germans made their gigantic attack in March 1918.[*]

I was most interested in the Pre-Roman 1500 BC burial ground about one mile from Cranwell. I took a day off to visit this with trench instruments and worked heavily on a part that was undisturbed. I found a complete skeleton with an excellent set of teeth. It was in splendid condition and had evidence of several injured ribs. I was also most fortunate in finding several pieces of lapis lazuli and odd pieces of rare jewellery. I cleared up all the area of my diggings and left no evidence of my all-day (10 a.m. to 6 p.m.) activities. I intended to make further visits to this "Brigantine Burial Ground" – I hadn't seen any members of the public during the whole day! I cycled back from the Lincoln Road to Cranwell and had a bath before dinner and after dinner had a most interesting chat with several RAF Archaeologists in the anteroom!

In the late autumn I had several thrilling days shooting with Bertie Sutton and members of the Cranwell shoot and was fortunate to receive invitations from local Lincolnshire gentlemen, especially Sir Neville Henderson, Commander Ancotts, the Countess of Londesborough, Sir George Whichcote and Captain Reeve.

On one day's shooting at Aswarby Park, a German bomber flew over and dropped a large bomb which did not go off. It landed in a large oak tree and its ropes got entangled in strong branches. I told the keeper to let it stay there as it was dangerous to attempt to move it.

---

[*] "I am not too sure about these lectures in a W.W.2. context. I *am* sure his colleagues would have been fascinated by his W.W.1. stories."

# Chapter Ten

## BY TROOPSHIP TO SOUTH AFRICA, WINTER 1942

*Extracts from diary*

*C*ranwell College. Receive urgent message from RAF Medical Headquarters in London that I am appointed SMO for convoy trooping duties L12 and must report to RMS Devonshire (29,000 tons) at the Liverpool Dock as soon as possible. I will have six RAF Medical Orderlies to assist. I have interview with Jock Halley and tell him I must depart within 48 hours to proceed to Liverpool. I am told it will be in tropical regions and I fill in forms for tropical kit. Told I could have 48 hours leave so I leave Cranwell for Liverpool and report to L12, leave my kit and tell Capt. I will be back in 48 hours. I catch last train for Glasgow en route to visit Fiona in Helensburgh. Snowing all day as I have happy time with Fiona (aged 10) who is very lively and well. Do some useful shopping with her and have very happy day. Fiona, in her colourful Hungarian frock does several attractive dances. Sheena and Fiona see me off at Helensburgh station and I catch night train from Glasgow to Lancaster where I arrive at 4.30 a.m. Intensely cold and I share Porter's room. Catch early train for Boston and arrive at Westfield, my sister Mary's home, in time for early tea and we all journey to Giggleswick School to see Simon. The chapel is superb and marvellously situated. Greatly enjoyed visit and Simon well. Eric and Mary motor me to Lancaster and I finally arrive Liverpool and report late to L12. I have an attractive cabin as SMO and have Croner as my steward.

I make extensive tour of ship with Captain and I feel accommodation far too crowded, especially in "deep hold" fore and aft. Feel I will face many hygiene problems re. ventilation. There is excellent hospital on ship with six beds. Spend all morning doing critical examination – many blocked "scuppers". Took afternoon off to make extensive examination of superb cathedral which I greatly enjoyed. Was able to attend Evensong. Superb organ and choir excellent. Arrive back on L12 early evening. F/Lt Maurice (Marlborough) my Deputy SMO and Fl.Lt Hoffman (Physiotherapy) arrive. General Greenslade and Col. Brett at our table.

I continue with extensive examination of "scuppers". Most of plumbers scratching their heads. They can't find solution. (Superb view of Cathedral from ship.) Put in for seven dozen Elsans (portable lavatories). Plenty of WRNS arrive to brighten trip. Excellent shop and barber on ship. I write 17 letters at night. The ship is crowded with over 3,000 troops and I make night visit to all sleeping quarters. I tell Captain I am NOT satisfied with two deep holds as they have inadequate ventilation and smell badly as on previous trips these two holds contained an enormous number of cattle hides. Send three men ashore for hospital treatment. I go with Captain to visit the extensive kitchens and inspect cooking of meals. Inspect the several mincing machines – very important. I observe the "super sewer", the River Mersey performs perfectly every day! Scuppers still continue to be blocked daily, also many lavs! There is a great shortage of hot water and Captain makes an effort to get this corrected. At 12 noon we finally leave the Mersey and pass down the Lancashire coast. A wonderful sight to see all this mighty fleet and naval escorts. There is a tremendous glut of paper which blocks the scuppers and the lavs. I get a lovely view of the whole celestial heaven; stars superb.

We have had games organised and the troops seem to enjoy this addition to the daily routine. We have the thrill of seeing a Sunderland flying boat circle round the whole fleet. Still have problems with ventilation in crowded dormitories. This is a problem and we struggle with this to get relief. A chess tournament causes much interest and delight. It is interesting many airmen from the two stuffy holds are now sleeping on deck and getting much more comfortable nights. The Chaplain held Communion this a.m. at 7 in the WO's mess.

We are still heavily engaged in blocked scuppers most of morning and I do a complete very long night exam of all billets and took me two hours. I went on bridge for first time in full moon – marvellous sight of gigantic convoy. Sirius (Canis Major), simply glorious riding the clouds, defies the moon. Bed 1.30 a.m.

Superb Commando raid by on St Nazaire, Bay of Biscay, destroyed dock gates; explosions put out dock one year. 15 Huns shot down. It is lovely to see the Southern Cross and the Alpha and Beta Centaurs.

We complete extensive spraying for droplet infection and still spend much time on general hygiene and arranging the sleeping on decks for airmen from stuffy holds. We are rapidly approaching the heat zone. I find fan very comforting in my cabin. WRNS greatly enjoy organised dance with excellent band.

We are busy in hospital – all six beds occupied, mostly gastro enteritis cases. Hoffman is appointed Director of PT and Sergeant Pelter (5 British records) useful on PT on upper deck. Daily parades most successful. We have now got most of A4, 5 and 6 sleeping out. Long walk round most of billets late past midnight. Troops sleeping well although very hot conditions. Many cases of sunburns – have given instructions on care to prevent this injury. The swimming bath opens today – very successful and most extensively used. Full moon rises over Africa – superb sight. Many of the troops don't understand great power of the tropical sun and get severe sunburn. I give talk on radio on the care needed. Discipline with young airmen is poor, as they don't realise they are entirely responsible for their own severe burns. They rest on deck and are exposed to power of the sun. See many flying fish and porpoises.

Hoffman gives me excellent treatment for my shoulder. I make extensive examination of the all kitchens and especially mince meat and preparation of food as we have great increase of enteritis on sick parades. I arrange for special sterilisation of mincing machines and ship's kitchen. We are now approaching Freetown and whole fleet is anchored. Greatly amused by black man diving for money. He can see coins in sea and collect them successfully. Gen. Greenslade leaving for special air flight to Middle East. A shore M/O S/Leader visits us and glad to be shown round. He arranges to take to shore (for hospital) airman with fractured patella.

"Bumboats" – visit our ship with masses of ripe bananas, which we haven't enjoyed for 2 years. The stars are now most impressive as I see Canopus, Southern Cross, Procyon (little dog), Capella as Officer Wright gives me grand tour on the bridge. It is light until 10.30 p.m. and I have most interesting hour.

Several parties of troops go on shore leave in Freetown. Heat is now intense and first case of prickly heat. Many troops do not take notice of Hoffman's instructions. He thinks this lamentable. Batman is leaving ship to go to AVM Champion de Crepagny (special appointment). Have to lecture my MOs re. alcohol as they are able to get a large amount from the canteen. Stars are now grand and I greatly enjoy nightly examination of the skies. I have great thrill in getting a glorious view of the constellation of Scorpio; Antares simply superb. I met a Wren on the ship who lives in Rhu and knows Sheena's Mitchell relatives well.

Hoffman is taken ill with great pain in right loin and we have to admit him to hospital. Symptoms, strongly suggest renal colic and I give him injection of morphine which relieves him. He still has disturbed night and he remains in bed. Improves slowly during day – remains in hospital.

We have grand concert on Upper Deck – mixed choir sing splendidly and several violins play.

News tonight on wireless states first girl (in ATS) has been killed in England. She was killed by splinter from shell. I meet Mr Dennis on ship who was Games Master at Forres where Michael was at school. Airman Deighton, of Yorkshire tells me all about Java. He tells me that Japanese Emperor has to send his Imperial Shinto Robes to the laundry after British air raid!

Have a busy day with MOs selecting about 40 airmen for shore hospital. I see Canopus early in afternoon, far south. Captain is very pleased with the general cleanliness of ship. We lead Port line of ships in the convoy and I see an albatross following the ship. All very quiet on the ship. It is St George's Day. Very clear. I get first view of Table Mountain, Cape Town, 34 miles away in golden dawn. I know now what Vasco da Gama felt on first view of Cape of Good Hope. Great thrill as we enter the big basin. We anchor at 10.30 a.m. and I let all MOs go on shore to see Cape Town. Local inhabitants demonstrate great hospitality. Lifts everywhere for troops. I stay on board on duty.

### St George's Day

All WRNS leave ship with much regret. General Smuts invites us to lunch tomorrow. Hoffman posted to EFTS[*], near Pretoria. I go with Hoffman to movies and see Greta Garbo in film – a really super cinema. Folk most hospitable. We meet Gen. Smuts for lunch at the Civil Service Club; have super lunch and then we all go to the Grand Opening of the Rugger season. There are three matches during the afternoon and last match (after tea is served on the grandstand) is between Inter-State XVs. Super Rugger; I see Hoffman off to Pretoria and then Dr Sichel motors me to his home in Kenilworth to meet his family. Dr Sichel is Eye Consultant to Cape and does all special RAF treatments. I meet all Sichel family. Next day Dr Sichel arranges for me to make a superb 170 mile trip in mountains through five passes. We see tons and tons of glorious apples and pears all rotting in orchards, even the pigs won't eat

---

[*] Empire Flying Training School.

*them. Excellent lunch in mountains, lovely drive back via Stellenbosch and arrive ship at 7 p.m. Then go to cathedral for Evensong and spot Cranwell Chaplain in nave.*

## Cape Town

*I get permission to sleep ashore so go and take up residence at Assembly Hotel in Cape Town. Have busy day shopping in superb shops in Adderley Street. Send Barbara and Mary a dozen pairs of silk stockings.\* Helpful shop assistant says she will send stockings and that they will get safely to UK. Get Fiona some excellent models of Elephant and Michael some precious foreign stamps for his collection. Call and meet Dr Robt. Macdonald on introduction of Sqd Leader Campbell, RAF Hospital, Torquay. He is ex-Magdalen College Oxford and Guys Hospital. Gave me delightful visit. I have a very enjoyable evening as Mrs Sichel takes me back for dinner. See photo of Henneker-Gotley as Captain of England Rugger XV at Oxford. Stars wonderful and get a superb view of Scorpio in all his glory. Call on Mrs Baxter, wife of Lord Mayor of Cape Town. Grand old Scot, Mr Baxter, picks me up at Assembly Hotel. Have lunch with family and we visit Rhodes Memorial. Visit Rhodes' house, Grote Schuur which is now gifted to SA for the residence of FM General Smuts – lovely trees and shrubs. See oranges, lemons and olives in Mrs Baxter's garden which is full of many delightful flowers. I greatly enjoy visiting this lovely house and family. Zulu driver takes me back to hotel.*

*I visit Botanical Gardens with Mrs Sichel and Annette. See locusts for first time. Have tea in lovely grounds. Went to Museum, see ancient paintings on stone and several skeletons of dinosaurs. Also excellent reproductions of natives and bushmen in plaster. Then visit art gallery where I see delightful collections of Dutch art and fine Durer etchings. I am most impressed by marvellous specimens of Grevilla Roberta and Araucaria Excelsa. See many blue doves in trees. Superb morning. Walk around gardens in Town. Lunch with Mr Sumierin, father of Roy who was at BNC. Also meet speaker of SA Houses of Parliament. Have lunch in delightful club in Adderley Street – what superb lobsters! In afternoon ascend Table Mountain in cable car. At summit get glorious view of Cape Town, the port and Atlantic Ocean. Cable railway very thrilling. See many lizards and attractive flora, greatly*

---

\* Which were unobtainable in England during wartime.

enjoy visit at top. Spend two hours enjoying this. Make descent in cable car. In afternoon I visit Mrs Bertherin of special Cape Liquor Van de Hurn. She gives me great welcome as her son was a pilot in No 7 Squadron RFC at Proven, Belgium, in 1917. I spend afternoon with her and greatly enjoy her lovely garden. When I say "au revoir" she gets her brother to get me a bottle of Van der Hurn, to take to ship.*

I return to ship as Captain is keen to move to "roads" for tests. I identify many new stars. Stay on boat for night and have superb and glorious view of Cape Town and Table Mountain: Scorpio wonderful. Lovely Cape flowers including Protea in my cabin.

Heard Ch. J. Brown was killed by bombs in Norway. Great friend of Frankie Rhodes (BNC). I'm reading book on Cecil Rhodes, seems very like Frankie Rhodes, (1920 BNC. with me). We return to Port after long day of special tests.

Several enjoyable visits to the Sichel family and they take me to the Diocesan College, Cape Town to see Mrs Sichel's son. Meet several of the teachers, all ex Oxford and now enjoying teaching jobs. This is a lovely College and there appears to be an excellent spirit prevailing. They have a superb 1st XV Rugger.

I went to the bottom of Adderley Street to have a good view of The Snake Pit and I was amazed at the large number of Black Adder serpents. Small black boy collects Black Adder snakes for the curator and he gets £1 each. Now here is a true story of the crafty wee black boy about 14 years old. Late one night a policeman went to get a night view with his electric torch. He switched on his electric torch and to his great surprise he spotted a wee black boy crawling in the pit floor among the snakes. The boy was catching black adder snakes and putting them into a bag: he did not worry about the poisonous snakes. He rapidly escaped from the snake pit and carried off the bag. A few days later he appeared at the Curator's House bringing three black adder snakes and collecting his £1 per snake. This is quite remarkable as it is quite clear that he was frequently going at night and collecting snakes and later was taking the stolen snakes back to the curator to collect his £1s. It is remarkable that this wee boy did not mind the darkness of night and crawling around the snake pit amongst several varieties of snakes, all poisonous! The Curator had not the slightest idea that the snakes were from his special snake pit.

---

* Yet again Peter demonstrates he was an early exponent of the art of "networking"!

I spent several hours on the ship in my cabin arranging my purchases and having many happy hours with Dr Sichel, who gave me two very entertaining books – My friends the Baboons[*] and The Soul of the White Ant – *for the voyage.*

My final excitement in Cape Town was a visit with Dr Sichel to the main hospital which was a superb building and was in the middle of the great Heart Transplant Operations carried out by Dr Barnard[*] . The Laboratories were wonderful and operating theatres a joy to behold. This Hospital, named "The Grote Shuur" is very modern in every aspect and beautifully situated. I had a final walk down Adderley Street and did some shopping before going on board to join the ship. We were expecting some wounded from the Great Desert Campaign. We had some special medical orderlies posted to the ship and we made ready with preparing for the arrival of the wounded for return to UK.

I am greatly enjoying Natural History of Selborne. *It is much warmer and very enjoyable and I find the delicious oranges a great delight. In Khaki drill again for daily uniform – very enjoyable. I am greatly enjoying* Life of Cecil Rhodes *by MacDonald. All the wounded are very happy and doing well. Medical orderlies doing splendid nursing duties.*

Attack in Madagascar is going very well. Much naval activity reported in far north which suggests another convoy is en route *for* Archangel[*]. *Amazing shoals of flying fish, wonderful sight, much soot from funnels of ship. Much hotter. I stitch two ratings up after diving in swimming pool and striking bottom. Churchill makes an excellent speech which we hear on ship broadcast. Good news from Malta, 72 axis planes destroyed in three days.*

Wounded are in all stages of convalescence and some have very severe wounds. Cape Town and Table Mountain look very delightful from ship which is now just outside basin and we are moving out to sea at high speed. We have enormous stock of super oranges and Captain says "You can have as many as you like." Very heavy swell and an albatross follows us along. It does not take any notice of gun fire. We get final view of Table Mountain and Cape Town. Get report from Navy. We capture chief port in Madagascar. Expect Vichy will revolt strongly.

See Ursa Major for first time since left Freetown. Special

---

[*] See poem at end of book.

[*] He is confused here: these heart transplants took place there many years later.

[*] Archangel – port in Russia to which the Allies sent war supplies for the Russian front.

*bulletin* tells us all about Singapore. Most dramatic. We "Cross Line" at 2.00 hours. The Ship's canary escapes through open Porthole and after flight over Atlantic it alights on the upper deck in lounge. All windows closed and we recapture the bird. I lecture RAF sergeants on altitude flying. It is Vigil of the Ascension. Case after case of oranges disappear. Talk about Sir Charles Sherrington's chimps and the disappearance of bananas.*

Play deck tennis with captain, then medicine ball and PT. Plot stars during the night watch, most exciting and enjoyable. Meet Lt Hun RN who has been on destroyer with Barry Kent (Radlett patient) and says he is an excellent cadet. All my Cape flora very colourful in cabin, especially Proteus. The old ship is sailing splendidly and I note by my navigation of the stars, Canopus and Alpha and Beta Centaurs, we are sailing due West towards Brazil. I tell navigation officer I note this reality and he is amazed at my knowledge of the heavenly bodies. We did this to give the German U-boats off African coast, as wide a berth as possible.

I make great effort to conclude The Outward Report. How I revel in hot salt bath after games. Now also write report on this voyage. I volunteer to do Anti-Submarine observation spell of duty – several hours – do this every day with one of the ratings. Spend part of night with 3rd Officer Wright on the bridge doing special patrol of stars. Blue sea, sky extremely blue. Report on radio, one Australian pilot shot down five Junkers in the Med. I remove a large sebaceous cyst from airman's scalp with local.

At 19.00 hours Polaris is 15°. I see Capella as she sinks in mist. We have many battles with deck tennis most enjoyable. Had very disturbed night so arise at five a.m. and go on bridge. Venus greets us with all her glory. Superb. Lines of golden sea weed coming with tide from Gulf of Mexico! See Vega and other northern gems better as we sail steadily northwards to Britain.

Wonderful sight, grand old ship in huge swell. This is advent of NE Trades. I did 28 stretches of C deck on windward side to get perfect view of waves. The good old ship takes the big stuff perfectly. Never slept until four a.m. Noises and rolling incredible, worst night for ages. Ship in gale. Chicken rissoles bring on return of gastro enteritis. Very rough all day and much colder. Had acute attack of diarrhoea. Little relief from drugs all day!

Superb bombing on German battleship as she attempts to return to Germany from Norway. Put clocks on half an hour

---

* As related in Oxford chapter.

tonight. Still considerable roll on ocean and it is much colder. Better after hot salt bath. Still carry out anti-submarine patrol and did FFT on all the ratings and RAF. Bed early as clocks go forward one and a half hours as we head eastwards. Very cold, lots of birds. Think we are only about 500 miles from Ireland. Big raid by RAF on Mannheim. 40,000 incendiary bombs cause immense damage. Wonderful to see cheery faces of soldiers as they approach home after two years away. All the wounded in hospital doing well, especially the Royal Marine, who has many wounds and still in bed. We hold final smoker; what singing! Terrific evening greatly enjoyed by all on board.

## 22nd May 1942

Fiona 11 today. This is exciting day as we sight Ireland and Mull of Kintyre, and Goat Fell, Arran just after lunch. Only 75 miles from Fiona. The ship finally arrives at Stranraer. We prepare special stretcher parties for wounded. We say good-bye to Royal Marine who has cleaned all his buttons and looks superb when we dressed him and landed him ashore. Orders for all to disembark, except permanent staff to remain on ship to go south at midnight. Rain all day as ship leaves Stranraer and is due to sail to Newport Mon. Turning past Isle of Man, what an empty ship.

Clear up all final jobs and many forms. We turn east round St David's Head. Finally arrive at 18.30 hours. What a day, gale and storms. Pilot arrives on board. It is Empire Day. We are anchored off Barry. Pilot says wind too high to take us in. Broadcast from Durham Cathedral Veni Creator sung perfectly. Dr Abington preaches a superb sermon – greatly enjoyed.

Our ship has been stranded on sand bank. There is much excitement at nine p.m. as huge fires seen in Bath and Bristol in middle of Hun air raid. We hope we are not a target. I go to bed early. Very cold.

No tugs to get to grips so we are anchored for the night.

## 27th May 1941

Anti-aircraft barrage balloons fore and aft. We wait all day and then nine tugs arrive. High tide at 6.50! At 6.30 bow is clear and then five tugs at stern give "Cock o' Doodle" siren to declare we are free. I have full tour of engine room and most impressed by *marvellous concentration of energy. Chief Engineer Nichol takes me round. This example of marine engineering a masterpiece of economy of space. One hour later, pilot takes us into Newport Main Dock. Hurrah! End of Voyage. I have 17 packages of luggage and have many farewells. I leave ship and join taxi at 12 noon. Down to 38 West Park Road and meet Aunt Emily and Uncle Ernie and Cyril. All well and I leave them fruit.*

*Travel to Marlborough to see Michael. Meet House Master who tells me Michael is not at Marlborough at present as he is in Nursing Home in Glasgow\*. Operation for appendicitis. Unfortunately, I have left case of Cape oranges with his House Mistress and cannot manage to get the case returned. I rebuke House Master and tell him his matron will not return oranges and leave very disgusted.*

*Travel to London and take sleeper to Glasgow from Euston. Call to see Michael in Nursing Home and visit Sheena and Fiona. Michael cheery and appears well. Leave him some Cape fruit. Have to return Cranwell tomorrow and report for duty. Have long chat with Michael and Fiona re all the thrills of South Africa. Give Fiona small ebony elephants. Michael thrilled with excellent collection of foreign stamps.*

*Take train to Grantham via York – long and tedious journey. Arrive Grantham 9 p.m. and take taxi to Cranwell. End of Voyage.*

---

[*] A good example of communication difficulty in wartime.

# Chapter Eleven

## BACK WITH FIGHTER, BOMBER AND TRAINING COMMANDS 1942-1945

*Extracts from diary*

*29th May 1942 – a typical day at Cranwell*

*Ten p.m. – Just arrived back at RAF College, Cranwell, from the trip to South Africa (as SMO to Transport L12) via Newport Mon. Felt very tired and ready for bed and was soon asleep. My batman called me 7.30 a.m. 30 May 1942 and I took Sick Parade in College and reported to Group Captain Jock Halley. He was delighted to see me back and reported that the college training Course was doing well.*

*I was keen to see more night flying by the cadets. I found night meal for pupils at 11 p.m. was well prepared. Experienced pilots from RAF Station acted as tutors. Special search-lights provided the bright beams for the taking off and landing techniques. I interviewed several pupil pilots and returned to the college at 5 a.m.; went to bed for three hours and my batman called me for the college sick parade at 8 a.m., most successful.*

*I had breakfast at 9 a.m. and then went to the Station Hospital and did a sick round with the duty RAF sister. I saw several WAAF from local stations that had otitis media and I treated some sick WAAF with inflamed ears with good results. A few airmen from the main station had been admitted to the hospital with chest infections. I arranged for chest X-rays to be carried out to assess the extent of infection. I also examined some patients in the out-patients department.*

*I visit AVM Bertie Sutton and his wife Peggy at Headquarters and stay for dinner. I have most interesting chat re. L12 convoy and visit to S Africa. Bertie thinks that I will be moving soon to another station and I tell him I have had three very happy years at the College and enjoyed three superb seasons in the various excellent shoots. It was most kind of Lady Sutton to have Michael and Fiona to stay as their guests. They enjoyed their stay and Michael had one flight in a Miles Magister with Sqd/Ldr Macilwaine. I also wangled a night flight in an Oxford for us both. Michael was fascinated to see the sun come back up on the horizon as we climbed. Shortly after we landed the night sky was full of our bombers as they took off from local aerodromes for a big raid on Germany. The drone of their* engines persisted for quite a while after their dim shapes had vanished to the east. Michael and Fiona had great fun with the Sutton boys and enjoyed the huge station swimming pool. Fiona had made excellent progress in the swimming pool under the instruction of Flt. Lt. Lord NZ Air Force now instructor at Cranwell (later killed in action). I went to East Camp aerodrome to visit the signals school and saw a huge aeroplane fly off with large number of boy cadets of the signal school taking the air for a signals course. This is a very active unit for the signals pupils under the command of G/Cpt Gould. There is also a large school for the training of WAAF in East Camp. There must be 1000 WAAF doing special administration course before being posted to RAF stations.

Sunday morning matins is carried out under John Jagoe, Chief Chaplain and the huge hangar is packed with RAF personnel and large number of WAAF. Singing is most enthusiastic. Organ performs splendidly.

## Kenley – With Fighter Command

### August 1942

Signal arrives from medical headquarters Air Ministry. I am posted to RAF Fighter Station, Kenley. Air Cdre Batchy Acherly, Station Commander. I make many farewells in and around Cranwell. Farewell to Peggy and Bertie Sutton and Jock Halley at the RAF College.

Very exciting to see round fighter station. Visit CO who gives me warm welcome. I visit unit for inspection of fighter planes and pilots. Pilots all kitted up at the ready and relaxed in deck chairs near their planes. I have cheery talk with many of the pilots. While I am there, about 11 a.m., alarm sounds and pilots rush to their planes; air mechanics very smart and immediately stand by planes and help in starting them. All are soon airborne and message arrives stating that German planes are en route for English mainland. Large formations of enemy bombers with fighter escort over English Channel at over 20,000 ft. Kenley Fighter Squadron is very soon in formation, climbing fast – a marvellous sight. Soon out of sight and much activity by the ground crews preparing for next alarm. This is most important as I make inspection to hangar to see planes being repaired by special air crews and meet many of ground staff.

The Officers' Mess was most palatial and dining-room had an extended platform and a five-piece orchestra played for dinner every *night. I made an inspection of the Squadron's sick quarters which had recently suffered an enemy attack. One medical officer had been killed. I had a long interview with the Station Commander, Air Commodore Batchy Acherly whose twin brother was also an A. Cmdre and Fighter Station Commander. I took sick parade next morning and examined some air members of the Kenley Station who were in hospital beds with chest problems. It was a fine day and fighter air crews were all ready at the* rendezvous *sitting in their chairs close beside the parked fighter planes.*

*The Fighter squadrons made two extensive sorties against large German formations of bombers and fighters at well over 20,000 ft and claimed two German bombers in attacks over London.\* I had interesting conversation with the CO and Adjutant and arranged some lectures on Air attacks and enemy formations\* .*

*The German air force was already in action and fighter and bomber crews were airborne at 11 a.m. high above Calais. The alarm signal was given and the pilots were speedily in their fighters and airborne in a few minutes. I continued with my general inspection of the fighter station and was busy giving injections to members of the station in the afternoon. We received an alarm signal in the late afternoon giving us the news that our Stn Commander was ditched in the English Channel. He had engine failure and he was picked up by Air-Sea Rescue after 1 hour in the sea. His twin brother, Air Com. Acherly, visited Kenley in the later afternoon. It was amusing to see the behaviour of Batchy's dog, who was certain that this Air Com. Acherly was NOT his boss, and would not make a fuss of him. We received a message that our CO was safe and landed on the south coast.*

*Batchy's brother remained with us for dinner and left before Batchy returned to Kenley Station about 10 p.m. He was still in his flying kit and did not demonstrate any distress with the result of his forced landing in the English Channel. The orchestra continued throughout dinner and played excellent selections. I made an extensive inspection of night dormitories and everything was in good order.*

Enemy air attacks continued every morning over a wide area of the south coast and several fighter stations were bombed. Special air attacks were

---

\* If my memory serves me correctly most Fighter Command activity at this time consisted of sweeps over Occupied Europe.

\* I think this is unlikely.

carried out by RAF patrols over the French coast on the air missile sites which were being prepared for FM Goering's attacks on London. (Once I was visiting Bertie Sutton in the Air Ministry, when one of these heavy mortars exploded in the centre of London. Some of these flying bombs were fired on by fighter planes and they were destroyed during flight and made to crash to earth.) Lord Dowding had three Fighter Command Groups which he controlled from the Headquarters of Fighter Command at Bentley Priory. These squadrons were specially sent on special duties to attack the German squadrons of bombers and fighters as they left their bases on the French coast.

Every day on the Kenley fighter station was extremely busy and I carried out morning sick parades and worked in the sick quarters. The Fighter pilots were very active each day. I was greatly delighted to see the sudden spontaneous action of all the pilots as they dashed to their machines as soon as the alarm sounded. I had an interesting conversation with the CO on his recent ditching in the English Channel. His engine packed up and he was unable to get his machine to make a landing on a near coastal aerodrome, so he had to ditch in the sea. His survival kit served him well and he was almost an hour in the water before he was picked up by the Air Sea Rescue Squad.

**Notes by Michael Wilson**

Sadly my father's memoirs finish here, but I will do my best to fill in the rest of his life story, letting him tell it himself with extracts from his letters to me and my family.

He omitted to mention that, much to our alarm, he volunteered to join the special British Expeditionary Force which was to go to Finland to help repel the Russian invasion in 1939. He was equipped with special white uniform for the snow. Much to our relief his participation in this enterprise was cancelled.

He must have been promoted Squadron Leader fairly early on in the war because he was Senior Medical Officer at Cranwell. Extracts of two letters flesh out details of the sort of SMO that he was:

From Air Vice Marshall Willock, Officers' Mess, Cranwell:

*16th July 1942*

*Mr Dear Doc*

*I was surprised and disappointed to learn that you had been posted so soon after your return to Cranwell.*

*I can however readily understand your being pleased to get to Kenley with the "fighter boys" and it is really a case of Cranwell's loss being Kenley's gain!*

*I want to thank you very much and very sincerely for all your excellent work at the College and your many kind acts in the locality.*

*I expect Medical Officers must often feel that they are "back room boys" and that their efforts are not fully appreciated, but I can assure you, Doc, that I realised and appreciated what a powerful influence for good you were with those boys at the College, apart from your valuable professional ability and qualifications . . ."*

And when my father died in 1990 I received this letter from a retired Bishop:

*". . . I was the Chaplain at the Royal Air Force College, Cranwell at the beginning of World War II and I shall be ever grateful to your father for his wise council and pastoral care of my wife and myself, then a newly-married couple with a young baby and woefully ignorant of so much medical knowledge that is now taken for granted.*

> *I especially remember the simple yet profound talk he gave us both about the responsibility we had taken on when the baby was on its way . . . "*

In my father's desk I found an envelope labelled "Special War Poems". This sample evokes the feelings of a fighter pilot at this time:

> I think that it will come, somewhere, somewhen,
> In shattering crash or wavering sheet of flame;
> In the green-blanket sea, choking for air
> Amid the bubbles transient as my name.
>
> Sometimes a second's throw decides the game;
> Winner take all, and there is no re-play
> Indifferent earth and sky breathe on the same
> I scatter my last chips, and go my way.
>
> The years I might have had I throw away,
> They only lead to winter's barren pain
> Their loss must bring no tears from those who stay
> For spring, however spent, comes not again.
>
> When peace descends once more like gentle rain
> Mention my name in passing, if you must,
> As one who knew the terms, slay or be slain,
> And thought the bargain was both good and just.
>
> *Seamus Haughey*
> *(Royal Canadian Air Force, Killed in action 1943)*

Occasionally he was called upon to preach sermons to the packed RAF church and, in contrast, to his brother-in-law Harry Broughton's congregation in tiny Farndale in the Yorkshire Dales. My sister and I were at the Church and he so warmed to his subject that we thought he'd never stop! I well remember on that visit to Farndale there was a ferocious German night air raid on Middlesborough. We could see the night sky lit up with fires and hear the detonations of the bombs.

We had one weekend leave with him in an hotel at Balloch on Loch Lomond. We were hauled out of bed to do PT on the flat hotel roof before breakfast. Ugh! Later we hired a rowing boat and went to an island on the loch. A storm arose, and we had an immense job to row back to the boat station where we arrived fearfully late, exhausted and drenched!

My father's game book reminds me that we had several wonderful holidays with Wooda and Bill Paterson at the Ord. Sometimes Jane and Jim were on leave from the forces to add to the pleasant holiday. His Game Book tells of days in the stooks shooting pigeons, hours in the stubble and potatoes shooting partridges and hares, as well as a memorable day after grouse at Novar and in the Balnagowan Forest. Always recording with joy when my efforts were rewarded with success. Then on August 31st 1944 he records "Took Fiona out for a walk in 4 acres of potatoes. She shoots a hare at 30 yards with .410 single barrel. Her very first shot. Then shoots another with her second shot. Isn't Michael surprised!" (Fiona was 13).

I am not aware of any ladies in my father's life at this time, but my mother met Commander Jack Hunt RN in 1943. They were married in May, my dear Grandfather giving away his daughter for the second time, in so far as, being divorced, it was allowed. Tragically, Jack was killed three months later, when Captain of the Dockyard in Algiers during the North African Campaign. After a German air raid he was towing a blazing ammunition ship out to sea with a destroyer, to try and save the city. Both ships were blown to pieces before the destroyer could cast off. But the city was saved. Jack was an outstandingly fine Christian and had spent most of his leaves helping to run Church Missionary Society youth camps, many of them for deprived children.

As far as my father's RAF career was concerned I do not think he was long at Kenley before being posted to Bomber Command at Lindholme. His Game Book tells me he was there by October 1942. I remember his being very distressed at the heavy losses being sustained by his bomber crews in their raids deep into Germany.

By October 1943 he was based at Cargen House, near Dumfries, promoted to Wing Commander and back in Training Command, Senior Medical Officer of 50 Group and (later?) 29 Group. In this rôle he covered many air bases in the North of England and throughout Scotland, usually by air, and I suspect frequently with a trout rod tucked into his kit. The mess at Cargen House was a convivial place and my father had some wonderful companions there. With Athol Murray he spent many weekends walking in the Lake District. He also enjoyed some notable geese stalking, but drew much more pleasure from seeing and hearing these majestic birds than from shooting them.

In April 1945 on leave he was guest of Miles Brunton on the Oykel. He describes a "memorable fish" as follows:

*On leave. River summer level. Fishing 11ft vibration rod and greased line. Wood's pattern. Smallest size. Went out after dinner in slacks. 1st cast to George Pool at 8:40. Sun brilliant N W Wind. Fish rose to first cast with small March Brown – Rose twice more – waited 5 minutes – changed fly to small Blue Charm. Classical Wood's take first cast. Off commenced the fireworks!! Fish felt securely hooked. Hectic dash to tail of pool. Much jumping. Saw he was a lusty salmon. Lots of dashing about for ¼ hour. Simply could not give him stick as cast so fine. Whistled as I saw Mr McDonald on bridge – no saliva left. At 9.15 fish dashed down stream to Deep run. Very difficult to get on steep face of rocks as I was alas in nailed shoes. 10 minutes in deep pot hole. Much grating of cast. 9:30 p.m. back in George Pool – felt I had him and then darted into gulley at exit of George Pool on far side. No waders – Manage to move him back into George's at 9.50 had him near gaff. Fish again crossed to far side gulley. I had to take off coat and haversack and cross river – water very cold. I wound him back into pool –*

*recrossed river to left bank as fish dashed to head of pool. Then after 5 mins he shot back yet once again to the far side, so had to cross again to right side, had to poke in gulley to move him – a lusty fish. Again back in George – played him with a short line and held him up stream. Had him near gaff 4 times. No Mr MacD on bridge now!! At last have him on his side and he rolled over and I gaffed him at 10:15 16½ lbs. Final thrill, fish slipped out of my hand at top of bank and hurtled like a toboggan down steep bank into water. I dashed down path and collected fish from the edge of George Pool. It was almost dark as I heard voices of "search party". Was met on bank by Miles and Jim Risk. A lovely hen fish.*

*Post Mortem. Hook securely anchored in vault of mouth towards side – cast terribly frayed and almost through. Moral Don't take smallest rod for night fishing. Take Dog whistle – but it was a wizard fish and an unforgettable 1½ hours. Then in the "wee room" the mist quickly thickened and I did enjoy a gargle of Glen Fiddich and a grand bath to relive those 90 golden minutes all over again and wasn't George\* surprised in the morning!!!*

This was his 86th Salmon.

In August 1945 the war ended and, being a doctor, my father was among the first to be demobilised, not, I suspect, without some deep regrets at parting from the special men and women with whom he had shared six years of his life.

---

\* George Ross, a lovely man - the ghillie.

# Chapter Twelve

## RETURN TO A GP'S LIFE . . . Radlett 1945-1971

My father was a very fit 50-year-old when he was demobilised. He enjoyed renewing old acquaintances and making new ones. He came to terms with the introduction of the National Health Service, though he had some pithy things to say about the abuses some people quickly discovered. He lost a number of patients through refusing to prescribe free items, like corsets, for perfectly healthy young women. He particularly enjoyed maternity work and was soon delivering the next generation babies in the village. Indeed his statistics for babies brought into the world rivalled his impressive score of salmon! He could be awake and fully alert the instant his phone rang to summon him to a case. He was also elected first Chairman of the Royal Air Force Association in the village.

I have delved into the disorderly array of memorabilia collected over numerous moves of house and country over the past five decades, and offer you extracts from some of his letters to span the latter part of my father's long life.

**1948**

*Grove House,*
*Radlett*
*Sunday*

*. . . Your hen pheasant was a tremendous treat for us and provided a rare banquet. Most tender and as I sadly parted with the last fork full of tender flesh I had the vision of the "airborne filly" soaring through the oaks and the thrilling report of your gun with the exciting sprint to collect the prize!!! . . .*

*In the Train*
*Monday*

*. . . Uncle Bill and Auntie Wooda kindly called for me and my LUGGAGE on Sunday at Oykel, so it was grand to have a day at Ord, all fresh and bathed in warm sunshine. I even went for a 12 mile ride with Fiona this morning and nearly met my Waterloo*

*when Winston bolted off like a demon and was in supreme control for three miles. Now I can hardly sit down and he did give me an anxious time as he was travelling at an incredible rate and had I fallen off or taken a toss on the hard metalled road – well – even hospital might not have accepted me!!!*

My father's dear friend, Bertie Sutton, died at about this time. I think he would be honoured to have one of Bertie's obituaries included in his memoirs. This is the one I found among his papers (three suitcases full!):

Air Chief Marshal Sir Wilfrid Freeman writes:

*Although the obituary notice of Bertie Sutton showed that he achieved considerable success and reached high rank and position, it scarcely does justice to the effect he had on the intellectual development of the many RAF officers who came under the influence of his stimulating personality and intellect. For many years at the RAF Staff College at Halton, Cranwell and in India his unusual knowledge and appreciation of literature and art and his ability to impart his own enthusiasm to others had a profound and lasting effect on the lives and minds of many officers. Those who came in contact with him never failed to benefit therefrom, and must always be deeply grateful for the avenues of interest he opened up for them. Like his father, Canon Sutton, he enjoyed the open air and every form of sport; a fearless rider to hounds, as he was a fearless pilot in the war of 1914-18, a keen shot, and a good fisherman, and a more than competent poacher.*

*There have been and probably will be greater RAF officers than Bertie Sutton, but there will be none more deeply loved and admired for his intellectual gifts, wide reading, and human understanding.*

Peter presented an Official Standard to the local branch of the RAF Association in memory of his 7 Squadron chief. It is kept in Christchurch, Radlett. At the memorial service to my father, the congregation were invited to gaze upon the standard – " . . . now draped proudly to the memory of two gallant gentlemen." A very touching tribute.

**1949**

*The Haven*
*Oykel-land*
*Thursday P.M.*
*April 1949*

... I need not mention how much I missed your cheery company on the river to-day ...

... This is really a wee note to welcome you on your arrival at BNC and to wish you the best of luck for the Trinity Term. My mind and heart are too full to tell you how much this joyous holiday has meant to me. We have shared in a rich realm of hearty and thrilling sport. We have had many heart-aches over our losses and disappointments – but the thrills are abundant. Never will I forget the landing of your first fish (Even Miles Brunton from his sick room sent you congrats this afternoon) that initial view of your bent rod at "action stations" sent me off like Zatopek in the Olympic 5000 metres. I ran 300 yards with my fish, feeling as light as a cream cracker biscuit!!! I gazed at the spot this evening and felt how supremely lucky we are to have known the beauty and peace of this unique sanctuary. But age will never dim the golden hour we spent together last night. I know too, how long that memory will last for you. Dear Huddy gave you a marvellous "nursery school" and your days on the ever-responsive water of the Brora matured your casting and approach to the rod technique.

... As the sun went down on the majestic splendour of the hill – I saw you running into the heavenly glow and your isolation in the fiery sunset with the noble peak of Canisp and his companions to enhance the scene was beyond description. Such is the treasure of our memories of the loveliest holiday I have ever known. Can we ever forget too, the incredible thrill of that hour on the Einig Falls and "The Perch" as the defiant Einig electrified us with the speed and awe of his ageless power?...

*Radlett, Sunday*

... When I arrived at Gordonbush the river was low and I fished with my 12ft-rod and fine line – this was grand sport and one 15 lb fish gave me as good a time as your acrobatic fish in the Einig Falls Pool. The small rod handled the fish beautifully and the cast seemed as thin as my hair. However, I tailed the fish after nearly 1/2 an hour with a salute from about 20 greylag geese, curlews and mallard ducks. Then the rains came and I saw the magic rise of a Highland river – that thrilling episode of the fluvial sparkling river suddenly awakening, until the full majesty of a roaring spate assumed command. I quickly changed my instrument from a 1st violin to a cello and I drove home in a thrilling sunset with five silver fish in the boot and I had communications with five other fish!!

Then followed that dusky bath in the golden peaty water and as I stretched and revelled in the luxury of that bath I caught all the fish over again and most of the ones I lost!! Then, believe it or not, my hostess had arranged for us to have salmon and roast grouse for dinner!! Mrs T[*] has over 100 brace of birds and two deer in her deep freeze. The moors were so bountiful last season that I noted the game book recorded nearly 2,000 birds and the river produced over 1,000 salmon . . .

. . . I stayed the night at Ord and lunched with Jane at Heathfield and Phil motored me to Inverness. Jim had just sold 150 young sheep @ £9/10/- per head at Tain – a useful cheque!! Lambing is in full swing at Ord and Cadboll . . .

**1950**

*Grove House*
*Park Road*
*Radlett*
*Herts*
*29 1/50*

. . . Work is simply frantic and I'm doing a "mountain" but carefully expending my energy under the relentless pressure. A spate of very critical cases is a drain on one's energy . . .

. . . I'm glad you enjoyed The Creation – I am at present revelling in Beethoven's IX Choral which I have in an album of 9 records given to me by W/Cd Simms, Musical Director of the RAF . . .

. . . I had a lovely day out shooting last Monday and after the long rest my gun performed to the tune of six pheasants all with single shots from the right barrel!! Travelling down wind in crisp air and sunshine the "swing" worked according to plan and it was

---

[*] Jessie Tyser, his generous hostess over many years.

*a day of "cocks" only, otherwise I think I would have had over a dozen. Then, the only driven partridge of the day was a crisp finish of the season. Now I must put some wool in the trumpet!!!*

*Gordonbush*
*Brora*
*Sutherland, NB*
*19 iv/50*

*... I longed for you each day at Oykel where <u>you</u> could not have failed to land 1.75 fish per day. We had lovely water all the time and beat the 77 last year by two. Our total of 79 for 6 rods was commendable as three of the rods had only battled with trout on the "dry fly". Still, Harold and Elizabeth Ridley collected 7 fish each. Huddy recorded 15, Dr Mimpriss 19 and the wily old Dr. 25 – I landed all my fish in thrilling solitude (except 1) and my final fish (my 200th) was on "greased line" in the Big Scallopie. This fish was a gem as I was deep in the pool – the gigantic pillars of limestone loomed above and 700 feet aloft the ravens watched me battle and gave vocal support. The pool was placid and the sweet note of a tiny warbler welcomed the first pair of sand martins (15 iv/50). I watched my "S" bend in the line vanish down the pool – then the unbounded thrill to witness the double s bend of the line suddenly bend and whirr through the water. I daren't strike or move – I gazed high up at the ravens and the whizz of the reel told me he was on – then he shot about everywhere and leapt out of the water time and again. Can you imagine a more joyous spot with those mighty rocks to play a fish and I finally tailed the silver beauty just above the Wee Scallopie.*

*I got another from your point in "The Washerwoman" also on greased line and believe me I don't think any mortal in Great Britain revelled in his bath as much as I did that night. I hope the fish arrived safely on Tuesday to welcome you home from the south so that you could have a feast before returning to the city of dreaming spires ...*

*Radlett*
*8/7/50*

*... I was greatly pleased with your letter and it revived all the unforgettable thrills we shared in the wonderful Strath Oykel – Einig. I can safely say these happy days together were the happiest I*

have ever spent. Time can never erase from my memory the thrills of your four exciting fish. I have re-enacted those scenes many times since my return. The capture of your first Einig fish was the supreme moment of my fishing career. With the celebrated "Perch" almost awash and the roaring Einig falls in all their glory – I was crouching on a shelf of ageless rock adjacent to the Grey Wagtails' thrilling nest. Then suddenly the whizzing reel as contact was made with an adolescent Einig fish and "action stations" was sounded.

Then you were presented with a priceless memory and I can still see that 5ft leap as your lively fish made his desperate effort to part company with your own selection of that wee March Brown. It was shocking for me to miss with the initial effort of the gaff. But only the grey wagtail was there to witness the retreat from the Perch with fish secure at last. This fish was worth a dozen spring fellers and on the light rod and greased line a fish from "The Perch" is to my mind the supreme triumph.

But the ravens saw another view which happily you almost shared in solitude. Again your wee March Brown lured a fish and a salmon too at that. I wish I had seen the early stages and the "take" in glorious "Wee Scallopie" – but that memory is yours alone. It was not until my "radar" picked up your call, so tremendously exciting, that sent me off on the 400 meters – I know I arrived breathless but it was the perfect finish to land a fish in that "monsoon."

Then "the Gremlins" provided that glorious fish from "Georges." what a fighter – again the heavens opened and the pool was in wizard order – so much was added to the thrill as your captive dashed upstream to the head of the boiling torrent – I greatly enjoyed this capture and your commendable handling of the fish – as I know you had parted company with 3 or 4 previously. Yes, a fish from "Georges" is a gem when high above, perched on the ancient wall – that delicious note of the wren is carried on the wings of the wind and mingles with the roar of the torrent. Perhaps our final fling was to you the richest surprise. After that fruitless day – awful gales and relentless rains – the tyrant "Senior" forced his son to go forth. For "Skuith" had the gift awaiting, the lure of the Torrish and I was confident despite a swift rise would not deny us. That was a glorious finish and a worthy battle – how my heart leapt and bumped as I saw your fish heading for the Buck Run. It was a grand capture and very skilfully done. On reflection we might have had three fish that night as we both had more than enthusiastic offers from the Washerwoman.

*Heaven, it's away past midnight and a storm rages – surely the pitch at Lord's will not be evil for Oxford tomorrow after Oxford's grand effort . . .*

Grove House<br>
Radlett<br>
12 xi/50

My dearest Michael

Your thrilling letter with all its exciting news filled me with delight and pride and I hasten to send you my warmest congratulations on your superb running. To get your selection with the Oxford III team is a most valiant effort and I think I am more thrilled than you could possibly be. Further, when all are so keen, with a host of runners, your selection is all the more creditable . . .

. . . Cuppers must have provided you with the greatest thrill ever, in your sporting career and I'm certain the worthy place of your several (Brasenose) teams was in great measure due to your own keenness and inspiration. I had calculated that from the form of trials and the galaxy of talent in other colleges the best you could hope for was VIth or VIIth in the Cuppers. What a field there must have been at the start with 200 eager runners and I would have loved to have been in the crowd at the finish to cheer you and your teams home.

It is clear that BNC with the high placings of your II and III teams gives you the premier position in the inter-collegiate duels. I have pictured your lively imaginations during the thrill of cuppers, when running to your last atom of energy, your vibrating vision spurred you to further effort and how tremendous it must have been to find you could crash past so many in that last ½ mile and to register such a worthy place with so few breasting the tape in front of you!! How you must have revelled in that bath afterwards and with the mental and physical hazard of the dislocated toe I don't hesitate to say your own running was tremendous -Bravo!

But soaring to the stratum of final joy is the reality of your being selected to run for Oxford III and at your first effort running so well. I was most thrilled to read of your exploits . . . You have now registered on the scroll of your memory that priceless treasure which will provide you with golden hours in the years ahead. Your Cirencester trip and run must have given you endless thrills and I only hope you equalled your effort yesterday when running at

*Cheltenham. I shall await details of the run with uncommon interest . . .*

*Michael and Fiona at the Caledonian Ball, 1950.*

*Grove House*
*Radlett*
*Sunday 11 pm*

*. . . Fiona is thrilled with Thomas's and is also most comfortable and happy at the hostel. Simon\* and Hawkie have just returned from London as Simon motored Fiona back with a multitude of medical books and half a human skeleton . . .*
*. . . I have had three cracking days shooting, 50 head of game*

---

\* Mary's son, Peter's nephew - also a doctor.

each time and I am having some thrills with the driven partridges as they are so wild. Last week I went with the Kearsley's party and we got 42 pheasants and 8 partridges and some various. It was most amusing as "PIXIE" was on top form and insisted on following me everywhere and much to the amusement of everyone she retrieved **all** the Pheasants to my hand irrespective of the gun who shot them and by her devotion and behaviour she was convinced I had shot the lot!!! ...*

Balnagowan Arms Hotel
Oykel Bridge
By Lairg
25/IV/51

My dearest Michael

I was most thrilled to receive your welcome and entertaining letter last night and Huddy promptly investigated the literature of the Ice Age caves near Inchnadamph and was tremendously entertained by your diligent researches ...

... Yesterday was a memorable day and will remain long in my memory and will last until the final setting of the sun. The sun was gilding the high tops still snow-mantled and the marker stood at 2 feet at the bridge. I wandered off in solitude and the prospect looked grim as I gave the celebrated Washerwoman and Junction a strenuous flogging with every variety of fly – but NOT a touch. So I wandered on to the lower beat and passed many sheep all so weakly with no food and all looking totally unable to cope with the strain of lambing. The mortality will be about 50% and nature is ruthless in claiming a terrible toll.

Two buzzards were away to the left and I heard the raven call with his raucous note from high up above the Upper Scallopie. How perfect the pool looked so I selected a fly and entered the pool with a splashing waterfall 600ft up in the thrilling ravine and the ageless rock all so thrilling on the far side. I had high waders and the temperature was 40 deg. but I decided to give the pool a worthy cast. The raven gave me a radar call and exactly opposite the angler's rock the reel suddenly screamed with excitement and then a most lively fish shot about the pool with much high jumping. I had to cope with him 15 minutes – but oh how glorious in that lovely

---

* He was sometimes invited to shoot at gundog trials. A singular tribute to his marksmanship.

*pool and I led him to the lower track and tailed him there. It was a lovely fish 8 ½ lbs with sea lice attached. I then passed the scene of your triumph last year – but the Wee S was a blank although it was given three flies. Now I went on to draw the Long also blank and crossed the rocky path to reach what I term* the Pastoral Symphony (Rock-Langwell). *There I lunched and felt the afternoon would give me many thrills. It did!!!*

*After food, I greased my line and selected a small fly and never did I witness such thrills. Oh how I longed for you to be there – this is what happened: – 8 1/2, 6 1/2, 9 1/2, 8 1/4, 7, 7 1/2, 8 1/4 lbs. Seven clean fish all landed solo: Upper Scallopie (1) Rock (3) Black Eye (1) Stone (2). My record for a day on the Oykel. Then can you imagine the hotel front at 7.30 p.m. with 18 on the concrete!!! Somehow the bath that night was perhaps the best I have known and as we now have new beds in all the rooms. I slept until the tea arrived at 7.30 a.m. . . .*

*Balnagowan Arms Hotel*
*Oykel Bridge*
*By Lairg*
*Sunday 29 1V/51*

*My Dearest Michael*

*As you may guess we have just returned from the Sunday trip, to the "Western Realm" of beauty. We were presented with a new aspect of natural beauty. Ben More, Canisp, Suilven and Stack Polly were all mantled in heavy snow and your conqueror B More looked all the more unconquerable in the golden glow – I pictured your scene of last midsummer and wondered how you succeeded in getting so near the summit on that NW face. What a thrill you must have had. Then the Limestone region of Elphin looked grim and presented us with evidence of starvation, as we could see ewes lying dead with the lamb hardly born. High above, the hoodie crows and gulls soared in anticipation of an orgy. Quinag refused to allow us a fleeting glimpse of his ageless summit and persisted in cloaking himself with cloud above the snow-line. But it was a thrill and how much we missed your companionship.*

*The Sabbath, of course, is a wonderful interlude for fishers and gives me a much needed rest of body and limb.*\* *The week closed last*

---

\* No fishing allowed on Sundays.

*night with our score at 77 and I have had 23 fish on the scales. Last evening I was alone up the Einig and got a grand fish to take my fly from "the Perch". The Einig was angry and was tumbling down in fury and I only had a wee bit of rock to balance on. About 100,000 stalwarts were shouting themselves hoarse at Wembley at that moment — I thought of this and the incredible contrast to my isolated thrill. But again, I was thwarted and in twisting round to make for the adjacent schist we parted company and I'm certain had you been there with the rod I would have gaffed this delightful fish. So I left the Perch after this grand thrill and went to the Einig Run, 100 yards below the falls. So far, my score had been zero for the day and a biting N. wind revealed the presence of an Arctic front and I felt I would wander home without a fish.*

*I quietly fished the run and all was blank — then I spotted a snout just breaking the rough surface at the very tail of the pool. I changed my fly for a wee Green Highlander and approached the pinpoint with beating heart. The fly circled the final swivel and I waited that breathless moment — spontaneously came that thrilling tug. I daren't strike and whizz went the reel. Twice the line went down to a few yards of backing.*

*The distant falls roared defiance and urged the fish to do battle. Then off darted the fish at express speed towards the "Bent," 80 yards of line out and off I started to keep up with the fish. Then I had 10 minutes of the most exciting time I've known. I couldn't do a thing about it. I had to wade past trees and branches — but still the cast held fast and I was now fighting the fish 50 yards down stream in a roaring torrent. At last I steadied him and his silver side rode the crest of the rapid water — now 15 yards and he tried again to bolt. I saw I was only 100 yds from the Bent and it was now or never — with the point of my rod in branches I wound him in and I got a friendly swirl to float the fish past my gaff — I missed!!! and Einig defied me still. How I gasped!!! I disentangled my line from the tree as the fish was tired — now I waded out and guided the fine prize between me and the bank. He was mine at last and I sat down near a cheviot ewe and lamb and the Einig rolled on. The walk home was a feast of memories and I rested a while and gazed from the high bank down the Washerwoman towards the spot where you landed your 11 lb fish, April 20th 1949 . . .*

*. . . All the migratory birds were coming in and lots of jolly wee wrens almost fly through one's waders. The grey wagtail appeared on Wednesday and lots of deer frequent the bank in search of food . . .*

*A fine catch.*

Gordonbush<br>
Brora<br>
Sutherland<br>
Scotland<br>
11 V/51

... *A thrilling final day with 3 lively fish on the wee rod just the perfect finish to a wonderful holiday. I have tailed all my 11 fish here and the melting snow has kept the fresh fish running. These spring fish on the 12ft-rod have roared my pulse up and high jumpers never broke the fine tackle once. But they fought to the last and had to be fairly whacked before I could tail them. The greased line "take" is a most exciting affair and even Mrs Tyser was impressed at last. But she prefers the more muscular technique. The ghillies have seen nothing like it and gasped as they watched the juddering line streak out across the pool and then the spontaneous aquabatics. This last week by the pastoral banks has been wonderful. The full Highland symphony laid on. The wild geese chorus and legions of curlews and moorland birds – then the hungry lambs – it was superb -finally the cuckoo reached here last Monday. Then at night, the mighty peat fire and that stimulating bath and the treasured memories of the day as one stretches in that peaty water. Colin Dalrymple, the Earl of Stairs's son, has been my companion this week and one of the Gibbs, both grand company . . .*

**1952**

*Sutherland Arms Hotel*
*Brora*
*Sutherland*

*. . . Huddy (now 77) is in fine form and his usual charming self – his tackle is incredible with every rod almost in pieces and his lines like treacle!!! An absolute scream to see John George Edward's[*] face when he unpacked – it was tremendous. . .*

*. . . How can you expect me to write to you with Huddy[*] telling Walter Mimpriss all about the saw fly and how it lays an egg in a hidden grub buried 1" deep in the hardest wood. Huddy has just related that this incredible insect penetrates with a hair tube 1" long, down through this hard wood and having plotted the insect, actually lays its egg in the vitals of the unsuspecting grub!!! . . .*

*Gordonbush*
*Brora*
*19 iii/52*

*. . . The river is the lowest that ever Mrs Tyser has seen it in March for 30 years. Then at 11 am the rain came in earnest and in 4 hours it was up at 2 1/2 feet and still rising rapidly. I knew that the rapid rise would put the fish down but the prospects for the next few days*

---

[*] The ghillie.

[*] Huddy, Dr A C Hudson, was a fellow of the Royal Zoological Society and used to love to take his friends to see unusual special exhibits at London or Whipsnade zoos. To see him eating his breakfast before going on the river was priceless. He was under the impression that he could get on the river more quickly if he tackled his porridge, kedgeree and toast and marmalade simultaneously, discoursing the while on some learned subject!!

*are excellent, so I should have abundant sport with all the new arrivals from the sea. It is thrilling in the upper river, cock grouse are most numerous and battle all around me. Then the curlew trumpet sonata is in full swing with Golden, Ring and Green plover all adding their musical gems. But the greatest joy is the chorus of over 100 Grey Lag Geese which are constantly playing around and landing within 150 yards of the pools. This is a great joy to me and the whole scene is enriched by the stream of wildfowl who are busy arranging for the spring nuptials . . .*

*Grove House, Radlett. (Photograph taken by Humphrey and Vera Joel.)*

## 1955-58

My sister, Fiona, married Alan Bond, a Kings Dragoon Guards Officer in 1955. They were posted to Malaya. I married Rosemary Gammell in 1958, having spent 3½ years in Cuba and Colombia. My father was fascinated by our letters from these countries and in spite of never having been in tropical lands could imagine our daily routines and surroundings with remarkable accuracy. He was supportive and deliciously intrigued by my romance with Rosemary, which due to an emergency posting to Chile had to be concluded in three months, from first meeting to marriage.

Grove House gardens. (Photograph taken by Humphrey and Vera Joel.)

*Peter poses among his dahlias.*

In 1958 "Hawkie" a dear friend, and my father's housekeeper for many years, died of a tumour. He was to have considerable difficulty in finding a suitable replacement.

**1958**
In August Rosemary joined me in Chile, three months after we were married.

> Grove House
> Radlett
> 15th September 1958

> *Dearest Rosemary*
>
> *A wee letter all for your dear self to tell you what a gigantic thrill the arrival of your letter gave to me. Thank you a thousand times and you can imagine I have read it several times . . . Of course I have pictured all the manifold joys associated with your early days in your new home and I can see M. fairly sprinting home*

*from the office.*

*But I did enjoy so much reading about your initial days in your new home . . . Little Elsa sounds a gem and this must give you and M. great joy with her care and affection so willingly given. I look at the* Esso *map every night and know my way round every* Via *and already, I have all the banks pin-pointed and will follow all your trips and local excursions . . .*

*. . . Spring will be bursting forth in your realm and every day will reveal new thrills in your garden. I can picture the excitement you will find each time you journey forth on your weekend trips. All the new sounds of birds and local scents will delight your heart. The news of the piano has greatly thrilled me and I know M. will revel in the evening recital as he stretches his weary limbs and listens to the talented offering of harmony. It is most fortunate you have found a good instrument and you can gladden your heart during the long hours of isolation. It is so vital to keep your joints and technique up to scratch and I know how much you will enjoy playing to Michael . . .*

*A favourite rhino enjoying Peter's pears.*

*... This year my pears are better than ever and M. will tell you that this statement from me is of some import. I have bagged 200 pears and another 100 are in daily peril of the impudent tormentors, the Tom Tits!!! On the rockery our massed cyclamen are like a mighty ballet, quite a sensation and to-day about 200 most beautiful butterflies were feasting in the riot of Michaelmas daisies.*

*Next week wee Sarah will be 1 and there is much excitement in Johore Bahru as the packing gathers momentum. – They can now say "we sail for home next month!!!"*

*A country doctor's lunch-time break.
Relaxing with Juno and Rona.*

**1959**

*Grove House*
*Radlett*
*9.vii.59*

My dearest "TRIO"

*Imagine the spontaneous joy which swept into my mortal frame when bang in the middle of my Handley Page Surgery at the aerodrome this morning, Hetty put through a phone call and said "Oh Dr, here is a cable for you, I'll read it at once." So the nurse handed me a pencil and I wrote down the tidings of great joy. So my dearest ones, let me send you my most loving greetings and I do rejoice with you over the safe arrival of precious wee Crispin Hugh . . .*

*. . . To return to the most thrilling news, of course I send you dearest Rosemary, my warmest congratulations in your skill in presenting me with unbounded joy, in the gift of a precious Grandson. I will be quite honest and say that yesterday high noon I left the intense heat of the garden (102 deg. in the greenhouse, 85 in the shade) and returned to my peaceful bedroom to offer meditations for special help and comfort for you, as I had a profound feeling you were in labour and your delivery was imminent. So you can imagine what I felt like this a.m. when the joyous greeting cable arrived . . .*

*. . . Day dreams have filled my mind all day and I have pictured the arrival of wee Crispin for his feed and the sweet maternal reconnaissance of just every feature of your precious baby. I could see you holding him at arm's length and MAW with flushed cheeks beholding his son for the first time. I do hope you had a moderately short labour and now you feel comfortable with the United Dairies working to your personal comfort and the satisfaction of rearing wee Crispin. It is incredible to realise the wee chap will be almost a week old before this letter reaches you . . .*

*. . . Now dearest Rosemary, a further offer of thanks to you for your excellent entertaining newsletter which is so absorbing I can really enter your realm. As you know I love reading all your news, however local and I'm so glad to learn you feel stronger. Crispin looks a wee pet and how greatly I grieve I am unable to see him as a baby. I adore that snap of you both and think it is a gem and I carry it everywhere. Your spring season seems to be rushing ahead and the warmer days will suit you all and greatly benefit Mother and Son!! . . .*

**1961**

*1960. Fiona's family grows: Amanda's Christening,
with Sarah and Rosalind (right).*

In 1961 after a long and companionable courtship, interspersed with plenty of outings to London, Paula Colyer accepted my father's proposal of marriage. He was 66 and she was 54. Paula made her Peter work very hard to win her and he was by no means her only suitor. He searched diligently for a suitable engagement ring and to his delight he found an antique emerald and diamond one in Tessiers, New Bond Street. To their great sadness, one could almost say bitterness, because of my father's (totally innocent) divorce, they could not be married by the Church of England. A Registry Office had to suffice. Rules are rules, but to such a devout man and woman of such integrity, the hurt was very deep. He seldom went to church in Radlett thereafter, but on our visits loved to take us to early morning Communion in the little Church at Aldenham.

*Peter and Paula's wedding, 1961.*

Having been re-introduced to Paula during my summer leave, I was back in Chile. But Rosemary, Fiona, his sisters, Simon and a clutch of special friends wished them well at a happy party in the Café Royal. After a honeymoon in Sicily, Paula moved from the Red House to Grove House, and soon became an important and much-loved member of our family. To us she seemed, both in looks and in some characteristics, remarkably reminiscent of my mother.

To my father, his marriage meant a modification to his lifestyle, most especially to his holidays. At the time of his marriage his game book recorded 446 salmon. His generous hosts were one by one passing away, though he still received and accepted regular invitations from Jessie Tyser to fish the Brora. Paula found Jessie T somewhat overpowering and usually spent these weeks with the Patersons or at home.

For many years they enjoyed summer holidays on the continent and ranged as far afield as Yugoslavia and the Holy Land, often with friends. The pilgrimage to the Lands of the Bible, to both Old and New Testament holy places gave my father great joy. Though both had super friends of their own it was lovely for them after long years on their own to be able to share these experiences.

My father continued to practise in Radlett until his retirement in 1966 at the age of 71. His good friends and patients, Mr and Mrs Dick Bott and Mr and Mrs Leslie Kent (the artist) organised a wonderful party for him, attended by some 250 people. He received a book on Greek archæology and a cheque for £839:9s, a very generous sum indeed in those days. It was a heart-felt and warm "thank you" from families for whom he had cared over a span of forty-five years, including the war.

*Peter and Paula in the garden at Grove House.*

He and Paula remained in Radlett for a few more years. He attended some private patients (a nice gesture from his partners) and Paula continued her work in charge of an industrial medical centre.

*Grove House*
*Radlett*
*Shrove Tuesday 1968*

*My dearest "All"*

*We have just returned from our <u>most</u> enjoyable visit to Forres and let me say at the outset we found Crispin in tremendous form and he is obviously very happy at School . . .*

*. . . We arrived at School at 10 a.m. and found about 6 other cars with parents ready to contact the lucky boys who clustered round the windows . . .*

*. . . Before morning service we were welcomed by Mr Strange in his study and he told us Crispin was very happy – doing very*

*well in class and considering he was almost a week late he had settled remarkably well. Crispin sat with us in the gallery of chapel and we had a delightful service. A short drive round the sea front before lunch and then we claimed our table at the Wolferton Hotel. The first salmon of the season was on the menu and Crispin demolished a lovely grilled steak with much relish. As the sun was bright, we soon found our way to Corfe and to the museum there to see footprints of Dinosaurs . . . thence on to Studland where we had a stimulating walk on the wide stretch of sands . . . I found a huge patch of virgin sand and much to Crispin's surprise I made extensive drawings of the Queen Mary, Elephant, Crocodile, Aeroplanes, etc. etc. Crispin remarked several times "You must be the best drawer in the world Grandaddy." Then back to Corfe for tea before we returned to Forres, to hand him over at 5/15 p.m. The most happy day was ended all too quickly and in a few seconds he had dashed off to join his new friends – cheery and happy . . .*

*. . . I feel I must say with much pride, that your Crispin put up a most commendable show – we can all be proud of him – he speaks extremely good English, has a wide vocabulary\* and has beautiful manners. He told me, quite quietly, "Grandaddy I scored 4 goals in one game."*

*Doc with Dick Bott, admiring one of the gifts at his retirement party. Note our evergreen doctor – he was 71 at the time!*

---

\* Born and brought up in Chile.

**1970**

Grove House  
Radlett  
XVIth Sunday after Trinity

My Dearest Michael

It seems impossible that at this moment you are in NY and probably walking round the Metropolitan Museum of Art, whereas only 7 days ago we were all revelling in the sunshine at Thornford. I hope you found your visit to Germany was profitable and helpful to you in your business realm. I guess you were impressed by the marked efficiency of the German business machine and found the whole country organised and efficient . . .

. . . The boys would have a unique Sunday together at Forres and Andrew would delight in meeting Crispin at odd hours and I guess he was not slow in making friends and getting down to some football practice on the playing fields. His first letter will make you roar with laughter . . .

. . . I thought the Christening Service was delightful with wee Alistair performing perfectly. Actually on this vacation we seem to have seen so much of you all and the time doesn't seem to have rushed by like past leaves. I regret we didn't manage more social delights together, but personally I enjoyed the quieter days in the home and Cinders* really did pull out ALL the organ stops on the Kitchen Front. Poor Flash is quite lost without you all and keeps wandering around the various bedrooms and finding balls in every quadrant of the garden!!! . . .

. . . A most thrilling finish to the County Cricket Championship – well almost a finish (as Surrey and Lancs are playing the final match which has had all Sat. washed out by rain). Colin Cowdrey and the Men of Kent have pulled off a most staggering triumph as they were BOTTOM of the championship only 2 1/2 months ago and I can't see either Surrey or Lancs collecting 26 points in their last match. Cuttings enclosed for your interest and enjoyment. In S. Africa the final rugger test has left SA winners and thus the All Blacks have been dethroned. But the whole of the Tests have been a shameful display of brutal, disgusting foul play with blood and slaughter and many serious injuries and the refs. seem powerless to control and no-one was sent off!!! . . .

---

*Our nickname for Paula.

At this time a new entry in his Game Book indicates the start of series of happy holidays with Joe Paterson (no relation) and Death Bullmore fishing the May Fly season on Lough Curra and other loughs in Ireland.

My father always felt Death was one of the great unsung heroes of the Second War. By his invention of special night landing flare paths, Wing Commander Bullmore saved the lives of countless bomber crews who had hitherto crashed in fog. His flare paths enabled lost or badly shot up aircraft, often with radios out of action, to locate an airfield and land safely. By his drive and persistence he cut through the frustrating red tape and achieved acceptance for his scheme. My father always held that he should have been decorated.

In September 1968 he records with pride that Paula landed her first trout in Connemara. But her name ceases to appear thereafter. Fishing was not Paula's scene, but my goodness she could produce mouth-watering dishes with fish or game birds in her kitchen. Her Peter was forever awarding her "Gold Medals" for her culinary efforts for him and their friends. And before Paula was given charge of any pheasant or partridge, Flash, their lovely yellow Labrador was given a work-out: "Seek, seek, seek" and "Hi-lost" searching for birds hidden in the garden! Dogs loved Peter, not least I suspect because he had a cunning habit of sending scraps their way with a deft flick of the wrist, hoping his hosts wouldn't notice!

*Michael and his family on a Brazilian beach in 1971.*

**1971**

*Second Sunday in Epiphany*
*17.1.71*

... I'm so sorry for you all in this tremendous heat and those vile mosquitoes at night. How I would declare war on them with the Flit gun ...

... I had a super morning's shooting on Wed. I couldn't make the whole day as I had 3 most acute cases which I couldn't leave for more than a few hours. I had great luck in the draw and I started at No. 10 stand and being cocks only I had a most exciting time and one I didn't expect at the end of a long line of guns. But to my surprise I had most of the cocks over me and probably 40-50 hens – what a time I could have had if it had been "free for all" I think I would have had 15-20 birds. It was most exciting picking out the cocks and I shot 6 at this stand and when I left at lunchtime we'd got about 60!!!

I had about 20 birds over me at one time and I nearly twisted my neck off trying to pick out the cocks. Such tremendous fun. I came home at lunch time with 2 brace of pheasants and 2 hares in the boot of the car. Didn't Paula and Flash rejoice!!!

The first snowdrops are out – such lovely flowers and they are so exquisite in form and design. I whisper as I look at them, "I'm looking into the face of God" ...


*Once more returning Shrovetide bids us hail*
*The Feast of Pancake and the flow of Ale*
*In Brasenose held, prime revel of the year -*
*Day of unmatched, unmitigated Beer.*

*AD 1850*

*Shrove Tuesday 1971*

*My dearest all*

Just as you are sitting down to lunch there is a lively colourful scene in the old college hall – yes much merriment, as the new ale verses of 1971 are presented and the pancakes are rushed in to the "long-haired hearties" (as I'm told 75% of the chaps are long-haired and scruffy.)!!! This quite regrettable style has to be tolerated *for the present, but I don't doubt for one moment the quality of the grey matter beneath the mop of hair is quite as fertile as in days of yore! . . .*

*. . . Of course you know we won the final cricket Test at Sydney but I am going to send on the complete reports as the whole match was simply tremendous. The final day was breath-taking and I saw the fall of those 5 vital wickets. In fact the whole of the final day via satellite, the picture was superb – the atmosphere intense and with the opening overs I felt Australia would get the runs and save the series, especially as England had 3 members of the side injured. Then Illingworth sent down a string of super overs and bagged 2 vital wickets and then the Aussies' tail crumbled and I got so excited Flash thought I had changed my species. The pictures were so perfect – one could follow the ball from the bat to the fence and then we were given a repeat (in slow motion) of each wicket as it fell. Bravo to the boys and now "The Ashes" will soon be back at Lord's.*

*You will be interested to know that to keep myself in a calm balanced state, I make a detailed inspection of the marvellous fish fossil from Brazil literally every day – this gem gives me endless and tremendous joy – again many, many, thanks . . .*

*. . . The sun still shines in our stricken land and my hours have been greatly brightened this evening when Aunt Nella phoned, giving us the good news that she had spoken to you on the phone. How splendid and grand news to hear the flight out was comfortable and all is well. I can picture the morning visit to your colourful market – AND your breakfast table crowded with a vast selection of wonderful fruits. Oh for a slice of PAW-PAW. Aunt Nella was in grand form and is going down again this Sat. and will have the thrill of seeing Crispin playing in the FIRST XI (Bravo and really most commendable for his age.) This will be a real stimulus to Andrew. I also hear Crispin is doing very well in the academic field . . .*

*. . . I expect Richard is greatly enjoying "The Elders"\* and will give them a chat in Spanish – I can also picture Alistair now highly mobile and mostly in the prone position. I don't expect he is an energetic "rocker of cots" as per Richard! . . .*

---

\* Rosemary's parents.

*Grove House*
*Radlett*
*11 iii/71*

*My Dearest All*

*England seems to be a different place to-day — even the birds are singing merrily and scarlet PO vans are once more darting around the countryside. So after the long weeks of stagnation and frustration we can now resume normal relations and as I said in my PS yesterday our first mails have been delivered. I can well imagine dearest R how you have longed to receive letters from the boys . . .*

*. . . I am thrilled to read you are enjoying such success with your orchids. I have 1 Cymbidium almost to bloom (6 flower buds) but my Azaleas are a sensation and the front lobby is a blaze of colour and delights one and all. The spring flowers in the garden are glorious and we have had the finest February for many a year. Even the white-headed blackbird you have seen so many times is revelling in the colour banks and is on the nesting site again . . .*

PRESS BOX TV Set Radlett 7 xii 71 (He was almost 77).

## Special Rugger report on Oxford v Cambridge

All is set for a thrilling match – the stands crowded – the whole touch-line area – crowded with enthusiastic Prep-school boys – the band playing and a fine crisp, December afternoon. There is little to choose between the two sides although press reports favour Cambridge to win. Oxford have brought in a big American lock forward as they are too light to combat the heavy Cambridge scrum – this is a calculated risk, as Neville 6'3", has only played in two rugger games previously. The Oxford Capt Owen Jones has recovered from his attack of hepatitis, contracted when playing with the Ox and Cam. Touring XV in S America.

Here come the teams – emerging from the tunnel beneath the Royal Box – Cambridge the first and there is much cheering – then the Dark Blues trot out – more lusty cheering. It seems strange to me that 75% of the teams have long tresses of hair and massive side whiskers – surely this suggests we are in for some gladiatorial combats resembling ancient Rome. Here is the Ref. Mr Lewis of Welsh-Wales! He looks at his watch and Oxford winning the toss kick off to a gigantic roar from the stands and "treble" yells from the side enclosures . . . Thus for 20 minutes it was all Cambridge and my blood pressure rose to astronomical heights.

*BUT* this is the important factor. The Oxford line HELD. Oxford could have lost the match in that first 20 mins and the scoreboard showed 0-0. Then, as Cambridge had won so much of the ball – scrummage – line out and a succession of rucks – the miniature Oxford scrum half – received a good clean ball and out shot the ball to the Oxford centre and now for the first time in the match Oxford found themselves in Cambridge territory. A scrummage 35 yards from the Cambridge line found the Ref had penalised a Cambridge front-row man. To my surprise I saw the Oxford Capt detail Douglas, a *front line* forward, Newcastle and Univ., to take the kick. A breathless hush left Twickenham with its packed stands, absolutely silent. With meticulous care Douglas prepared his pitch for the kick and seemed to stand at least 10 sec with head bent and almost in meditation – the great silence erupted into a mighty crescendo of roaring cheers as the ball soared high up through the centre of the posts. Now this was the very stimulus needed to reveal an Oxford resurgence. They organised their scrum into a perfect machine, with the limping Yank always in the fray and 15 minutes later they won a line out. The ball reached the Oxford lines. Swiftly Heal shot the ball past his left centre and the ball appeared to reach the wing – but Cambridge rushed to block the hiatus – but the spirited Oxford back row rushed into the fray and somehow Carroll (from stand-off) appeared outside – the ball was somehow flicked into his hands and he dived over for a tremendous try. Here I was transported to realms unrepeatable and roared with delight. Flash, totally unable to comprehend my extraordinary behaviour. The Kick, again by Douglas, right from the touchline, only just failed BUT imagine the psychological effect on Cambridge, who should have been 15 pts up in the first 15 mins, to suddenly find themselves 7 points down . . . The scoreboard read Oxford 10pts Cambridge 0 and the whistle blew for half-time.

[Your correspondent had to take a drink here.]

As the first half found Cambridge "all over" the Oxford XV now we saw the absolute reverse of the first 10 mins of the second half. After 5 minutes Oxford wheeled on the opposing put-in and the Oxford back row paved the way for Seymour to boot the ball on and beat 2 Cambridge men in the run-in, to touch down for Oxford's second try. Here the whole Oxford XV rose to the heights and the miniature scrum half, Heal, now put in some superb kicking and the Oxford back-tackled with ruthless efficiency and with victory assured we now witnessed unforgettable moments, with Cambridge swept into oblivion and rushing into error at every turn. Everywhere from line-out to ruck the Oxford XV seemed to produce latent energy they just ran the ball everywhere with revealing confidence . . . The whole Oxford scrum swept in for the maul. They won it and ran the ball right. 50,000+ were now standing and roaring their heads off, as Jones came up from full back and joined in the line to create an overlap – he made no mistake and took his pass at top speed and the last I saw of him was a horizontal dive over the line in the corner and the Ref's arm raised high in the air for the final try. Here, with incessant cheering the weary Douglas arrived without being told, to take the kick and right from the touch line he almost converted his gallant Captain's thrilling try and the ball hit the post high up. Here the final whistle blew and Oxford had won a thrilling match, the largest winning score since before the war.

| | |
|---|---|
| Three penalty goals – three tries | 21 pts |
| to One penalty goal | 3 pts |

Note. Oxford's third successive win.

**1973**

After a two-month visit to Brazil:

*Grove House*
*Radlett*
*Easter Day 73*

My Dearest "All"

We are still in a stage of what one might call "Rehabilitation" as, until this a.m. we both did not awake until 9.45 a.m.!! The climate is not what one would expect from a late Easter, as very cold NE winds have swept in upon us ever since our arrival. But as Rupert Brooke wrote long years ago. "Oh to be in England now that April's there." is a superb reality – notwithstanding the cold, the whole garden is massed with glorious colour – and the scent of narcissi follows one round the paths and the rich song of the blackbird compels me to stop and listen to his rich "oboe" solo . . . that gallant soldier poet died on St George's Day, on the very eve of that disastrous attack on the Dardanelles. His great friend, who helped to bury him on Skyros, found time to write a hurried letter to his mother, but long before it reached England his loyal companion in arms fell mortally wounded from a Turkish sniper and joined that gallant company in the realms of glory. It is not hard to imagine the reunion of these comrades as "they crossed to the other side."

I pictured you all this morning, as you joined company with so many friends at your dear Church (our 1300 hours) and the reading of the Easter Canticles at the lectern. Yes, I could clearly see you standing there and it is hard to believe that, at this time next week, you will have parted company with your lusty sons and even before this letter reaches your hand.

On Good Friday the 'Three Hour Service" in Aldenham Church was the most beautiful devotional offering (but I do wish the church hadn't been so cold) . . .

 . . . This letter should be an expression of our very profound thanks to you both for giving us such a wonderful and unforgettable holiday. Every day revealed some measure of your great kindness to us and as you know we are tremendously grateful for such bountiful generosity. I have had ample time for reflection to contemplate the wonderful time we have had . . . By your gifts to us on our TWO trips to Brazil I have seen more of you and your family in these four years *than in the last 40 years and this has meant <u>so</u> much to me. I have seen <u>all</u> the boys in every stage of their young lives and with my fertile memory I have treasured memories that will last until the shades lengthen. So please accept our warmest thanks for your great kindness to us – and look how we revelled in your dear company as we sped along the wonderful roads on those long journeys up to the farm and Campos do Jordao. In the treasured nine weeks we did so much together and just think that through your kind agency I actually met "James Bond" for the FIRST time!!* Your skill and generosity in taking us to the Ballet was a real joy and was like a dream to witness the glory of Covent Garden in the heart of your great city of São Paulo . . .*

Forgive the inclusion of parts of the following long letter. For the fishers among our readers it will give pleasure. Bear in mind Peter was 78 ("a well mended kelt," he called himself) and Mrs Tyser was 80.

*Gordonbush*
*Sutherland*
*Vigil of the Ascension 1973*

*My dearest All*

*As you know I posted your letter this a.m. and just before going down to breakfast I noticed the skies had darkened and rain suddenly broke upon us like a monsoon. For an hour it "poured" rather like the rain storms we saw in Brazil and I knew the "burrns" would be overflowing within an hour and by mid morning I felt the river would be hopeless for fishing . . . Of course, fishing was hopeless as the fish had other ideas and as I stood by the stones the "piscatorial" scramble started.*

*I've been on salmon rivers before when spates have suddenly erupted, but never have I seen salmon running in such numbers before. It was literally a race and the fish were so eager to get up to the upper spawning beds, they ploughed through the rising stickles with backs and fins out of the water and often 3 or 4 abreast. Scores of fish were racing up the river from Snag to the Flat and I should think by noon there must have been 200 splendid lively fish in Phedair. I went up to the Falls and it was terrifying to see the power of the mighty torrent. It was quite remarkable that the river could have risen so rapidly and by 1 pm the river was bank high and*

---

[*] We took them to a 'Bond' film. Paula didn't enjoy it much but Dad certainly did!

*Phedair Stone was covered. I lunched by the mighty river and the roar of the falls was remarkable and I could see fishing would be hopeless for the day as branches, huge logs and debris were being swept along – But I rejoiced inwardly as I felt by tomorrow sport would be excellent and the blank days forgotten. It was fine all afternoon and I felt what a wonderful sight a Highland river is in full spate . . . So now my dearest ones, I'll drop down the shutters of mine eyes and greet you on the morrow.*

*Later: Ascension Day. Nicky McNichol soon had me fitted out and said, "The River's in grand 'orrrder'." and I simply could not wait to set off. As I drove down the drive I shouted with delight and recited James Hogg's immortal verse on old Scotia and went straight for Balnacoil where I met Richard[\*] who had just arrived from Kintradwell. He very kindly took me to Struan Run – which as you know is just below the Falls pool and immediately above the glorious wee Struan Pool. I stood on the rock just above the small "run in" to Struan and the holding area is no bigger than a squash court. We selected a small Hairy Mary, only size 7, and action stations was launched. I had only 6 feet of line out and within 2 minutes I felt a mighty tug and the reel was "singing" and the fish shot past me within a yard and made straight for the Falls pool. I simply could not check him and the line whizzed away right down to the backing. NOW the passage along the rough river, bang on the edge of the speedy torrent and holding the fish was stimulating in the extreme and with Richard's help we finally arrived at the Falls, with the fish shooting around at great speed. Here we had a thrilling battle and it was marvellous with the huge torrents roaring in and fish jumping everywhere. We were 10 minutes getting this fish under control but I felt he was securely hooked and with Richard holding my "tailer", it was after he made 3 final runs in the huge pool that I reeled him firmly in and Richard soon had him securely on the rock and yes Sir!! We were in business at last!! Of course, without Richard's help I should probably have lost this fish, as I couldn't play this lively fish – hold the tailer and scramble along the narrow rock edges. Richard then went to the high rock above the falls (Mrs T won't let me go there without Alistair) and I went down to Struan. The pool was in glorious order. Away down at the Flat Jessie T was playing a fish and in half an hour had a brace on the bank and 100 yards above me Richard was already into a fish. I launched my fly over Struan and would say here I am using only a*

---

[\*] Richard Tyser

light 12' rod (Much less tiring for 70+).

Fish were jumping everywhere and so near to me, they splashed my face and spectacles. Very soon my reel was singing again and I had a lively fish shooting all over the pool. Landing a fish is not easy with the irregular rocks and I had to walk him up which he didn't like and after much jumping and 3 attempts I finally reeled him in firmly and tailed him speedily with the tailer. Richard got 2 fish from the Falls so the Trio had 6 fish by 11 a.m. and it was a glorious morning.

Just as I was carrying this silver gem to the little van Mrs T drove up and issued firm instructions from "the Bridge". "Dr W go along to the Flat, it is full of fish and with the strong W wind behind you you will do well." So off I went rejoicing and the pool looked superb and in glorious order, with 150 yards of perfect fishing. Fish were moving everywhere so I continued with my little Hairy Mary – so small I felt for such big water – but Richard remarked "for the end of May the water is about 3 deg. WARMER than the air." Mrs T went off to her beloved "Jessie Pool" and Richard to lower pools.

Curlew and plover and cuckoos greeted me as I presented my gradually lengthening line to the head waters of this lovely pool. Half way down – casting my fly far over, a mighty tug and the whizzing reel confirmed that I was in contact with a lively fish. He made a long dash right to the head of the pool and into the swift torrents. I was, of course, talking to myself at this stage combined with mixed thoughts of the Ascension and Caledonia stern and wild. So along this high grassy bank I firmly walked him up and after a couple more spirited rushes his silver side showed up and I reeled him by hand. I simply couldn't believe I had 3 fish on the bank. At this stage Richard joined me for lunch at the Hut and what a lunch: superb salmon sandwiches, half a roast grouse – York ham, a bottle of beer and a Thermos of grand coffee.

[At Snag 2 pages and 3 fish later] . . . Not a bit of it, he set off again up stream at high speed and before I realised it he was jumping out of the water right at the head of the pool and my line was out well into the backing. I raced along, along the grassy bank and got abreast of him and gave him much pressure and walked him 30 yards down stream to a better landing – when he was almost at my feet and apparently ready for tailing, the hook parted company and I had anguish but saluted a gallant fish who had battled so bravely as he floated to freedom. I sat down in the warm sunshine and took the tea haversack out of the wee van and what a sight to see

*6 silver beauties lying in the 2 fish baskets. Two cups of hot china tea was just the thing at this stage, as it was 17.50 hours. I felt I would finish this memorable day by returning to the Flat. Jessie T had gone home and Richard was up at the Falls. The Flat had dropped a couple of inches and I re-tied the wizard little Hairy Mary. The cuckoos and curlews were joining in a lovely avian duet as I launched the line over the lovely water. I soon had a lively tug but no contact but it told me fish were still interested. Sure enough, a long cast far over the main stream swung into the likely lie and in a jiffy he was on and what a battle to finish the day. Could I land my seventh fish of the day, my first time ever at Brora??? Such a battle and I felt anxious as he jumped and jumped and jumped. To my relief he tired and I laid on the pressure so he couldn't make another dash – I reeled in rapidly and he came right over the stones and with a shout of triumph I tailed him firmly. My 7th fish for the day was on the bank. How I longed for you two dear souls to be with me to share my joy.*

*It was now almost 1900 hrs as a truly happy and moderately senile piscador drove the van down to G Bush, and that marvellous peat bath was all ready to receive my rather tired limbs. Yes that bath and the relaxation in the hot water was glorious and I blessed that wee fly, which Megan had tied 10 years ago, as it had caught me 7 silver beauties.*

*The surprise of to-day has staggered me. Only 2 fish caught by Mrs T are the sole entries in the famous game book for the first 3 days of the week. The arrival of your grand card inspired me and gave me great joy. That heavy rain was for just 1 hour yesterday am did the trick and just think of it, there are 23 silver beauties on the slab tonight.*

*I fear I have tired you – but I had to put "IT" all down and it's now past mid-night, so I will now to my bed and post this opus in two separate envelopes. The river will drop rapidly and scores of fish will go over the Falls, but there will be some likely "takers" on the morrow for me.*

*All is silent in the Strath and all asleep except me but very, very soon I'll be dreaming.*

> *With all my dearest love to you all,*
> *From your loving Dad and P. Puck*

These fish took my father's tally to 547 salmon, which he was to extend to 555 by the end of his holiday. He was only to catch two more salmon, in

1978, as guest of Death Bullmore on the Torridge in Devon.

The next day in a letter headed THE GLORIOUS FIRST OF JUNE my father described how he caught six fish.

> *. . . a cock grouse saluted this 15th victory from the Sutherland territory above Stockan; thus, my dearest ones, ended my unforgettable "SAGA OF THE STRATH" and what a holiday – early frustration – then sudden and spontaneous joy and now 15 fish, all thrillers, and 9 dramatic losses – all precious memories. How I have loved writing these pages to you – I may have wearied you but in the writing you have both been very near to my heart.*
> *Your loving Dad and P. Puck*

He continued to shoot regularly until his 80th year, especially as guest of Eric Pearman at Boxbury Farm, of Dick Bott, and with Simon, his nephew, at Waltham Abbey. His Game Book records this of his last shoot:

> *After lunch long belt of kale delivers the birds. Given VIP treatment by Eric Pearman and best stand in dell. Flushed birds fly high. I collect 4 cocks 4 hens at this stand, all in front. What a thrill for the advent of my LXXX anno! I get view of birds 400 yards up slope and by the time they reach me they are flying very fast and in stratosphere.*

# Chapter Thirteen

## RETIREMENT IN ROCKBOURNE

In 1974 Peter and Paula finally left their friends and beloved patients in Radlett, and for nearly a year were based with Margaret Facey, Rex's widow, in Ringwood. After a long search they found a lovely bungalow near the village of Rockbourne in Hampshire, where they were to spend ten very happy years. My father finally laid aside his stethoscope and medical bag 48 years after he started his practice in Radlett.

I have painted a picture of him as a doctor in the Foreword. He was a real old-fashioned, dedicated and caring country doctor, much beloved by his patients. Let them have the last words:

> "A trusted and valued confidant in time of trouble."
>
> "Loving care and tenderness."
>
> "Cannot think he ever did or ever thought a mean act."
>
> "He dispensed his gift of making people happy, even if he could not always cure them."

And as Bill Strickland ended his address at the memorial service in Radlett (sixteen years after he left the town):

> ". . . and we know he is now at Peace, having by his example revealed his acceptance of what Christ proclaimed as the greatest Commandment – to praise God and love your neighbour as yourself."

My father often quoted this poem as he talked of his dreams for a somewhat impecunious retirement (alas, I haven't been able to trace the author).

> Far from the bondage of bricks and mortar
> Far from the hurry of urgent deeds
> Give me to live by the running water
> Running water and whispering reeds
> Let it be where there are mills and patches
> And water meadows where King Cups grow;
> And bridges to lean on from whence one catches
> A fugitive glimpse of the Trout below.

> In a little cottage with friendly neighbours
> With books and a rod for my simple needs
> So shall my soul find rest from its labours
> By running water and whispering reeds.

He had to wait a long time, until he was almost eighty, but this wish was happily fulfilled in Rockbourne.

**1975**
Up at Oxford for a dinner:

> *Marshfield*
> *Rockbourne*
> *Hants*
> *vii x 75*

> *... On Sat. morning I saw the colourful BNC flag flying in the breeze from the Tower. Imagine my indignation, when, squatting on the pavement immediately below, I saw about a dozen scruffy "Marxists" handing out vicious propaganda pamphlets and selling "Worker" Daily. Only 20 yards away on the morning of 21st March 1556 Archbishop Cranmer was rushed along the pavement from St Mary's Church and burnt at the stake in the Broad. A ghastly reality that so many of the young "Freshers" are being "roped" into this dangerous creed ...*

After a visit by Andrew:

> *Marshfield*
> *Rockbourne*
> *28 xi/75*

> *My dearest "All"*
>
> *In fact I can say "Quatro" for this morn!! ...*
>
> *... We greatly enjoyed looking at the excellent photos of your trip on the Amazon and Andrew gave us superb descriptions of your epic holiday. So you can see how greatly we enjoyed every moment of your dear son's visit and didn't he enjoy Paula's Bramble and Apple Pie -- yes! and brambles gathered by his very own Mum in our local woods!*
> *We pictured your home this weekend without your beloved*

Elsita and wondered how she found life in her native Chile . . .

. . . I hope MAW you had a successful trip to the west and the ancient city. Your responsible job is now so packed with urgent problems – never ending – that I can see you never get a "let up" – even at home problems of business keep knocking at the door of your "higher centres" . . .

. . . The builders are getting along fine . . . When this final alteration has been completed we will be able to unpack our possessions and then get "domestic order" really under control. We will be altogether more comfortable and things will be settled in their final places. But I simply can't tell you how radiantly happy I am in this haven of peace and beauty – I see joy just everywhere inside and outside and under the stars I watch the triumphant passage of my celestial friends and bless my Creator for giving me the priceless gift of my precious senses . . .

**1976**

> Marshfield
> Rockbourne
> Sunday next before Advent
> "Stir-up Sunday 76"

My dearest "All"

The hectic week is almost over and Cinders had her op. (rt. leg) on Thursday a.m. and all went well and I collected her at 6 p.m. A chat with the surgeon convinced me that she would be confined to her bed for about a week . . .

. . . I went to Walhampton at noon yesterday and collected Richard who was in great heart. He took me to inspect his books in his class room and I read all his history essays – having been awarded 3 stars. Grand little essays, full of merit and most commendable – then off he went with the whole school to the Chapel, where they had half an hour Carol practice in preparation for the Carol Service to be held in Lymington Parish Church in two weeks' time. The pupils sang really beautifully and I had a good look round the music room which is most perfectly laid out, gives the pupils splendid details of the whole field of music, including a complete set of coloured prints of all composers from Vivaldi to 20th Century composers. There are illustrations of ALL varieties of musical instruments . . .

. . . Richie, bless him, seemed to sense the nature of Cinders' infirmity and this afternoon we had a lively game of bowls with conkers and little red apples. Cinders, from her bed, revelled in the battle. . .

. . . I fear this delay in healing and having to stay in bed 10-12 days will prevent us from going up to Fiona's next weekend for Jonathon's final recital at St John's. I couldn't possibly go and leave Paula in bed alone in the house. I am managing to give her the nourishment she needs and likes, lots of fruit and coffee and hot water bottles 4 hourly!! I will now have to phone Fiona and give her this disappointing news . . .

. . . Cinders sends you all much love and warm greetings and I know (secret) that she anticipated "Stir-up Sunday" by making you a super Christmas Pudding before she went to Hospital . . .


On a visit to Rosemary's parents:

*Wynchard*
*Thornford*
*27 ix 76*

*. . . A lovely greeting awaited us and what a glorious hour I spent with dear wee Alistair – drawing animals and reading stories. Then tomorrow – "The Vigil of St Michael and All Angels", Rosemary is taking us to School to see Andrew playing with the Colts in a Rugger Match – How I wish you were with us for this grand event . . .*

*(Later)*

*. . . After lunch we all moved to the rugger pitch and saw the Colts in action with Andrew playing a leading part in the scrum. Very soon The Colts took the lead and Andrew scored 2 grand tries in the first half with Rosemary raising her voice to "Diana" in wild rejoicing. How I wish you could have seen Andrew in action and against the wind (second half) he scored a most thrilling try. For a forward his speed was quite remarkable. He cut through the middle and with four opponents thrusting after him he sped across the 25 and grounded the ball between the posts – a super, super try which Grampy and AGW acclaimed with enthusiasm. I once did a similar thrust when playing for BNC against Oriel in 1921 – and Ripley Oddy, the Oriel Stand-off (Rugby) exclaimed, "Damn that little man."!!!*

Fiona and her family c. 1972.
From left to right: Amanda, Rosalind, Fiona Sarah and Jonathon.

*Marshfield*
*Rockbourne*
*7 xii/76 Tuesday*

*My dearest "All"*

*To us, how quickly the time is coming to a close, but, to you I expect it drags on far too slowly. However, think of it, this letter will be brought to SP by vary special courier – none other than the lively Richard. I can see him arriving, clustered on every limb with luggage and packages and on Friday Paula and I will be going over to Romsey to take our Xmas consignment . . .*

*. . . Now dearest R I do hope you have now reduced those thumping "headache attacks". You want to be fit for your manifold activities these holidays. We will picture you all revelling in your early summer sunshine and I know you will get very much help from all your boys. With the arrival of his 3 brothers young Alistair will enter a realm of delight and demonstrate is 2 precious "ivories" to C, A and R . . .*

**1977**

*Marshfield*
*Rockbourne*
*xxvii vii 77*

*. . . In the presence of a sensational sunset I take my pen and write . . .*

*. . . Today we were visited by a whole family of young Pheasants with mum in strict control, and during lunch we had a delightful view of the family as they enjoyed the peace and feeding ground of the orchard. No doubt your miniature partridge friends will be feathered and able to take wing for short flights. Since your departure we have had dry weather and continued to enjoy the most bountiful harvest of both strawberries and raspberries. Paula's border is now blazing in a riot of new colour, with clusters of exquisite phlox and several mid-season flowers and the Dahlias are all coming into bloom. Most strange NOT seen a single wasp this summer and last year we were invaded by swarms in the Rasps.*

*Fiona, Paul and Rosalind are now in* Pippa's Song *in the Med. and Mandy and Jonathon will join them next week. Sarah is now established at the Norwich Hospital and seems very happy there and Rosalind (just before she left for her holiday) decided to accept the appointment at St Thomas's Hospital and will take up duties end of September. I am glad she has decided on this, as she has been given an important post and will have a most interesting time with the rehabilitation of very sick patients of all ages . . .*

*Now re your ? relating to my Gt Gt Uncle who was a Don at St John's College Oxford. He was a Classics Don, Ordained and held the College living at Cheam in Surrey. I think probably he spent the Long Vacation there and put in a Curate during his absence. This was quite the custom in early Victorian days. I will be able to give you further details after I have had a chat with Barbara. Cinders has just been in to say tell "them" that I am deep freezing broad beans. 5 super bags but I would add, the old man spent 1 1/2 hours "shelling" them and aren't my digits stained!!! Also a super lot of rasps in the deep freeze – all ready for your lusty sons next term.*

*Just before I put out my light each night I reflect at length on all the supremely happy hours we spent with you on that unforgettable visit . . .*

*. . . HM is still going the "rounds" on her Jubilee tours and to-day had a remarkable reception in Birmingham and Coventry . . .*

*Marshfield*
*Rockbourne*
*Hants*

*LXIII Anno Guerra*
*"Young lads off to prison!!" (Scarborough on mobilization)*
*4.8.14*

*My dearest All*

*Strange things happen to me. I took Mrs Clarrie home this evening after her day of domestic activities here, and there in front of me was a coloured calendar in the kitchen, showing a view of Knaresborough Rly. Bridge and Station. Here, at this very spot, 63 years ago we, the XIVth Foot (5 W Yorks) entrained for Active Service!!!*

*Yes! Dearest R. your mammoth and entertaining opus has arrived safely and is full of **so** many news items we long to know – many, many thanks for giving us such interesting details of your* new home, and the good news that all the boys are safely home and are delighted with the flat. Bravo to Andrew on his match away down in Rio – splendid news and just the triumph to spark him off to "set about this wee white ball in earnest." Please give him our warm congratulations . . .

. . . Here Autumn dawns with all the rolling hills and huge fields a glorious sight – rich gold and a record crop – the wheat is an astounding colour and the straw a record length – just over our northern fence there is a splendid crop of oats over 4' high and almost ready for the "combine". I'll be sorry to see it cut and ready to be baled. We have just had the last feast of super raspberries – I took off the net this afternoon and within seconds the wily blackbirds swept in to feast on a few berries I left for them. Cinders's border is now more glorious than ever and my sweetpeas are 7' high and massed with glorious blooms.

Forgive this short report on "The Exciting Cricket Test" from Trent Bridge at Nottingham. I saw almost all the match on the late night summary – most superbly shown on the super colour TV – again, our warm thanks. Tis hard to believe but the old country **won** this most thrilling and exciting Test, so are now **two** up in the series and would have also won the first match at Lord's but rain prevented us. Be it known unto you that England have not won a Test at Trent Bridge for 47 years AND England have never been TWO up at this stage since I was 10 years old in 1905!!! A "Test special" is on the way to you and you will read what a difference Boycott's return to the England Test side has made. His skill against a battery of very fast Australian bowlers was most thrilling to watch and apart from a little luck he scored 187 runs for only once out. His cover drives made me rise from my cosy chair like a trout after a mayfly. The English fielding was superb and their catches quite the best I have seen for years and years.

A first PC from Fiona reports all well from "the Med" and Mandy and Jonathon will have joined up by now and think if "IT". This sister of yours has had a radio telephone installed on the boat and "it's a great success."

Dear Parents both, may we wish you much joy in having your dear boys all around you for these summer holidays – happy hours together in your new home and many blessings rest upon you all . . .

*Marshfield*
*Rockbourne, Fordingbridge*
*viii x 77*

*... So I sincerely hope that Crispin is now reassured and optimistic over his prospects and much encouraged by his short weekend exeat with you after the Blundells Match. I have been thinking of you this afternoon on leave and revelling in the rare delight of seeing Crispin battling on the rugger field, his knees plastered with grand English mud ...*

*Marshfield*
*Rockbourne*
*xvii xii 77*
*"Der Tag"*

*My dearest All*

*"Anno 83" has been a day of unending joy from early morning until this late hour and at sunset hour, your Dad rang up from Thornford to give us the wonderful news that Crispin had been accepted for Oriel ...*

*... I simply must now record what a wonderful year this has been "family wise" for me. For almost 9 months I have rejoiced in your presence here and in Brazil and can rightly say I have seen more of you than in the last 25 years!! ... Especially we thank you for your help and advice re the new extension to the garage ...*

*... The New Year will see many problems arriving with each morn for you, but my dear boy, I beseech you to face each hurdle with courage and patience supported by the great help of your own beloved. As each day passes it will be nearer the great and joyous emancipation – so hold fast and may you be given health and strength to face the closing spell of your busy domicile in S. America."*

**1978**

*Rockbourne*
*x iii 78*

*My dearest All*

Here, in the UK it is incredible what a transformation has developed in our midst. Just everything in nature heralds the glorious season of spring – scores of lovely crocuses and lots of little rockery gems lift their heads in salutation and dozens of industrious honey bees are queuing up to make pillage on the velvet buds -then there are about a dozen superb daffodils in bloom. But, I regret to report that our special cock pheasant made a ruthless attack on Paula's very special white crocus and cut the blooms right to the ground. Further on the nature front (mice raiding the greenhouse) I have cracked the century now recording my 102 victim! . . .

. . . Here the much-needed help of Clarence has been denied me as I had to take him to Salisbury Hospital to see the skin specialist – huge fungating verruca of his left foot – result – urgent admission - operation. He had not said a word to Mrs Clarence and how he had managed to work I can't imagine and wearing heavy gum boots – attending 100+ calves and hard work – hedging – yes indeed, a tough. Fortunately I insisted on examining his feet and my suspicions led me to take my razor along with me to his cottage. I removed a lot of callus – like the crust of the Cairngorms. Quite the worst month of the whole gardening year to be without a gardener: so I must await and hope Clarence will be fit for action before Easter . . .

*Marshfield*
*Rockbourne*
*xv iii 78*

*My dearest "All"*

. . . It was nice to see Sarah who looked well but was rather subdued but still that sweet gracious young lady. She had just passed her "Intermediate" Exam – did very well 76%. We did not venture into her private realm as there was so much chat relating to the property. Ros looked radiant – loves her work at Thomas's -is full of confidence and obviously doing most useful work. Mandy rather stale with the manifold energy expended on the final run-up to the early summer "A" levels. Paul is most diligent in doing his "commercial" bit for me in seeing I get the best chances in the sales of my various possessions.* . . .

Rockbourne<br>Visitation of the Blessed Virgin Mary

. . . I know that I posted a letter to you only yesterday but I simply must express my profound gratitude to you for sending the opus magnus – superbly presented and edited by dearest R . . . I will it treasure all my days. You have presented us with a classic in description and narrative – packed with absorbing interest from beginning to end. Every member of this epic adventure will have treasured memories, which will never fade and I still shudder to think what could have happened to any member of the party, especially the "Colts"!!! The coloured print of "Safari Party" is highly entertaining and brings me right into the picture – Crispin looks like a STAR in a Western thriller and the Amazon heroine is swallowed up by the shade . . .*

. . . I had such a surprise when planting courgettes on the compost heap – quite suddenly a glowing pink hen pheasant strutted from the hedge – quite fearless and kept me company for 10 minutes. Then after a fortnight of great havoc by Master Mole on Cinder's borders at last this PM I caught the culprit AND previously the trap had sprung a dozen times without success. Cinders will rejoice, as scores of lovely plants had been uprooted – but such is the havoc that I fear another brace of moles are revelling in our subterranean regions!!! . . .

iv iv 78

. . . What joy for us as the morning mail brought your welcome and thrilling letter with lots of exciting news which kept me bouncing up and down all day. Many thanks and at the outset let me send our warmest congratulations to Andrew in his superb triumph in

---

* Paul was Fiona's second husband. My father was selling some treasures to pay for a sun room and to widen the garage, as Paula found the original garage impossible to negotiate! I would like to mention here that my father took a keen interest in his grandchildren, their achievements and problems. He was rewarded by the great love and appreciation they had for him.

* All six of us went on a safari to the Pantanal swamps in the Far West of Brazil, which was then almost unknown.

being awarded his School 1st Hockey colours. This is a unique triumph for one so young and especially in such a large school and I do rejoice with you on his commendable success. Further, we must add that this last term had long spells of appalling weather – many days when sport, esp. hockey on heavy pitches was unplayable; so Andrew's 8 goals from short-corners was a triumph of super skill. Bravo!

Now, I take the trumpet and blow a blast of high salutation to Richard for his notable triumph in being top of his form. When we think he was quite an invalid with his debilitating boils (for quite a long spell) his scholastic efforts are most praiseworthy and we send him our warmest congratulations. You must be highly delighted that he has now organised his higher centres to first-class performance . . .

. . . Here April has dawned in all the glory of an English spring season and all nature is revealing unending joy and the song birds are in endless chorus – I have found 2 wrens' nests – gems of construction and all the other birds are most industrious, with the blue tits working overtime in their nesting box – high entertainment for us during meals. The garden is already a blaze of colour with a superb display of Polyanthus – Daffs and all the rock plants – a most incredible transformation from snow, ten days ago, to patches of rich colour just everywhere. I am very much behind in the vegetable garden – still so wet and difficult to get on with the vital planting of potatoes and vegetables . . .

. . . Give me your views as to what to decide about the rifle? You were the last to use it when with me and shot 2 partridges in one shot in 1943 when at Dumfries and the day Fiona fell into the RAF Sewage Plant!!! . . .

. . . Heavens it's past midnight and the 5th of April is here so (with all humility) I would remind you that 41 years ago I had that mighty thrill of landing my 30 lbs fish at Brora and now the worthy monarch is holding court at Thornford! . . .

*Marshfield*
*Rockbourne*
*v.v.78*

My dearest "All"

I would like to write at length on the interesting and absorbing points of your epistle, but I crave your indulgence as on this

*Friday night we are busy preparing for an early morning departure to proceed to Newhouse Farm, where we are going to join in the celebrations for Amanda's 18th birthday this weekend ...*

*... Fiona and Paul are only just home from the Med. They had a frightful voyage with storms and gales and only themselves to control the boat for 36 hours non-stop. Yes, just their two selves. Really a most commendable effort from Corsica to the French Riviera. The Med can be a very stormy realm – when it likes. Ref. Acts; St Paul's journey!! Most difficult for them, with one to cook and feed and only a lone navigator at the helm and gales tearing away at the sails!! The two nights must have been ghastly. Pippa's Song is safely back in the UK and at Hamble not far from Richard at Walhampton.\**

*Marshfield*
*Rockbourne*
*As from Monday P.M.*

*... Yesterday Andrew and I went over to the Hamble to see Fiona's new yacht – a really splendid boat and we went for a sail down the Solent. Of course it was a real joy for Fiona, Paul and Rosalind to see Andrew and I know he was very delighted to see the Family, quite at home on their super yacht. Fiona, Paul, Ros and one other will set sail on Sat. for the Canaries. Sarah, Mandy and Jonathon will join the boat at ports en route. All will return from Las Palmas early August – leave the boat there and finally return in early November 78 for the crossing of the Atlantic to the West Indies and USA. The boat is a joy and a masterpiece of construction and was the sensation of the Boat Show. . . . I am sure Fiona will get a profitable sale in USA. Out on the Solent yesterday she sailed superbly and should perform well in tough weather. Fiona has decided to sail her across to the far west AFTER the hurricane season ...*

*... As we parted company Fiona presented me with Jonathon's two new records released on June 1st. Both received high grade reviews and his Jubilee record made at Eton (before his voice broke) is a superb presentation of some lovely compositions –*

---

\* They were selling *Pippa's song* to raise funds in order to pay for a more suitable boat in which to cross the Atlantic.

his lovely voice comes over like a skylark's. The second record was made at St Johns Cambridge just before he left to go to Eton.

Our guest returns to Canada on Friday and I can say we will be mightily relieved, as we are both quite exhausted with the endless requirements of this total invalid. She is so demanding and needs much entertainment all the while . . . We have taken her out to lunch almost every day. Cinders providing a **cordon bleu** *dinner her final night. As you can imagine I have had very little time to do some vital work in the garden, (this lamentation is private just between YOU and ME!) . . .*

*All well in the garden on our return and pheasants everywhere – what a relief I'm **not** a poacher!!! . . .*

*Marshfield*
*Rockbourne*
*9 vi 78*

*. . . Here I also have a joyous event to report. As you know Andrew has (I am happy to report) arrived for his half term exeat looking very happy and fresh after his exams. I met him at Salisbury Station at 9.50 and what a rush of cheery boys to scramble into the awaiting cars. Here was your son superbly clad in the glorious 1st XI Blazer and in the bright sunshine looking like a young Greek god. He early related to me that he had put up a good show in his exam papers and was full of confidence to do battle with the remainder of his exams on his return after the weekend (Monday pm). He told me with much relish that he had broken the school swimming record three times this week for the 50 metres Butterfly and hoped to do well in the school swimming sports next week . . .*

*. . . What fun it will be to hear all the exciting episodes from Crispin's adventures in the Andes, Andrew has given us many absorbing stories of the Safari and we have just seen his excellent collection of snaps. I still shudder to think that you were far too near some lethal snake, jaguar or oversize alligator; quite apart from the piranhas . . .*

*Marshfield*
*Rockbourne*
*22.00 hrs*
*Mid-summer's Day 78*

My dearest "All"

*You will hardly believe me, but in the last 10 minutes I have seen Brazil HIT the post 3 times in 30 secs and such corking shots from Roberto each one rebounding well beyond the penalty area. The Polish Goalkeeper didn't know where to look. Brazil have got this game sewn up and will surely reach the final . . .*

*. . . I have a new avian friend – a supremely beautiful cock pheasant who visits me every day – struts around the lawn and cackles away to me without fear or anxiety. Then to-day we were visited by a sad and pensive pair of French partridges, who have obviously had some tragedy with destruction of their nest and eggs - last year they proudly conducted 14 lively chicks down the drive and visited us several times. The cuckoos and blackbirds are now silent. The robins have hatched a second brood and the goldfinches and pied wagtail are nesting within our border but so far I haven't detected their nests. As I entered the strawberry net this a.m. I was reminded of you last year at this very time and I collected a super basket of exquisite berries. Bountiful crops of broad beans – new potatoes and lettuces give us rich vegetable nourishment. Raspberries will gladden our hearts and delight our palates at the end of the month. Cinders is thrilled with her herbaceous border and even Van Housen [sic] would have to work hard on his canvas to do her justice – one glorious delphinium is like a Red Indian Totem Pole!! . . .*

*. . . Our generous hostess – the venerable Jessie Tyser – is 85 to-day, going strong, but not shooting, but still landing her own salmon. I know I'm right that MAW owes her a great deal for helping to bring "THAT LITTLE ENGLISH ROSE" into his life! Even all the Arctic Gremlins and the deep snow around Pictish Castle couldn't say him "NAY!" I can still see the blizzard sweeping in upon them as they alighted from the train at Fearn Station and Jim escorted them to his cosy fireside at the Moss! That's many moons ago . . .\**

---

\* My father was convinced that we had become engaged that day. I didn't finally win Rosemary's hand until Easter Sunday, a few weeks later!

*Marshfield*
*1.vii.78*

... Here in the UK the AA Championships produced sport equal to the Olympics. I will never forget the 10,000 metres which was run in a terrific downpour, with the track flooded and splashing like a water polo match. Brendan Foster broke every record and beat the world record holder of this event – to see him running superbly in the pouring rain with the Kenyan on his heels – lap after lap – was incredible and then his last 4 laps were staggering. Really the finest 10,000 metres I've ever seen. It's a miracle that his running shoes lasted the course and such appalling weather conditions were all against records ...

... This afternoon at Wimbledon there was a match unique and breathtaking. Sue Barker v a 6 ft Yank teenager and the packed centre court (record crowd) erupted. From a hopeless position with defeat looming, the young golden-haired Devon girl put on her spurs and weathered the storm. This huge Yank Amazon (16) uses an oversize racquet which in itself is terrifying ...

... July has just dawned and this means that soon after this letter reaches you, Richard will be bursting into your midst and with his very arrival, you will be preparing for your wee Alistair to undertake his first journey to the UK and his advent into Prep School ...

*Marshfield*
*xix vii 78*

... Fiona and her co-mariners have made excellent progress and crossed "The Bay" successfully and should be in Lisbon today. Jonathon broke up last Thursday, his xvth birthday and flew to Lisbon this weekend. Leaving Lisbon about now they set sail for the Azores. This should give them extensive experience of the mighty ocean. Ros will return in 3 weeks (her holiday from hospital) and Jonathon and Mandy will go on to the Canaries returning with Fiona and Paul to the UK by air in late August ... They will complete their Atlantic crossing in November ...

... We loved your description of your company of humming birds. You have been justly rewarded for your enterprise and care for the welfare of your super avian friends. This a.m. early, the local farmer commenced combining the huge field of rape and the young pheasants sat on our fence and wondered why this mighty machine *should disturb their habitat. They looked quite alarmed.*

*Your masterpiece about your epic Pantanal safari, still keeps me spellbound. The new copy is a joy to read and thank you again for giving me this treasured literary gem. Bar and Harry have revelled in reading the thrilling pages and are full of praise for your courage and specially for you dearest R . . .*

*Eglos Rose*
*Pendower*
*Cornwall*
*xiv.x.78*

My dear Michael

*. . . I must reflect once again what unbounded joy you brought to us during this leave – for me it filled every moment with treasured memories which I can enjoy into the winter days. Cinders rose to the occasion and produced wonder meals throughout your visit and then the succession of delights – every day; as we feasted on the musical visits to Salisbury Cathedral; two visits to Walhampton and a happy pilgrimage to Oxford, so we could picture what wonderful days await Crispin, as he embarks on his academic career in the glorious college of Oriel. I feel truly thankful that I have been spared to enjoy these memorable days . . .*

*. . . The real news here is that Cinders is having a real rest and rejoicing in all the manifold delights which Cornwall presents . . .*

*. . . I phoned earlier in the week to Mr Southern at the Thorburn Museum and he was so kind to give me a PRIVATE appointment on Th. 2 pm. Never will I forget his most generous hospitality and he was thrilled with your letter and the print of your picture . . . He took us round every gallery; we had 1½ hours of rich enjoyment – I've never seen such a rich and priceless display of exquisite avian painting and his moorland scenes left me gasping. How I wish you could have been with us. Mr Southern responded to my enthusiasm and profound appreciation as we made an intimate inspection of dozens of pictures. I had time to take in all the genius of Thorburn and look intimately at his master painting of every variety of game bird – ducks and all the hawk species etc. I can never thank you enough for leading me to this unique collection AND if I am spared <u>we</u> will return and enjoy these wonderful*

*paintings together** . . .

. . . We will be thinking of you very much during this spell of your hectic activities with the visiting Firemen and all the urgent problems associated with your far-flung empire. We wish you a smooth and successful passage through this stormy sea.*

*We are greatly refreshed by our holiday here and the unusual routine. Both Cinders and Mac have prospered in this restful atmosphere. Take care of yourself and may the whole Company of Heaven surround you in all your activities . . .*

*Marshfield*
*Rockbourne*
*25th October 1978*
*Feast of St Crispin*
*Soisson, Circa AD 288, Martyr*
*Also battle of Agincourt, circa, xxv x 1415.*

My dear Michael

*A glorious sunny day with all the leaves turning gold – such is the advent of this historic day. I can even add another item of joy and interest to Crispin's Day, I landed a lucky salmon from the R. Nith, 13 lbs many moons ago. And yet another joyous event this very day when our Sovereign Lady Elizabeth II attended the consecration of the glorious Anglican Liverpool Cathedral. It was a most memorable event, with all the Bishops of the Northern See attending and the Archbishop of York preaching an excellent short Sermon. After the service HM The Queen carried out a cheery "walk about" amongst hundreds of citizens and children around this noble building. During the service a most pleasing event – the RC Archbishop of Liverpool presented the Cathedral with a Bible, a welcome gesture in this city of tension . . .*

*. . . Very frequently we have been thinking of you during this momentous fortnight – knew you would be having a really tough time and with several of the "big guns" visiting, felt you would be constantly in the firing line. I imagine that Bothwell Street will keep you "batting at the wicket" until I hear the first notes of the Cuckoo next spring!!! . . .*

*. . . Crispin has written me a most happy letter from Oriel and*

---

* I am very sad to relate that due to the pressures of the recession (1993) many of the paintings from this wonderful collection are being sold by Sotheby's.

*was delighted with my letter of welcome. He is obviously very happy there and getting his teeth into the problems of the School of Geography. I wouldn't be at all surprised to find him running in the Freshers Cross Country!!! . . .*

*Marshfield*
*Rockbourne*
*xiv xii 78*

*My dearest "All"*

*I expect when this letter reaches you, you will have Crispin and Andrew bringing you much joy and wee Richard and Ali will be flying over the NE tip of your vast country and only a few hours away by air. Your sister and her co-mariners will be resting and revelling in the manifold delights of the West Indies. As I write Jonathon will be just about joining up with the family in Barbados. He left London this morning . . . We received a letter from Fiona yesterday a.m. and apparently the last week of the voyage (2850 miles in 25 days) was very tough with storms – huge waves 25' high – very dark nights and the top-sail with the mast spreader and pulpit damaged so they had to finish the voyage without the mainsail. Fiona quotes, "It was like ski-ing down a glacier." They were all sick for the first 5 days! I am much relieved that Ros is such a competent sailor – shades of Sandy Allan! She will have been invaluable to Paul and Fiona. Surely a super effort by all. I expect you will receive a letter from Barbados before you receive this . . .*

*. . . invitation for us to visit you for six weeks at the end of January. Yes! Yes!! Yes!!! We will be very thrilled to come and visit you again. Think of the added secret joy for me to be in your precious company again. As you say the warmth and sunshine will do my joints good and Cinders revels in the super sunshine and heat. Our passports and vaccinations are up-to-date! . . . In less than two months I will lift up mine eyes to behold the wonders of Scorpio!! . . .*

*. . . Scotland put up a superb battle against the All Blacks and very nearly won as they were hammering at the NZ line in the last 5 mins and gave away the match with a charged down kick as the Scot tried a drop at goal. Then an All Black dribbled the length of the field and scored between the posts . . . Cambridge easily won the Varsity match. The Oxford scrum was the lightest I have ever seen and the Sherborne 1st XV scrum would have pushed*

*them off the pitch – in fact Andrew's merry viii would have mopped them up!!!*

If it was my father and Paula's turn to despatch one of our sons to Brazil for the holidays, on unpacking their suitcases we would discover a little package of flowers, meticulously wrapped in damp cotton wool. Thus it was that as we sweltered in our Southern Hemisphere Christmas heat, a semblance of a cool Christmas at home would be generated by a little arrangement of winter flowers and berries – winter jasmine, holly and so on – to grace our dining room table. In the spring we would receive snowdrops, miniature daffodils and the like. Small wonder that on one of his visits to São Paulo my father was asked to address the Garden Club; an august body of erudite gardeners. Delighted to be in the limelight and to oblige, he did so, accompanied, of course, by the posy of spring flowers he had brought out with him.

*Marshfield*
*Natal Day xvii xii 78*

*My dearest All*

*Such a wonderfully happy day with the closing hours of the vigil suddenly transformed into unforgettable bliss with the sound of your voices in my ears, all so supremely clear. I couldn't believe the wonder of it all as I heard your voices and what a marvellous advent to my birthday\*. I do thank you with all my heart for your kind thought and with the early hours I shared with Cinders the thrill of opening the presents and birthday cards . . .*

*. . . Crispin's long letter to Cinders and me with special birthday greetings was a delightful epistle full of interest and all the manifold delights of his first term at Oxford . . .*

*. . . Another thrill for us as Aunt Nella made contact a few minutes ago and almost before I could "tune-in", the cheery and happy voices of Richie and Alistair gave us the stimulating news from Walhampton. What an excellent and lively school it is! Richie, "Grandaddy I was TOP of my form" and from the other phone Ali chimed in "I'm getting a `remove' to another form next term." It is clear that Ali has made a superb start at Walhampton and will bring great joy to you all. The wee boys are just off to London and are being conducted round shops and the West End, before*

---

[*] In those days transatlantic phoning was very expensive. We used it very seldom.

*entraining for the Airport. At this moment I expect Andrew is high in the vault of heaven and fast heading SW towards the NE corner of Brazil.*

*I wonder if you have now received a letter from Fiona? (I noted that they only saw 1 SHIP for the whole of their 25 days cruising). After a much-needed rest and after Jonathon's arrival* Flyttfågel *will head for Tobago, a lovely haven of beauty and peace, and they hope to spend Christmas at Bequia before sailing forth to Mustique-St Vincent-St Lucia-Martinique-Guadeloupe-Antigua (where Sarah and Allan join up with them). I know you will realise how lucky Fiona and mariners are to have this delightful yacht to cruise at leisure around this wonderful cluster of islands . . .*

## 1979

*Test Match special IVth T Match*
*Marshfield*
*11th January 1979*

*My dearest Michael*

*No wonder I've got indigestion after my breakfast, as only a few minutes ago on turning on the Radio I heard the dramatic news that England have WON the ivth Test Match at Sydney and this means they have WON THE ASHES, First time in Australia for ages.*

*. . . Fiona reports "another wonderful school report – with further distinction for Jonathon in Trials. He only needs two more distinctions in Trials to become an Oppidan Scholar. Sarah and Allan fly out next week to join up with the family at St Kitts and after their holiday they fly back from Puerto Rico with Mandy, who is returning to start her job. After Sarah, Mandy and Allan leave for the UK, Fiona, Paul and Rosalind leave on a long 12 days sail right across to Florida where she hopes to sell* Flyttfågel*?? I think with depression in the USA Fiona may not get anything like the amount she anticipated for the sale! . . .*

*. . . What a sudden surprise . . . Andrew has arrived at Heathrow, baggage delayed an hour so he can only get as far as Salisbury, so he's coming here by taxi for the night and Paula and I have prepared his bed and now Cinders is on the kitchen front and preparing one of her Schoolboy Banquets!!! . . .*

Rosemary and I were now based in Scotland.

*Marshfield*
*The Feast of the ever Blessed and glorious Trinity, A.D. 1979*

*My dearest Rosemary and Michael*

*A few minutes ago I had the thrill of that merry chat with you on the phone and do thank you for giving us that rich pleasure. I loved hearing about your enjoyable day in superb sunshine and esp. the manifold delights of your day afloat among the Hebridean Islands. The picture of those very lovely islands and the lochs is still very fresh and vivid in my mind, so I know how enjoyable those hours must have been for you both and esp. the picnic lunch with Phœbus blazing away above you. The crystal clear atmosphere of your northern realm is free of pollution and unlike São Paulo, so that is why you got a patch of sunburn on your torso . . .*

Michael and Rosemary in the Hebrides, 1979.
From left to right: Andrew, Michael, Crispin, Richard (behind), Rosemary, Alistair.

*. . . We have just seen a soul-searching documentary on TV showing all the grim realities of shanty life in São Paulo. I did not know conditions were so frightful and especially the very high*

*infant mortality. The pictures of shanty town life and conditions were very grim. Surely such appalling poverty and the hopeless outlook for the future is the certain road to a Marxist state. A government drive is of paramount importance and birth control urgent. I know thousands of workers are coming to SP each month and this dream of "Eldorado" brings hordes in to swell the population of the shanty areas. I suppose the new building sites, for hygiene etc., are totally unable to cope with the masses coming in from the country areas. As the film stated, even before the end of the century, SP will be the largest city in the world with 20 million population – a terrifying prospect . . .*

*. . . It seems incredible that Crispin is almost at the end of his first year at Oxford and will be heavily engaged with his Mods this coming month. . . ..*

## 1981

This was a splendid letter about a dramatic Test last day – he was 86 when he wrote it.

<u>sports special No. 2</u>
*p.m. xxi vii 81 From Marshfield, Rockbourne*

My dear Michael

*This day <u>I will never forget</u> and you will know the impossible has happened and the odds with the London bookies were 500-1 against!!! I know I posted to you this a.m. the sports special no. 1, with the early and mid-events of the II Test and tomorrow I will send you the FINAL reports. . . from the newspapers . . . on the most dramatic victory of England this evening has only happened ONCE before, i.e. when the side who were made to Follow On actually won the TEST. That was when I was a tiny infant in 1894. The famous Jessop at Sydney also made a century like Ian Botham and England won by 10 runs.*

*Bless the TV! I saw the whole of the Australian innings and they started as if they would knock off the runs without difficulty. The England Capt. gave the new ball to Ian Botham and suddenly he struck (1st wicket fell at 13, Wood) and Headingley came alight. It was clear to me that the crowded stands sensed drama and I started to talk to myself. Willis was switched to the Kirkstall End* and he charged down the hill like a man possessed. Dyson looked secure and so did Chappell and I felt most anxious as the score was over 50 and 9 Australian wickets left. I almost dashed to the cupboard for a dose of $C_2H_5OH$! Then suddenly the whole of the tense crowd erupted as Willis removed Chappell; the second catch by the wizard Taylor (wicket keeper) AND within minutes thousands of excited spectators were standing, waving flags and cheering like mad as in 11 balls Willis had taken 3 wickets, without a run being scored off him (that was 4 for 58).

Nothing now could control the masses in the stands and their sustained cheers could be heard in City Square, Leeds. Could England really be on the way to a memorable victory? By now Willis seemed to race up to the wicket with incredible speed and he gave away several NO BALLS and each one meant a run on the score board. Up popped Ian Botham again and he made a super catch at 3rd slip to dismiss Hughes 0. Yallop followed with a Duck 0 and believe it or not a 3rd Duck 0 was recorded when Border (a sound attacking batsman) was bowled by Old (Yorks – also played for England at Rugger). I was glued to the Box and watched every ball bowled and mighty was my relief when Dyson after 2 hours dogged defence was caught by Taylor -another victim for Willis. Hundreds of wee boys stood on their seats waving Union Jacks as if they had been at a Royal Wedding. I then watched Marsh, the powerful bat (Aussie wicket keeper) take his stance at the crease and he was the one man I feared could hold on and take Australia to victory. But to my great relief he did not last long – again Willis struck. Marsh made a mighty swing and a lofty ball soared towards the leg boundary where Willey (young Kent fast bowler) made a most remarkable catch. Three wickets now remained and Bright and Lillee took the score along towards the 100 and I could almost hear the hundreds in the stand biting their nails. The excitement was more intense than I have ever known. I suddenly realised one mighty important point. ENGLAND were holding their catches !!. At this stage I was popping up and down like a Jack in the box and here was Willis pounding away like one inspired. Again he struck and had Lillee brilliantly caught by Gatting. Drama and excitement was now intense and was aggravated when Botham returned and in his first over he saw Old drop Alderman TWICE. The Australians in their dressing room hardly dare watch the incredible scene at the wicket and I knew Australia were only about 20 runs off victory. I'm certain you could imagine what the crowd was like at this point and TV presentation was superb. To watch Willis charging up –

*over after over – was truly remarkable and finally Lucifer let forth all his thunderbolts and Willis knocked out Bright's middle stump. Then followed scenes never before seen by me, as Willis tried to run through the crowds to the Pavilion – Yes the old veteran had taken 8 Australian wickets in only 15 overs for 43 runs.*

*Bravo to the new English Captain, Mike Brearley – he was splendid. But no one will ever forget Ian Botham and Bob Willis. And remember I saw that incredible innings of 149 by Ian Botham – unsurpassed by anything I have ever seen in <u>my</u> long innings . . .*

# Chapter Fourteen

## THE DECLINING YEARS OF OUR PATRIARCH

**1982-1990**

Sad things began to happen. My sister, who with Paul was running a yacht charter business in the Caribbean, developed cancer; we believe partly provoked by stress of financial worries. This was especially sad as their beautiful old Brixham trawler had developed a fine reputation and was showing signs of breaking even. I can still hear the distress in my father's voice as he told me the news of the diagnosis over the phone. They had to come home, and after a typically stalwart fight, Fiona died in October 1983.

Early in 1984 my father's sister Barbara died; she had been a very "special" person to him, throughout their lives. Then in July, uneasy at the sound of Paula on the phone, we invited them up to Scotland for a second time following a very happy visit in June. They never made it. Tests showed Paula had a cerebral tumour. Her niece, Margaret, and John frequently cared for them at their home in Reading during the late summer, but Paula's condition steadily worsened. When Rosemary and I took her for a short outing by the Thames, we chatted about the plans for Peter's 90th birthday the next month. She disclosed that she had been saving up her pension to give him a "special" party, and that the funds for it were in an old tobacco tin under her fridge. She wished the party to go ahead even if she couldn't be there.

And thus it was. Paula died, with my father at her side, just a week before he was 90. We found the tobacco tin with £600 in it, and duly gave him a wonderful celebration with over 40 guests sitting down to lunch in a Thames valley hostelry. As we toasted "absent friends" dear Paula was very much in all our hearts.

After a long search, Bertie Sutton's daughter and Ros found the ideal retreat for my father. There was a vacant bungalow at Headbourne Worthy House, near Winchester, run by the Lywoods. In this cluster of perfectly equipped sheltered housing homes, my father found convivial company, comfort and the necessary degree of fuss to bolster his ego. Many of his treasures kept him company. He even managed some cooking, though if the Lywoods didn't watch him, his sole diet consisted of their pre-prepared shrimps duchesse followed by Ambrosia rice!

*Peter's 90th birthday celebrations, 1984.*
*Blowing his father's hunting horn!*

Here it was it was that he really got down to his memoirs. By chance I read an article in the *Glasgow Herald* mentioning that Lyn Macdonald, the distinguished World War I historian was writing a series of books based on vernacular accounts by veterans, and would be pleased to hear from any who had a tale to tell. So I put her in touch with my father.

The summer and Armistice trips to Flanders which Lyn organised proved to be the highlight of my father's final quinquennium. Once or twice a year he would sally forth, proudly bedecked in his medals, and join Lyn's party; a splendid mixture of nonagenarian veterans, deeply interested carers and enthusiastic W.W.1. students of all ages. "Lyn's Marauders" were all admirably shepherded along from rendezvous to coach, to ferry to coach and so on by the redoubtable Colin Butler. They would visit battlefields, join the moving ceremony at the Menen Gate in Ypres and make pilgrimages to several war Cemeteries. They were often fêted by the locals. How immaculately the cemeteries are tended by the Commonwealth War Graves Commission team! At the cemeteries Lyn's party would invariably lay a wreath or plant a poppy in memory of a relative or friend of one of the party.

*Flanders with Lyn Macdonald, La Bassée 1987.*
*From left to right: Norman Tennant DCM, Arthur Halstrap MBE, CSM Jack Coggins DCM, David Watson, Ralph Langley (wheelchair), Alex Jamieson, Peter (wheelchair), George Blaylock (Chelsea Pensioner), Johnny Morris MSM (in beret), Vic Simpson. (Photograph courtesy of Wilf Schofield.)*

After one such trip my father and I flew up to Scotland. The efficient chief stewardess on the Shuttle detected he was someone special. So imagine his delight when we were invited onto the Flight Deck of this "huge" 757. As he gazed at the incredible array of instruments his face was like that of a little boy entering Father Christmas's grotto for the first time. To his joy he was allowed to stay for the landing, giving him a wonderful story to tell for months. What a contrast to the cockpit of the little RE8 which had borne him over the skies of Flanders 70 years before!

And so it was that, thanks to Lyn Macdonald's patient and persistent research, in November 1988 my father ("The Doc" as he was known to Lyn's party) was brought face to face with the grave of his friend Walter Malthouse in Fauquissart Military Cemetery. This young man had been killed beside my father at Aubers Ridge seventy-three years earlier. How proud he was to be chosen to say the immortal words:

> Age shall not weary them
> Nor the years condemn
> At the going down of the sun
> And in the morning
> We will remember them.

*Doc at Walter Malthouse's grave after saying the immortal words. Note the West Yorkshire badge on tomb stone. (Photograph courtesy of Wilf Schofield.)*

But "Doc" would not play ball with the TV and radio reporters. He was supposed to shed tears of grief at the unexpected meeting with his pal, but after his initial exclamation of joy at the discovery, and especially that Walter had found a resting place of dignity, he reverted to the *sang-froid* of a retired Police surgeon and related how he had collected the shattered pieces of poor Walter in a sack and buried them.

Lyn Macdonald ended the obituary in her newsletter, "Dear old Doc, with his beaming smile and his dangling monocle and his refusal to be other than perfectly delighted with everything and everyone, will be long remembered."

During his declining years my father was kept going by visits and phone calls from family and friends, prominent among them his eight grandchildren, Margaret Facey, Harold and Elizabeth Ridley, Harry Broughton, Ronnie Hamand, John Young, the Jarvises from Rockbourne, the Williams family and Jane Durham (his Paterson cousin). A happy feature for him was the steady flow of chatty correspondence from his New Zealand relatives, and for the first time he actually met his brother's children Betty, Shirley and John, who all visited the UK for the first time in the eighties. All of these, and many more unknown to me, played their part in keeping him going and in providing the stimulus necessary to keep these memoirs growing.

In 1985 he went fishing for the last time, as the final entry in his Game Book recounts:

> 25 July    Loch Bayfield on Doug. Budge's grand loch . . . Fine dull afternoon, mild wind. Only offer all afternoon, a thrill for 90+.
>
> 3 lb 4 oz    Had a thrilling battle from boat, Jim Paterson with oars. At 4 pm had a sudden deep take on "Black Pannell" fly. Fish put up a very hard fight – all round and under the boat. Could see it was an unusually fine Brown Trout. Alas we did not have a net so I had to play fish firmly. Fish finally dived round boat both sides and under boat. Jim produced a large tin and at 3rd attempt I guided fish under pressure into large tin. Hoorah for Jim, he has fish safely in boat. My largest Brown Trout in 70 years of fishing. Doug weighs fish 3 lb 4 oz.

He no longer had a garden to tend, but every time he came to us in Scotland, winter or summer, in answer to a query as to what he'd like to do first, with a twinkle in his eye he would invariably reply "Let's go to the Garden Centre." He took an immense interest in the garden I was trying to create in the wilderness I had inherited and was a great help with pruning, planting and planning.

Eventually the Lywoods told us he was no longer able to care for himself and Judith L found him a vacancy close by at Marlands Retirement Home, where he was soon happily installed with a diminished selection of his favourite possessions. Here he continued to write, but more slowly and with some confusion. After a couple of brief sojourns in hospital, one day in April 1990 I was summoned from Scotland to his bedside. He passed away that night, and I was given a little notion of the love and affection even an old man can engender as not only the nurses on duty, but also those off duty, in their night attire, slipped into his room, kissed him gently on the forehead, and said "Good-bye Doc" with tears in their eyes. The gruff voice which answered our phone calls "Doc Wilson here" was finally stilled.

*Peter was a very proud grandfather and always knew what each grandchild was up to. He met all of them at Andrew's wedding in Romsey in 1987. Here are some who were there, including his first three great grandchildren. From left to right: Michael, Crispin with Catriona, Mandy with Edwina, Jonathon, Sarah with Abigail, Rosalind and Alistair.*

As we say grace before family meals on special occasions, we can still hear the echo of his voice intoning the Brasenose Grace:

> Oculi omnium spectant in Te, Deus! Tu das illis escas tempore opportuno. Aperis manum Tuam et imples omne animal Tua benedictione. Mensae coelestis nos participes facias, Deus, Rex Aeternae Gloriae.

This was all remembered with well-nigh perfect accuracy over nearly seventy years.

As he was laid to rest beside Paula in the churchyard at Rockbourne, a cock pheasant, resplendent in his spring plumage, leapt onto the wall and crowed triumphantly . . .

*Peter with grandson Richard.*
*This last photograph was taken three weeks before Peter died in April 1990. He had been anxiously awaiting the safe arrival of Richard, who had been sailing the Atlantic before the mast in TS Astrid.*

I hope you have enjoyed the Life Remembered in these pages as much as I have cherished the flood of memories which have stirred whilst I have compiled them.

# Epilogue

We close Peter's story with two poems found among his papers, which reflect his personality:

Peter the warrior, physician and man:

> I would be true for there are those who trust me
> I would be pure for there are those who care
> I would be strong for there is much to suffer
> I would be brave for there is much to dare
> I would be friend to all-the foe-the friendless
> I would be giving and forget the gift
> I would be humble for I know my weakness
> I would look up – and laugh
> 　　　　– and love
> 　　　　– and lift
>
> *Howard Arnold Watters*

Words given to him by a friend in the trenches in 1915.

Ros, his eldest grandchild, gave him a birthday buffet lunch for his 95th (and last) birthday. He regaled us with this poem, which he had come across in South Africa in 1942. It is fitting that he should bid us farewell with these impish words.

Peter the philosopher and humorous raconteur:

> The Theology of Bongwi The Baboon
>
> This is the wisdom of the Ape
> Who yelps beneath the moon –
> Tis God who made me in His shape,
> He is a Great Baboon.
> Tis He who tilts the moon askew
> And fans the forest trees.
> The heavens which are broad and blue

Provide him his trapeze.
He swings with tail divinely bent
Around those azure bars
And munches to his Soul's content
The Kernels of the stars;
And when I die, His loving care
Will raise me from the sod
To learn the perfect Mischief there.
The Nimbleness of God.

*My Friends The Baboons. Roy Campbell*